Be a More Productive Scholar

Some scholars are highly productive. They break new ground and do it again and again. Their names and ideas are ubiquitous in scientific journals and scholarly books. They scoff at "publish or perish." To them, it's "publish and flourish." But how are they so productive, publishing hundreds of powerful works over their careers? Most graduate students, junior faculty, and even senior faculty have no idea. The methods of the productive are rarely taught and remain a hidden curriculum. Kenneth A. Kiewra interviewed dozens of productive scholars to uncover the hidden curriculum of scholarly success. *Be a More Productive Scholar* now reveals those productivity stories and methods by dispensing more than a hundred pointers for enhancing professional development and boosting scholarly productivity. Graduate students to seasoned scholars can benefit from this career-guiding advice.

KENNETH A. KIEWRA is John E. Weaver Professor in Educational Psychology at the University of Nebraska–Lincoln, USA. He has published six books and is listed among the top 2 percent of the most cited researchers worldwide. He has given more than five hundred invited presentations worldwide, and his teaching excellence has been recognized with numerous awards.

T0372698

Be a More Productive Scholar

KENNETH A. KIEWRA
University of Nebraska–Lincoln

CAMBRIDGE
UNIVERSITY PRESS

CAMBRIDGE
UNIVERSITY PRESS

Shaftesbury Road, Cambridge CB2 8EA, United Kingdom

One Liberty Plaza, 20th Floor, New York, NY 10006, USA

477 Williamstown Road, Port Melbourne, VIC 3207, Australia

314–321, 3rd Floor, Plot 3, Splendor Forum, Jasola District Centre, New Delhi – 110025, India

103 Penang Road, #05-06/07, Visioncrest Commercial, Singapore 238467

Cambridge University Press is part of Cambridge University Press & Assessment, a department of the University of Cambridge.

We share the University's mission to contribute to society through the pursuit of education, learning and research at the highest international levels of excellence.

www.cambridge.org
Information on this title: www.cambridge.org/9781009342520

DOI: 10.1017/9781009342513

First published 2024

A catalogue record for this publication is available from the British Library

Library of Congress Cataloging-in-Publication Data

Names: Kiewra, Kenneth A., author.
Title: Be a more productive scholar / Kenneth A. Kiewra.
Description: Cambridge ; New York, NY : Cambridge University Press, 2024. |
   Includes bibliographical references.
Identifiers: LCCN 2023049705 (print) | LCCN 2023049706 (ebook) |
   ISBN 9781009342520 (hardback) | ISBN 9781009342506 (paperback) |
   ISBN 9781009342513 (epub)
Subjects: LCSH: Education–Research–Management. | Education–Research–Vocational
   guidance. | Education–Study and teaching (Graduate) | Academic writing. |
   Scholarly publishing.
Classification: LCC LB1028.2 .K54 2024 (print) | LCC LB1028.2 (ebook) |
   DDC 808.02071/1–dc23/eng/20240110
LC record available at https://lccn.loc.gov/2023049705
LC ebook record available at https://lccn.loc.gov/2023049706

ISBN 978-1-009-34252-0 Hardback
ISBN 978-1-009-34250-6 Paperback

Contents

Acknowledgments

Thank you to those who helped shape *Be a More Productive Scholar*.

Foremost are my colleagues, my collaborators, who joined me in investigating productive scholars the past twenty-five years. They are John Creswell, Abe Flanigan, Saima Hasnin, Priya Karimuddanahalli, Doug Kauffman, Chris Labenz, Linlin Luo, Melissa Patterson-Hazley, Anja Prinz, Alexander Renkl, Jared Soundy, Jessica Walsh, and Helene Zeeb. I appreciate your dedicated work and collegiality, the fun times, and all you taught me.

Thank you Cambridge University Press for adopting this book and bringing it to life. A special thanks to David Repetto, Executive Publisher; Vinithan Sedumadhavan, Project Management Executive; Natasha Whelan, Senior Content Manager; Rowan Groat, Editorial Assistant; Joon Moon, Marketing Executive; and Penny Harper, Copy-editor. I am honored to have Cambridge University Press as my publisher.

Many thanks and much love to my supportive family: wife Christine, and children Keaton, Anna, and Samuel. You're my inspiration.

Of course, this book would not exist were it not for the über-talented and productive scholars whose stories fill these pages. You were generous to share your time, accomplishments, and hidden curriculum advice with me and others traveling along their scholarly paths.

This book is dedicated in loving memory of my parents, Frank and Winifred Kiewra. I appreciate all you did for me and all you taught me. I miss you dearly.

Introduction

Iron sharpens iron; scholar, the scholar.

William Drummond[1]

Publish or perish. Sure, there's that. Newly minted assistant professors understand they must publish, and likely publish a lot, to attain tenure. Graduate students understand this too, as they sow publication seeds well before graduation, hoping for an early harvest and fertile job prospects. But employment yearnings and tenure trepidation are not the only publication starters. Many scholars, green and seasoned alike, relish the scientific process – raising new and important questions, designing solution-seeking studies, and offering game-changing implications for practitioners. A few scholars are particularly good at this. They break new ground and do it again and again. Their names and ideas are ubiquitous in scientific journals and scholarly books. They scoff at publish or perish. To them, it's publish and flourish. But, how? How are they so productive? What separates them from the rest?

Meet the Productive Scholars

Colleagues and I sought to find out how expert scholars are so productive by investigating the best of the best in my own field of educational psychology. Beginning in 2000, I coauthored the first of seven qualitative studies investigating highly productive educational psychologists to understand their backgrounds and methods and to pass along advice to emerging and seasoned scholars alike. That first study[1] investigated the top three scholars emerging from a survey of educational psychologists. They were Richard Anderson, Richard Mayer, and Michael Pressley. The next study[2] identified and investigated the four leading educational psychology scholars at the time: Patricia Alexander, Richard Mayer, Dale Schunk, and Barry Zimmerman.

1

The third study[3] investigated a highly productive cohort of German educational psychologists associated with Ludwig Maximillian University of Munich: Heinz Mandl, Hans Gruber, Alexander Renkl, and Frank Fischer. The fourth study[4] investigated top female educational psychologists in Europe and the United States. They were Patricia Alexander, Carol Dweck, Jacquelynne Eccles, Mareike Kunter, and Tamara van Gog. The fifth study[5] focused on early-career award-winning scholars, recognized by the American Psychological Association and the American Educational Research Association (AERA), to unearth the roots of early success. Those scholars were Rebecca Collie, Logan Fiorella, Doug Lombardi, Sabina Neugebauer, Erika Patall, and Ming-Te Wang. The sixth study[6] explored successful graduate student scholars, namely four recent Graduate Research Excellence Award winners from AERA Division C, to understand which graduate school factors align with success. They were Hyewon Lee, Hyun Ji Lee, Carly Robinson, and Sirui Wan. A seventh study[7] focused on a single productive scholar, John Glover, by interviewing three of his former collaborators. I also conducted unpublished interviews with two AERA award-winning diversity and inclusion psychologists: Carol D. Lee and Zeus Leonardo. Finally, I also draw from interviews that Hefer Bembenutty conducted for his book on contemporary pioneers in teaching and learning.[8] Some of those pioneers I had interviewed previously (Eccles, Alexander, and Zimmerman) and others I had not (David Berliner, James Banks, Karen Harris, John Hattie, Marilla Svinicki, Brian Coppola, and Ivar Braten). A thumbnail sketch for each of these thirty-four productive scholars appears in the Appendix. This sketch serves as a source you can return to throughout the book to remember who's who.

For this book, I also draw from my research on talent development,[9] which includes (a) interviews with dozens of national and world-class experts or Olympic medalists, their parents, and coaches spanning numerous domains such as chess, baton twirling, rodeo, music, photography, swimming, fencing, spelling, and figure skating, to name a few, and (b) interviews with those still producing creative works in their wisdom years,[10] such as Rich Mayer (again), PBS news anchor Judy Woodruff, and the Wander Women who quit their jobs, sold their homes, and set off exploring the American wilderness. Finally, I draw from my own forty-year academic career as a six-time book author, top 2 percent most-cited researcher worldwide,[11] journal editor of

Educational Psychology Review, creator of the SOAR (Select, Organize, Associate, Regulate) Teaching and Learning Method,[12] chair of my college's promotion and tenure committee, and Academic Success Director at the University of Nebraska to offer a bit of personal scholarly advice.

This wide-ranging collection of talent stories and advice you're about to read transcends domains. What I learned investigating productive scholars in educational psychology likely holds for most productive scholars from astronomy to zoology. Moreover, *Be a More Productive Scholar* uncovers the pathways to scholarly success for emerging scholars at the graduate school or assistant professor trailhead, seasoned scholars well on the way, and those nearing their wisdom years finish. The book lends a hand to all travelers, including those from underrepresented groups encountering structural barriers to those seemingly born into their talent domains. Pathways as far-ranging as professional training, mentorship, work habits, research management, writing strategies, life routines, collaboration, support networks, failure framing, and many others are revealed using data, stories, advice, and quotations culled from my investigations of productive scholars, other talent-related work, and my personal journey.

Because each section in the book is meant to be self-standing and a quick go-to resource for readers seeking advice about a particular topic, some ideas, stories, and quotations appear more than once throughout the book because they are germane to more than one topic. Please think of such repetition as opportunities for increased learning, knowing that "No man ever steps in the same river twice, for it's not the same river and he's not the same man."[13]

Seek the Hidden Curriculum. Look at That. It's All Right Here

Rebecca Collie credits much of her scholarly success to the mentors who taught her the "hidden curriculum in academia," the insider knowledge that helped her avoid dead ends and saved her "years-worth of wasted time."[1] One bit of insider information Collie received dealt with how to interpret and react to journal reviewer feedback following a manuscript submission. In this case, she learned that a revise-and-resubmit decision with massive comments was actually a positive outcome. Her foot was in the door, and it was time to get busy making revisions and push through.

Collie pointed out that many assistant professors are not well versed on the workings of academia and have to "navigate the hidden curriculum on your own." Collie said, "You might wonder, 'Do I do it this way or that way? I guess I have to try it this way.' Then if it doesn't work, you have to go back and do it the other way."[2]

Collie's right. Graduate school mentors and senior colleagues might not have time to direct you, or falsely believe that you already know the ropes, leaving you to trial-and-error it. Or they may dispense unnecessary and ridiculous advice as a teaching supervisor did for me as I was about to teach my first college class as a teaching assistant. The supervisor said, "Don't be up there itchin' and a-scratchin' like some damn baseball player." Okay …

That's the purpose of this book. To reveal the hidden curriculum, the insider information needed to succeed as an academic scholar. Things your doctoral advisor and senior colleagues never told you or might not even know. And I promise, all the advice is much better than refraining from itchin' and a-scratchin'.

References

Introduction

1 Drummond, W. *BrainyQuote*. www.brainyquote.com/topics/scholar-quotes.

Meet the Productive Scholars

1 Kiewra, K. A., & Creswell, J. W. (2000). Conversations with three highly productive educational psychologists: Richard Anderson, Richard Mayer, and Michael Pressley. *Educational Psychology Review, 12,* 135–161.
2 Patterson-Hazley, M., & Kiewra, K. A. (2013). Conversations with four highly productive educational psychologists: Patricia Alexander, Richard Mayer, Dale Schunk, and Barry Zimmerman. *Educational Psychology Review, 25,* 19–45.
3 Flanigan, A., Kiewra, K. A., & Luo, L. (2018). Conversations with four highly productive German educational psychologists: Frank Fischer, Hans Gruber, Heinz Mandl, and Alexander Renkl. *Educational Psychology Review, 30,* 303–330.
4 Prinz, A., Zeeb, H., Flanigan, A., Renkl, A., & Kiewra, K. A. (2020). Conversations with five highly successful female educational psychologists: Patricia Alexander, Carol Dweck, Jacquelynne Eccles, Mareike Kunter, and Tamara van Gog. *Educational Psychology Review, 33,* 763–795.

5 Kiewra, K. A., Luo, L., & Flanigan, A. (2021). Educational psychology early career award winners: How did they do it? *Educational Psychology Review*, *33*, 1981–2018.

6 Kiewra, K. A., Hasnin, S., Soundy, J., Premkumar, P. K., & Labenz, C. (2023). Graduate student award winners in educational psychology: What made them successful? *Educational Psychology Review*, *35*, Article 90.

7 Kiewra, K. A., & Kauffman, D. (2023). John Glover: A long overdue account of his productive scholarship methods. *Educational Psychology Review*, *35*, Article 56.

8 Bembenutty, H. (2022). *Contemporary pioneers in teaching and learning*, Vol. 2. Charlotte, NC: Information Age Publishing, Inc.

9 Kiewra, K. A. (2019). *Nurturing children's talents: A guide for parents*. Santa Barbara, CA: Praeger.

10 Kiewra, K. A., Walsh, J., & Labenz, C. (2023). Moving beyond fulfillment: Wisdom years stories of passion, perseverance, and productivity. *Educational Psychology Review*, *35*, Article 20.

11 CEHS researchers among most cited scientists worldwide, May 2021. https://cehs.unl.edu/npod/news/cehs-researchers-among-most-cited-scientists-worldwide/.

12 Kiewra, K. A. (2022). *SOAR to college success and beyond* (1st ed.). San Diego, CA: Cognella.

13 Heraclitus. *BrainyQuote*. www.brainyquote.com/quotes/heraclitus_107157.

Seek the Hidden Curriculum. Look at That. It's All Right Here

1 Kiewra, K. A., Luo, L., & Flanigan, A. (2021). Educational psychology early career award winners: How did they do it? *Educational Psychology Review*, *33*, 1981–2018 (p. 1998).

2 Ibid.

1 | *You Can Do It*

If you can dream it, you can do it.

Walt Disney[1]

Wow! Look What's Possible

Let's hit the ground running before rushing off to scholarship.

No human had ever broken the four-minute mile. The barrier was both physical and psychological, even for well-conditioned track athletes. Then in 1954, 25-year-old medical student Roger Bannister finally cracked track and field's most insurmountable barrier. Bannister clocked the world's first sub-four-minute mile, beating the mark by six-tenths of a second. It's what happened afterward that is most surprising though. In the year following Bannister's barrier break, thirty-seven more runners trimmed the four-minute mark, including three runners in a single race. Suddenly, the unyielding barrier had crumbled. Before long, silver-haired grandmothers, Sumo wrestlers, and those running to catch a bus were beating the mark. Some were beating it many times, such as American miler Steve Scott who broke the four-minute barrier 136 times. Today, the world record in the mile stands at three minutes, forty-three seconds. Wow! Wow for barrier breaking, wow for Steve Scott, and wow for the current world record. Any doubt that record will fall?

Of course, the impossible became possible in other running events. Consider the marathon, a race just over twenty-six miles. The victor in the first Olympic games in 1896 finished in about two hours and fifty-nine minutes, a pace of nearly seven minutes per mile. That's some pretty good picking-them-up-and-putting-them-down, but nothing compared to what marathon runners are churning out today. Heck, my best marathon time would have earned me gold medals in the first six Olympics, even though I'm a middle-of-the-pack runner in modern times, with my best time lagging about half an hour behind the world record, which stands at two hours and one minute, a staggering four minutes and thirty-eight seconds per mile pace. Wow! Wow for marathon running and for record eclipsing. Any doubt that record will fall?

And it's not just an elite few who are accomplishing amazing athletic feats. It's also the average Joe and Jane, or should I say Dick and Courtney? Dick Hoyt was a sedentary man who had never run more than a mile, had never learned how to swim, and had not ridden a bicycle since he was six years old. It was then, in 1977, that his son, Rick, who was wheelchair bound and could not speak, typed a message asking Dick to push him through a five-mile charity run for a high school classmate. Dick mustered the motivation and stamina to complete the race with Rick but felt the pain for two weeks. Meanwhile, Rick felt exhilarated and wrote, "Dad, when we were running, it felt like I wasn't disabled anymore."[1] That sentence became Dick's motivation to push, pull, and carry his son to places few can imagine. In the ensuing years, until Dick's death in 2021, the pair completed nearly a hundred marathons, including thirty-two Boston Marathons; completed nearly three hundred triathlons (swimming, biking, running), including six Ironman Triathlons; completed hundreds of other races; scaled mountains; cross-country skied; and biked across America. Wow! Wow for the Hoyts' accomplishments. Wow for dedicated parenting. Sometimes reading your children a bedtime story or taking them to the park just won't cut it.

Courtney Dauwalter is a former high school science teacher who latched on to running to clear her head before work or to meet up with friends for a chat. Today, she is an ultramarathoner, defeating top men and women alike in some of the world's most grueling long-distance races of a hundred miles or more. In 2017, she destroyed the field in the Moab 240 Mile Endurance Race across the rocky peaks of Utah, which included nearly 29,000 feet of elevation gain and descent. Courtney's two-day and ten-hour finishing time put her an incredible ten hours ahead of the second-place racer, a man. Wow! Wow for ultramarathon runners. Wow for Courtney.

One more running figure. What did you accomplish outside of work in the past forty-six days, eight hours, and thirty-six minutes? Perhaps you got your car serviced, paid your monthly bills, fertilized your lawn, binged-watched a show on Netflix, and played a round or two of golf. Not a bad month-and-a-half. Now let me tell you what Pete Kostelnick did in that time: He ran across America. The 29-year-old financial analyst took off from work for a couple months and ran 3,067 miles from San Francisco to New York, smashing a 36-year-old record for running across America. To complete this odyssey, Pete averaged – are you sitting down, of course you are – over seventy-two miles per day, nearly three marathons a day. Pete ran about fourteen hours per day for six weeks. Wow! Wow for Pete and his astounding accomplishment. How are you feeling now about that two-mile stroll through the neighborhood?

Wow! Right? These running stories are incredible. Most importantly, they stretch your imagination about what is possible. They inspire you to do more. Now, let's stretch your belief system about what is possible among scholars.

When I investigated psychologist Michael Pressley,[2] he had published 126 articles over the previous ten years, about 13 articles per year. In that interview year alone, Pressley published eighteen articles and three books and edited two more books. He served as editor-in-chief for two journals and was on the editorial boards of nine other journals. He garnered two major awards. Oh, he was also department chair. Wow!

When I investigated psychologist Richard Mayer for a second time,[3] he had published 27 books and 329 articles in a career spanning thirty-eight years, and his productivity was on the rise. His ten-year productivity rate jumped from 95 publications between 1992 and 2001 to 150 publications between 2002 and 2011. That's fifteen publications per year over ten years. And, Mayer is not slowing down, having published eight books and 160 articles in the past ten years between 2012 and 2021.[4] Wow!

Okay ... now you say it! Wow! Scholars can accomplish amazing things.

Now, here is the point. You can too. Productive scholars are not born; they're made. Ditto for accomplished runners, chess players, baton twirlers, figure skaters, and musicians .... You name the talent area: All made, not born. Psychologist Benjamin Bloom[5] was among the first to investigate expertise when he studied the top 120 Americans in music, art, athletics, mathematics, and science. Bloom's resounding conclusion was this: What these talented people have accomplished, almost anyone can accomplish if conditions are right.

Be a More Productive Scholar reveals the conditions that make productive scholars like Pressley and Mayer so productive.

Conditions laid out in this book that you can access and control now that you know what is possible. Wow!

Recognize That Talent Is Made, Not Born

At first glance, it appears talent is born. How else could there be prodigies like Wolfgang Amadeus Mozart, Pablo Picasso, and Bobby Fischer? Mozart was playing piano at the age of three and composing at the age of six. As a child, Picasso painted masterfully. Gertrude Stein said that young Picasso "wrote paintings as other children wrote their A, B, Cs."[1] Picasso said: "I never drew like a child. When I was 12, I drew like Raphael."[2] Fischer became the youngest US chess champion at age fourteen. At sixteen, he became the youngest ever to attain the grandmaster title. It sure seems like talent is born, perhaps a gift from the gods as some believe.

Look a bit longer, though, and talent appears made, even among these prodigies. Both Mozart[3] and Picasso[4] were tutored by devoted fathers who were accomplished in their son's eventual talent domain. Leopold Mozart was an accomplished violinist, composer, and concert master who literally wrote the book on violin instruction the year Wolfgang was born. Picasso's father, Jose Ruiz Blasco, was a painter who taught drawing at various art schools. Fischer[5] had no parental chess lineage, but he was raised in New York City, a chess Mecca, where he was able to push pawns nightly with top-ranked grandmasters at nearby chess clubs. That's not all. Fischer was a child consumed by chess. He played on a pocket set on the bus ride to and from school. He snuck chess books inside his schoolbooks to read during class. He left school during lunch to play chess with a chess master who lived down the street. At age sixteen, Fischer left school permanently, dropping out of school to study chess full time. These prodigies made their talents.

Look longer still and it is evident that this talented trio did not become experts overnight. Their talents took many years to develop fully. Such is the case with all extraordinary creators. Psychologist John Hayes[6] studied talented composers and artists and found that all of them studied their craft diligently for at least ten years before producing a master work. True to form, Mozart's first landmark composition was penned when he was sixteen. Picasso painted his first master work when he was twenty-five. And Bobby Fischer captured the chess world championship at age twenty-nine. Had these extraordinary creators not worked so hard for so long, Fischer might never have dismantled Boris Spassky and the Soviet chess machine that had dominated chess for decades. Picasso might never have created the antiwar mural *Guernica*, which stretched eleven feet by twenty-six feet. Image renderings might have never left his sketchbook. And, Mozart might have never composed *The Marriage of Figaro*. The world might have only known *The Engagement of Figaro* or, heaven forbid, *Figaro's Finest First Dates*. Talent is made, but its making takes time.

This is great news. These and thousands of other talent stories, including those of productive scholars, confirm that the seeds of talent development rest in your own hands. You need only sow the seeds and, over time, cultivate their growth. But to do so, you must believe that talent is made, not born.

Talent Can Spring Most Anywhere

Among the productive scholars investigated, several hailed from well-educated families with deep education roots. Richard Mayer,[1] Erika Patall, and Sabina Neugebauer[2] all had fathers who were academics. Each told childhood stories about helping their fathers with scientific projects and traced their own success to those academic roots.

Several others, though, climbed to their field's highest branches despite having a fragile root system. Hefer Bembenutty[3] tells the stories of successful academics who rose from humble beginnings. David Berliner, an expert on teaching and learning, was raised in an old tenement in the Bronx. His father was a drug store clerk and his mother a secretary. Brian Coppola, a pioneer in discipline-centered teaching and learning, was the son of second-generation immigrants. His father was from a family of Italian cigar makers and shoemakers; his mother was raised on a poultry farm. John Hattie, well known for his meta-analyses on educational topics, was raised in a rural New Zealand home without a television or car. His father was a cobbler, his mother a movie theater manager. Hattie never traveled more than twenty miles from his home as a youth. James Banks, known as the father of multicultural education, was raised on a family cotton farm in Arkansas and experienced segregation firsthand. Growing up, he could only go to the Memphis zoo on Black Day, had to drink from a fountain labeled "colored," and could not enter the city library.

My own interviews and personal experience also confirm that a privileged path is not the only entry point to scholarly success. Tamara van Gog and Patricia Alexander hailed from working-class families and credited their nonadvantaged upbringings for their success. Van Gog said:

I've seen how hard people have to work and how you can only do extra things if you do additional work. My mother always stimulated us to do well in school as a way of getting ahead. And, my step-father was an early riser and often went to his vegetable garden before work. I think I got my hardwork habits from him because he made clear that if you want something, you have to work for it.[4]

Alexander similarly credited her "blue-collar" upbringing for her success:

I learned how to stand up for myself in life, which carried over into my work. I was never one to let anyone stifle my voice – at least not without a fight. I did not always expect to win, but I always expected to keep trying when something really mattered.[5]

Logan Fiorella,[6] meanwhile, admitted that he too did not have a family background that pointed him toward psychology and academia, let alone scholarly success. Neither parent completed college. In fact, Fiorella's path to scholarly success was more a stumble than a scamper. For instance, Fiorella "just happened to apply to the University of Central Florida because it was close to home." He naively majored in psychology because "that sounds interesting." Once there, he thought, "I guess I need to get research experience, whatever that means." That realization led Fiorella to "randomly explore different research labs and stumble onto the Institute for Simulation and Training" where he got his first research exposure. The lab experience sparked a general interest in research, but Fiorella "still didn't know what I wanted to do." He half-heartedly applied to Ph.D. programs in human factors but was not accepted. He remained at Central Florida to pursue a master's. It was during that two-year program that Fiorella was exposed to and drawn to the work of Richard Mayer on multimedia learning. Fiorella contacted Mayer to express his interest, applied to the program, and was accepted at the University of California, Santa Barbara with Mayer as his advisor. Fiorella found his niche without much forethought and without privilege.

My own academic journey was also one without privilege. My parents were high school educated. My mom was a cook in a local elementary school, and my dad operated a bulldozer following a stint in the military. I was a disinterested student until finding my stride in high school. I decided to pursue college, but without much forethought. I attended a small, little-known state college in New York without even visiting. My college days began a bit like *Animal House*, although I was never placed on Double Secret Probation. My first-semester grade-point average was 2.3, including a D in meteorology wherein the instructor reported my performance on the final exam as, "F minus, minus, minus," and asked if I was under the weather. Like meteorologists always get things right. I found my educational psychology element sophomore year when I took a class from Professor Nelson DuBois. The material was delicious, infectious, and Professor DuBois was a model of effective instruction. I wanted to do what he was doing. I stopped skipping classes and began auditing every educational psychology class on the books. Still, I had no idea about how to become an educational psychologist or about graduate schools. Fortunately, Dr. DuBois counseled me on the best graduate schools for educational psychology, helped me apply, and wrote a strong letter of support. With several acceptances in hand, Professor DuBois helped steer me toward Florida State University because of its reputation in instructional design, which included a stellar faculty headlined by Dr. Robert Gagné, the father of instructional psychology. Professor DuBois even helped me negotiate a teaching assistantship instructing undergraduates in educational psychology – just like him. Without academic roots, I had found the trail to academic training and potential success.

Believe You Can: Build a Growth Mindset

If you believe you can, you can. If you believe you can't, you can't. Belief matters.

Psychologist Carol Dweck,[1] one of the productive scholars I investigated, coined the terms fixed and growth mindset to represent the dichotomous ways people view their potential and ability to succeed. Those with fixed mindsets believe that their abilities are preset by biology and immune to experience. What you have is what you've got. Those with growth mindsets believe that their abilities are modifiable and shaped by experience. What you have is just the start. In one mindset experiment, students were questioned to establish their mindsets – fixed or growth. Students were then given a series of math problems, first simple then difficult. As expected, all students performed well on the simple problems. Regarding the difficult problems, fixed mindset students performed poorly on these and attributed failure to low intelligence or low math ability, saying things like "I'm not very smart" or "I'm not good at math," even though they had just solved the simpler problems with ease. Seeing the more difficult problems, they often gave up without trying. Meanwhile, growth mindset students performed well on the difficult problems. Their growth mindsets prompted them to embrace the challenge and work harder on the difficult problems, invent new strategies when needed, refuse to give up, and not assign self-blame when they did make mistakes. Their growth mindsets kept them believing they could succeed and succeed they did.

Having a growth mindset is better than having a fixed mindset, for two reasons. First, you'd have a mindset supported by science. Science has shown that abilities are not fixed; they are modifiable. Consider intelligence. In one study published in *Nature*,[2] researchers gave adolescents intelligence tests and scanned their brains. Then they tracked the students for four years, retested, and rescanned. Results revealed wide IQ changes over four years, with scores rising or falling by as much as twenty points. Twenty points is enough to move someone from the average intelligence category, where 50 percent of the population reside, to the gifted category, where just 6 percent reside. Researchers were convinced that IQ changes were not superfluous, because changes in IQ corresponded to changes in brain structure as shown in the brain scans. This is not surprising because many scientific studies show that experience changes brain structure. One famous study involved London cab drivers[3] who undergo rigorous training for years navigating the complex London streets before earning their cab license. Brain scans revealed that navigational training increased the size of the brain's hippocampus, where spatial navigation takes place.

The second reason that a growth mindset is better than a fixed mindset is because a fixed mindset is impervious to the two things that help people learn: skill and will. People improve as they learn new skills such as how to take better notes or how to solve algebraic equations.

People also improve as they increase their motivation, their will, to succeed. Fixed mindset folks shun skill and will urgings. They say things like "skills won't help me, I'm dumb, and I can't learn new skills" or "why try harder, it won't help, and I'm operating at my full potential." Even when someone is gifted, a fixed mindset limits them. They might say "I don't need to learn new skills, I'm already smart" or "why try harder, I'm a natural at this." Fixed mindsets are dooming. They leave one like an anorexic hermit crab afraid to grow, afraid to shed its protective shell, afraid to step into a challenging new world where much can be experienced and learned.[4]

Mindsets are particularly important for members of stereotyped groups. For example, African Americans are sometimes stereotyped as being low in intelligence while females are sometimes stereotyped as being bad at math and science.[5] Such beliefs are debilitating because belief matters. Even checking a box on a test to indicate race or sex or taking tests when outnumbered by students outside your stereotyped group can trigger the stereotype in one's mind and lower test scores.[6] Evoked stereotypes, though, mainly debilitate those with fixed mindsets. Growth mindsets override stereotyped beliefs. African Americans and females with growth mindsets don't believe in race or gender inferiority, and if they fall behind, they believe that they can work harder and catch up.[7]

Stereotypes not only debilitate performance, they yield surrender. They make group members feel they don't belong and drop out. Women and minorities are prone to give up on graduate school and academic careers, feeling like they are in over their heads and don't belong. Here again, a growth mindset can help ameliorate such beliefs. Dweck writes: "Prejudice is a deeply ingrained societal problem ... a growth mindset helps people to see prejudice for what it is – *someone else's* view of them – and to confront it with their confidence and abilities intact."[8]

In sum, it's smart to think about things such as intelligence, spatial ability, creativity, athletic and musical talent, and scholarly success like rubber bands. Regardless of band size at birth, bands can stretch, and stretch a lot, due to experience acquired along the way. Of course, mindsets are modifiable too. Here are three steps for making your fixed mindset a growth mindset:

1. Believe that ability is made, not born. All the talented people you know and all the talented people I studied made their talents. That

goes for luminaries like Mozart and Fischer and for run-of-the-mill folks like Pete Kostelnick. Pete was hardly a natural-born runner. He built his run-across-America endurance capacity one step at a time as he gradually upped his weekly training mileage to two hundred miles per week and to ten thousand miles per year, while working a full-time job. Remember what Benjamin Bloom[9] found: Almost anyone can do incredible things when conditions are right. The seeds of success lie in the palm of your hand.

2. Recognize and change mindsets. Recognize when you are operating with a fixed mindset and throw the growth mindset switch. Change "I can't publish two articles a year, there is not enough time" to "I will find and make the time necessary to work more on my research." Change "only the Mayers and Pressleys of the world can produce at such a high level" to "if they can do it, I can do it too."

3. Cultivate a growth mindset. Take stock each day of your process-oriented growth mindset perspective. Ask and answer questions like these:

   • What did I learn?
   • What mistakes did I make that I can learn from?
   • Where could I have tried harder?
   • Who can help me do better?

Take the Leap. It's Not as Far as It Looks

Even with a growth mindset, success might seem a pipe dream or a long way off. Among the talented children I studied, many of their parents never imagined such success was possible or saw it coming. One parent said: "If someone had told me 10 years ago that we'd be where we are today, I'd never have believed it." Another parent said: "When he started, we didn't know he was going to be this good. We weren't even hoping he'd be this good. It just wasn't on our radar."[1]

Productive scholar Michael Pressley spoke of the importance of believing that success is reachable and not so far away as one might imagine. Pressley said: "If anybody had told me when I was sitting in graduate school that I'd be sitting where I am right now, I probably wouldn't have believed it, but in retrospect, it isn't as far from there to here as I would have thought at the time."[2]

Pressley advises those in academia to scan the horizon of possibilities and fearlessly take the leap. Pressley retold this Joseph Campbell story to make his point:

A child comes before a tribal leader for his initiation into adulthood. The child must jump from a cliff. The leader nudges the child toward the edge. The child peers over the edge and recoils in fear. The sage leader calmly says, "Go ahead and jump. It's not as far as it looks."[3]

As you consider your path to scholarly success, don't be intimidated by those farther along the path, be energized. Know that they started in the same place as you. Ralph Waldo Emerson smartly said: "Every artist was first an amateur."[4]

Scan the horizon, take a deep breath, and take the leap. It's not as far as it looks.

It's Never Too Early to Be Productive

I have sat on a lot of search committees looking to hire new assistant professors. I am astounded by some applicants' publication numbers. Several boast double-digit publication numbers, and I recall a just-graduated-applicant CV stocked with more than twenty publications. Among the early-career award-winning scholars I studied,[1] Logan Fiorella entered the job market with ten publications, while Erika Patall entered with eleven. One of my own recent advisees had seventeen. How do they do it? Here are a few suggestions for early productivity:

- Focus on research and publishing. When you apply for academic positions, search committees are not going to review your transcript. It is helpful to have teaching experience and to be a good fit for the position. But above all else, search committees are determining if you'll be productive, be visible. An applicant with a strong publication record will often fit most any position.
- Don't wait to conduct research and publish. Hit your graduate training ground running. Get involved in collaborative studies right away. And not just with your advisor. Join in studies led by other faculty and students. My productive graduate advisee was a floater, seeking out other faculty collaborators across the university – even outside the university – working in areas of mutual interest.

- Be involved in multiple studies. Productive scholars are often involved in five to ten studies at a time, each at varying stages of completion.
- Carve out your own research area. Your dissertation should not be your first and only study on your pet topic. Initiate dissertation-leading studies years in advance.
- Don't let things drag out. Much graduate training leads students to believe that conducting research is a multiyear process. Nonsense. Quality studies can be designed, run, written, and out the door in a few months. Don't let your research projects stretch on like your commitment to learn the ukulele.

It's Never Too Late to Be Productive

Perhaps you think that you should retire when you reach a certain age, or when your eye bags threaten to swallow your nose, or when you fall asleep in faculty meetings (and you're the speaker), or when you don't care to wrestle with the next wave of technology advancements. Think again! I investigated productivity in the wisdom years (those typically marked by retirement) and found people in various walks of life shunning retirement and producing at their highest career levels.[1] Four-time National Championship coach John Cook, age sixty-six, was still guiding the Husker volleyball team into the Final Four and signing top-rated recruits. PBS *Newshour* anchor Judy Woodruff was still investigating and reporting the news at age seventy-five. And educational psychology professor Rich Mayer, age seventy-five, was accelerating his publication rate. His ascending ten-year publication totals over the past thirty years were 95, 150, and 160. In the past sixteen months alone, Mayer had published an astounding 44 works.

Seven years earlier, at age sixty-eight, Mayer could have stuffed his achievement awards in a couple dozen boxes and retired from his university position at full pay and benefits. Nope. Mayer shunned retirement and has, essentially, worked for free ever since. Mayer said: "I have no interest in retiring so long as my health remains good. I simply don't like the idea of retirement. I just don't understand it, and it rubs me the wrong way. My entire life I have tried to work hard and be productive, so then to suddenly say 'I'm going to stop produc-ing now' just doesn't seem right." Curiosity might have killed the cat, but curiosity and passion keep Mayer motoring. He said: "I enjoy what

I'm doing. My work makes me happy, and I'll keep doing it as long as I can. The thing that really keeps me going is my curiosity to pursue burning questions I really want to answer and to potentially discover something new and worthwhile."[2]

Effective time management strategies also boost Mayer's late-season productivity. He said: "It's really important that I segregate the day and week into specific time slots for accomplishing specific things, otherwise the day degenerates into a lot of junkie things that really go nowhere, such as answering email." True to his career form, Mayer preserves and allocates each morning for writing tasks. He said: "That's my most important work and that's when I'm most alert to complete it. If I can meet my daily goal of writing two or three pages in those morning hours, I'm super happy." Mayer schedules his classes and pushes his less demanding tasks like meetings and correspondence to the afternoon. He also preserves evenings and weekends for family time and relaxation, stressing that "family comes first" and that he "needs breaks to keep strong." Mayer does occasionally steal a bit of off-time to review manuscripts for several journals, admitting that doing so is "kind of fun and doesn't feel like work."[3]

Mayer is not immune to aging and recognizes its debilitating effects. Mayer said: "The aging literature tells us that just about everything is moving in the wrong direction as you age. Things slow down. Reaction times slow, senses become dulled, and cognition diminishes. These are not great things. Our bodies catch up with us. We weren't really designed to live this long."[4] To combat these effects, Mayer has four age-slowing defenses:

1. Accumulated Knowledge. Wisdom does not deteriorate, and Mayer draws upon his wisdom. Mayer said: "I can draw on my accumulated experiences conducting research, on my knowledge of the literature, and on my skills such as writing."[5]
2. Health Regiment. Mayer exercises daily, eats healthy foods, and makes sure he logs eight hours of nightly sleep. Mayer said: "As I get older, I find that I do not function well if I don't get enough sleep, but I find my sleep is more messed up. I like to nap and often feel ready for one around 4:00 p.m., which is never a good thing when our department schedules meeting or talks for that time."[6]
3. Workarounds. Mayer admits to a failing memory but uses workarounds to reduce forgetting. Mayer uses a monthly paper

calendar to record appointments, a yellow pad to list his weekly goals and plans, and Post-it notes to signal what he plans to accomplish that day. Mayer said: "This system keeps me focused on what I'm trying to accomplish long term, medium term, and short term."[7]

4. Avoidance. Mayer said: "I try not to think about retirement. I try to look forward, not back. I try to remain focused on my work. There is only so much time in the day to accomplish something."[8]

Productive scholar Doug Lombardi got a late academic start, which probably made him the first early-career award-winning scholar who received his award at a time he could contemplate early retirement. But, like Mayer, retirement is not on the horizon for Lombardi, who said: "I may be different from other early career researchers in that I'm a little bit older, my progeny are older, they're in college, so I haven't had to worry as much about family issues. [I love this work.] I'll probably die in this position."[9]

Don't Aim to Be a Productive Scholar

It is the quality of our work which will please God and not the quantity.

Mahatma Gandhi[1]

Productive scholars don't aim to be productive; they aim to produce important, high-quality work. Patricia Alexander said:[2]

Don't aim to be a prolific scholar; aim to be the best scholar you can be. Trying to be prolific might be detrimental because it can lead you down a path of producing without meaning, where the numbers take precedence over the influence. Aspire to true scholarship whether that leads to 500 publications or 50 publications. Be sure that each publication represents your best thinking, is influential, and impacts others.

Tamara van Gog said: "Productivity is nice, but it's not the production but what you have to say that ultimately counts. The contributions made are more important than the number of publications."[3]

"Have a few really impactful publications rather than many less impactful publications in not-so-good journals," Ming-Te Wang advised. "It's important to do groundbreaking work that moves the field forward and for people to know your work."[4]

Sabina Neugebauer also prioritized doing "my best work" over "productivity."[5] And Mareike Kunter sharply emphasized that "quality prevails!"[6]

The seeds for sprouting quality publications were planted in graduate school for graduate student award-winning scholar Hyun Ji Lee. Her advisors stressed publishing a few impactful studies of high quality rather than many less impactful and less rigorous studies. Lee said: "My advisors pursued impactful and high quality research and implored students to always do the same. They prioritized and modeled quality over quantity at all times. Their high expectations for all matters of research – from design to manuscript writing – taught me to strive to do high quality work."[7]

For me, the prevailing question I raise when choosing what to do is not "can this work lead to publication?" but "can this work impact how teachers teach, students learn, parents cultivate talent, or researchers become better scholars?" With such important outcomes hanging in the balance, only my best-quality work will do.

Be Productive Because You Love It: Follow Your Bliss

I love my work more than I love what it produces. I am dedicated to the work regardless of the consequences.

Novelist Naguib Mahfouz[1]

My first talent interviews were with parents of young chess masters. After learning how dedicated their sons were to chess improvement, I asked the parents why their children were so dedicated. All provided much the same answer: He loves it, he loves, he loves it. He's just passionate about chess. One parent said that he once took chess away for a time because the child was faltering in school and chess seemed the best bargaining chip for nudging the child back on course. Being torn from his love, even for a few days, the child was miserable. The parent said: "It was like yanking the soul out."[2]

When it comes to productive scholars, I found them much like the chess players. They work tirelessly because they love it. All would agree with writer Mark Twain who quipped: "Find a job you enjoy doing, and you'll never have to work a day in your life."[3]

John Glover loved his work. Former Glover student Alice Corkill said: "You could often hear John laughing in his office. He had this big booming laugh, and he laughed a lot … He was excited about his work, he was happy, he was laughing, he would joke around, and he was a fun person to be around."[4] So fun, in fact, that when Glover took the last of his daily bus rides to the University of Nebraska before changing institutions, his faithful co-riders threw him a party on the bus. They served cake and dressed in loud Glover-inspired plaid blazers to salute their fun-loving friend.

Scholar Doug Lombardi echoes Twain's wisdom: "I work all the time. But is that a bad thing? I don't think so. It's energizing. It's wonderful. I love it. I love what I do!"[5] When asked when he writes, Lombardi's work passion shined through: "What do you mean by writing? A lot of my writing is done when I'm taking a shower, washing my hair, or brushing my teeth. A lot of writing is done on my walks because I think about this stuff all the time."[6]

Scholar Michael Pressley was similarly engulfed in his scholarly pursuits. Pressley said:

Ideas are constantly on my mind. And the people I'm working with, I'm always talking to them about it. Sometimes, we'll just sit around for a day and a half and brainstorm, and those are interesting sessions … I seek out literature in the bookstores or library or I sit in my office and think about possibilities. I'm sort of always turning stuff over in my head, and then I'll run into things that sort of set off associations in my head and "click." I make sure I get those down.[7]

I knew Pressley was consumed by his work when he told me that he went to a movie with family but left to read a book in the lobby because he found the movie boring. I said: "Hey, wait! Who brings a book to a movie?"

Scholar Sabina Neugebauer loves the research process too. She said:

Uncovering patterns and making meaning of them has always been something invigorating and truly pleasurable. I get really curious about things and hooked on solving them. I become laser focused. I love what I do and become immersed in it … All my projects have sent me down roads connected by the same kernel of curiosity and the same passion for promoting educational equity.[8]

Scholar Rebecca Collie concurred, saying: "I truly value and love what I do. Therefore, it is not difficult to work hard and get things done."[9]

Scholar Patricia Alexander has followed her bliss. Alexander said:

I wanted to learn all I could about reading and learning – what goes on inside the head of students – and all those important constructs like strategies or interests intricately tied to reading and learning. I have always wanted to understand *why*. Such why questions continually pop into my head and will never be quieted. Seeking answers to those why questions are what drive my research and teaching – it is that questioning behavior and my passion for students' academic development that makes me an educational psychologist.[10]

Alexander believes that work and play can be one and credits her mentor, Ruth Garner, for showing her the seamlessness between work and play. Alexander spoke about a conference she attended with Garner: "We traveled all day, and at night we wrote manuscripts. Part of what I learned from her was this passion. You don't have to play and put work aside, it can be built into your life."[11] "Career is not just something that I do – it is who I am."[12]

Scholar Mareike Kunter nicely summed up the passion scholars feel for their work. She said: "I think academia is the most rewarding job you can have. You can do so many different things. It's intellectually inspiring, and you've got high flexibility and autonomy. So, if you're interested in pursuing an academic career, go for it!"[13]

Because if you don't, it might be tantamount to yanking out the soul. Follow your bliss.

References

You Can Do It

1 Disney, W. *BrainyQuote*. www.brainyquote.com/topics/you-can-do-it-quotes.

Wow! Look What's Possible

1 Reilly, R. (2005, June 20). Strongest dad in the world. *Sports Illustrated*, p. 88. https://vault.si.com/vault/2005/06/20/strongest-dad-in-the-world.
2 Kiewra, K. A., & Creswell, J. W. (2000). Conversations with three highly productive educational psychologists: Richard Anderson, Richard Mayer, and Michael Pressley. *Educational Psychology Review*, *12*, 135–161.
3 Patterson-Hazley, M., & Kiewra, K. A. (2013). Conversations with four highly productive educational psychologists: Patricia Alexander, Richard

Mayer, Dale Schunk, and Barry Zimmerman. *Educational Psychology Review*, 25, 19–45.

4 Kiewra, K. A., Walsh, J., & Labenz, C. (2023). Moving beyond fulfillment: Wisdom years stories of passion, perseverance, and productivity. *Educational Psychology Review*, 35, Article 20.

5 Bloom, B. (1985). *Developing talent in young people*. New York: Ballantine Books.

Recognize That Talent Is Made, Not Born

1 Gardner, H. (1993). *Creating minds*. New York: Basic Books (p. 140).

2 Evans, P. (2006). *It's not about the tapas*. New York: Bantam Dell (p. 127).

3 Gardner, H. (1997). *Extraordinary minds*. New York: Basic Books.

4 Gardner, H. (1993). *Creating minds*. New York: Basic Books.

5 Brady, F. (1965). *Bobby Fischer: Profile of a prodigy*. New York: Dover Publications.

6 Hayes, J. R. (1985). Three problems in teaching general skills. In S. F. Chapman, J. W. Segal, & R. Glaser (eds.), *Thinking and learning skills*, Vol. 2. *Research and open questions* (pp. 391–405). Hillsdale, NJ: Erlbaum.

Talent Can Spring Most Anywhere

1 Patterson-Hazley, M., & Kiewra, K. A. (2013). Conversations with four highly productive educational psychologists: Patricia Alexander, Richard Mayer, Dale Schunk, and Barry Zimmerman. *Educational Psychology Review*, 25, 19–45.

2 Kiewra, K. A., Luo, L., & Flanigan, A. (2021). Educational psychology early career award winners: How did they do it? *Educational Psychology Review*, 33, 1981–2018.

3 Bembenutty, H. (2022). *Contemporary pioneers in teaching and learning*, Vol. 2. Charlotte, NC: Information Age Publishing, Inc.

4 Prinz, A., Zeeb, H., Flanigan, A., Renkl, A., & Kiewra, K. A. (2020). Conversations with five highly successful female educational psychologists: Patricia Alexander, Carol Dweck, Jacquelynne Eccles, Mareike Kunter, and Tamara van Gog. *Educational Psychology Review*, 33, 763–795 (p. 776).

5 Ibid.

6 Kiewra, K. A., Luo, L., & Flanigan, A. (2021). Educational psychology early career award winners: How did they do it? *Educational Psychology Review*, 33, 1981–2018 (p. 1990).

Believe You Can: Build a Growth Mindset

1 Dweck, C. S. (2008). *Mindset*. New York: Ballantine Books.
2 IQ isn't set in stone, suggests study that finds big jumps, dips in teens (October 19, 2011). *NPR*. www.npr.org/sections/health-shots/2011/10/20/141511314/iq-isnt-set-in-stone-suggests-study-that-finds-big-jumps-dips-in-teens.
3 Maguire, E. A., Gadian, D. G., Johnsrude, C. D., et al. (2000). Navigation-related structural change in the hippocampus of taxi drivers. *Proceedings of the National Academy of Sciences USA, 97*, 4398–4403.
4 Waitzkin, J. (2007). *The art of learning*. New York: Free Press.
5 Dweck, C. S. (2008). *Mindset*. New York: Ballantine Books.
6 Steele, C. M., & Aronson, J. (1995). Stereotype threat and the intellectual test performance of African Americans. *Journal of Personality and Social Psychology, 69*, 797–811.
7 Dweck, C. S. (2008). *Mindset*. New York: Ballantine Books.
8 Ibid., p. 278.
9 Bloom, B. (1985). *Developing talent in young people*. New York: Ballantine Books.

Take the Leap. It's Not as Far as It Looks

1 Kiewra, K. A. (2019). *Nurturing children's talents: A guide for parents*. Santa Barbara, CA: Praeger (p. x).
2 Kiewra, K. A., & Creswell, J. W. (2000). Conversations with three highly productive educational psychologists: Richard Anderson, Richard Mayer, and Michael Pressley. *Educational Psychology Review, 12*, 135–161 (p. 154).
3 Ibid.
4 *Goodreads*. www.goodreads.com/quotes/11507-every-artist-was-first-an-amateur.

It's Never Too Early to Be Productive

1 Kiewra, K. A., Luo, L., & Flanigan, A. (2021). Educational psychology early career award winners: How did they do it? *Educational Psychology Review, 33*, 1981–2018.

It's Never Too Late to Be Productive

1 Kiewra, K. A., Walsh, J., & Labenz, C. (2023). Moving beyond fulfillment: Wisdom years stories of passion, perseverance, and productivity. *Educational Psychology Review, 35*, Article 20.

2 Ibid., p. 7.
3 Ibid., pp. 7–8.
4 Ibid., p. 8.
5 Ibid., p. 9.
6 Ibid.
7 Ibid.
8 Ibid.
9 Kiewra, K. A., Luo, L., & Flanigan, A. (2021). Educational psychology early career award winners: How did they do it? *Educational Psychology Review*, *33*, 1981–2018 (p. 2002).

Don't Aim to Be a Productive Scholar

1 Mahfouz, N. *BrainyQuote*. www.brainyquote.com/quotes/mahatma_gandhi_134719.
2 Patterson-Hazley, M., & Kiewra, K. A. (2013). Conversations with four highly productive educational psychologists: Patricia Alexander, Richard Mayer, Dale Schunk, and Barry Zimmerman. *Educational Psychology Review*, *25*, 19–45 (p. 39).
3 Prinz, A., Zeeb, H., Flanigan, A., Renkl, A., & Kiewra, K. A. (2020). Conversations with five highly successful female educational psychologists: Patricia Alexander, Carol Dweck, Jacquelynne Eccles, Mareike Kunter, and Tamara van Gog. *Educational Psychology Review*, *33*, 763–795 (p. 783).
4 Kiewra, K. A., Luo, L., & Flanigan, A. (2021). Educational psychology early career award winners: How did they do it? *Educational Psychology Review*, *33*, 1981–2018 (p. 1992).
5 Ibid., p. 2015.
6 Prinz, A., Zeeb, H., Flanigan, A., Renkl, A., & Kiewra, K. A. (2020). Conversations with five highly successful female educational psychologists: Patricia Alexander, Carol Dweck, Jacquelynne Eccles, Mareike Kunter, and Tamara van Gog. *Educational Psychology Review*, *33*, 763–795 (p. 783).
7 Kiewra, K. A., Hasnin, S., Soundy, J., Premkumar, P. K., & Labenz, C. (2023). Graduate student award winners in educational psychology: What made them successful? *Educational Psychology Review*, *35*, Article 90.

Be Productive Because You Love It: Follow Your Bliss

1 Csikszentmihalyi, M. (1996). *Creativity: Flow and the psychology of discovery and invention*. New York: HarperCollins (p. 107).
2 Kiewra, K. A. (2019). *Nurturing children's talents: A guide for parents*. Santa Barbara, CA: Praeger (p. 20).

3 Twain, M. *Goodreads*. www.goodreads.com/quotes/646569-find-a-job-you-enjoy-doing-and-you-will-never.

4 Kiewra, K. A., & Kauffman, D. (2023). John Glover: A long overdue account of his productive scholarship methods. *Educational Psychology Review*, *35*, Article 56.

5 Kiewra, K. A., Luo, L., & Flanigan, A. (2021). Educational psychology early career award winners: How did they do it? *Educational Psychology Review*, *33*, 1981–2018 (p. 2002).

6 Ibid., p. 2004.

7 Kiewra, K. A., & Creswell, J. W. (2000). Conversations with three highly productive educational psychologists: Richard Anderson, Richard Mayer, and Michael Pressley. *Educational Psychology Review*, *12*, 135–161 (p. 146).

8 Kiewra, K. A., Luo, L., & Flanigan, A. (2021). Educational psychology early career award winners: How did they do it? *Educational Psychology Review*, *33*, 1981–2018 (p. 1997).

9 Ibid., p. 2000.

10 Bembenutty, H. (2022). *Contemporary pioneers in teaching and learning*, Vol. 2. Charlotte, NC: Information Age Publishing, Inc. (p. 89).

11 Prinz, A., Zeeb, H., Flanigan, A., Renkl, A., & Kiewra, K. A. (2020). Conversations with five highly successful female educational psychologists: Patricia Alexander, Carol Dweck, Jacquelynne Eccles, Mareike Kunter, and Tamara van Gog. *Educational Psychology Review*, *33*, 763–795 (p. 775).

12 Bembenutty, H. (2022). *Contemporary pioneers in teaching and learning*, Vol. 2. Charlotte, NC: Information Age Publishing, Inc. (p. 100).

13 Prinz, A., Zeeb, H., Flanigan, A., Renkl, A., & Kiewra, K. A. (2020). Conversations with five highly successful female educational psychologists: Patricia Alexander, Carol Dweck, Jacquelynne Eccles, Mareike Kunter, and Tamara van Gog. *Educational Psychology Review*, *33*, 763–795 (p. 783).

2 | *Get Solid Training*

Wisdom ... comes not from age, but from education and learning.

Anton Chekhov[1]

Gravitate to Centers of Graduate School Excellence

When Harvard psychologist Howard Gardner,[2] of multiple intelligence theory fame, studied extraordinary creators in the modern era, he found that each had gravitated to a center of excellence, an intellectual hub where a field's best-of-the-best congregated, collaborated, competed, and created. For instance, dancer and choreographer Martha Graham sashayed from California to New York because the latter was the hub for dance, and writer T. S. Eliot transitioned from the United States to London so that he could join the Bloomsbury Circle, a group of talented English writers. Meanwhile, Mozart composed in Vienna and Picasso painted in Paris to center themselves among their field's most creative.

The productive scholars I studied gravitated to centers of excellence for graduate training. They sought out schools and professors that could best help them navigate their scholarly paths. Richard Anderson[3] received his doctorate at Harvard University where he was mentored by a famous psychologist linked to a long line of other famous psychologists, such as B. F. Skinner, rolling back to the dawn of psychology. Anderson was intentional in keeping the line of prominent scholars moving by advising strong doctoral students, turned professors, who, in turn, advised strong graduate students, and on it goes. Each year at the Annual Meeting of the American Educational Research Association, Anderson proudly displays his Starburst Chart, which documents his wide-branching and prominent family tree. Doug Lombardi is a proud third-generation branch on the Anderson tree. Lombardi's advisor at the University of Nevada, Las Vegas was Gail Sinatra, whose advisor was Mike Royer, whose advisor was Richard

Anderson. Lombardi commented on the significance of his academic lineage:

The research that I do today was influenced by Dick Anderson and all the legendary people who were his ancestors, people like Edwin Boring and Wilhelm Wundt ... When I talk about mental representations in my theoretical or empirical work, there's a lot of Dick Anderson in there. And when you think about my investigations of higher-order thinking processes, there's a lot of Mike Royer in there. What I do today is influenced by Anderson, Royer, and Sinatra. That's my direct line. But there are also the other associated folks, my aunts and uncles and cousins, who inspire, shape, and direct my career.[4]

Two other productive scholars I investigated also celebrate their Harvard roots.[5] Sabina Neugebauer said that attending Harvard exposed her to eminent scholars and an intellectual epicenter. Ming-Te Wang deemed his studies at Harvard motivational and inspirational. He said: "When you sit in the classroom and the instructor is some big name you actually read, like Howard Gardner and Robert Selman, it helps me to know that I can do it too. I can publish my work in top-tier journals too."[6]

Harvard, of course, is just one of many intellectual hubs, centers of academic excellence. Dale Schunk commented on his Stanford roots:

Being at Stanford was helpful. It was a wonderful environment to prepare for an academic career. The professors really took seriously the task of preparing future scholars. It was a wonderful environment because I was able to work closely with well-known people such as Al Bandura, Herb Clark, and Nate Gage. I was their research assistant, and all of them made sure that I learned what I needed to learn. I give the professors there a lot of credit for that.[7]

Tamara van Gog valued her graduate training at the Open University of the Netherlands. She said: "Because I was in an environment that was highly productive, well-known, and internationally oriented, I got to do a lot of symposia at international conferences with leading researchers and research groups from around the world. We were well connected at the Open University. Those connections helped my work and established visibility."[8]

Budding scholars wisely gravitated to graduate school centers of excellence to work with a particular mentor. Erika Patall gravitated to Duke University for her graduate studies because of what began as a chance occurrence. While she was working as a research assistant at the University of South Florida, Patall said that a colleague who had attended Duke "just wouldn't shut up about how awesome Duke was."[9] Patall investigated and applied because Duke professor Harris Cooper "was so deeply informing educational practice,"[10] which was Patall's passion. Similarly, Logan Fiorella gravitated to the University of California, Santa Barbara to work with Richard Mayer. Fiorella had come across Mayer's work while pursuing a master's degree in human factors at the University of Central Florida. Fiorella said: "I was especially drawn to Mayer's work on multimedia learning, his scientific approach of conducting simple and systematic experiments, and his clear writing style."[11]

How can prospective students identify graduate school centers of excellence and potential mentors? Perusing websites is one way. There you can likely read about faculty interests and productivity as well as successful graduates. Another potential source is research literature. In the domain of educational psychology, there has been a series of studies identifying the most productive universities and scholars. In 2022, the most productive universities for educational psychology were the University of Maryland, College Park; Vanderbilt University; and University of Texas at Austin. The top scholars were Richard Mayer, University of California, Santa Barbara; Patricia Alexander, University of Maryland, College Park; and Logan Fiorella, University of Georgia.[12]

Sabina Neugebauer recognized the privileges that accumulated for her and others at brand-name, research-rich institutions, including prominent scholars as advisers, a wealth of infrastructure for innovative projects, and essential financial resources. She recognized that even her early-career award was privilege-linked, as only those who have previously won the award, such as her advisor, can nominate others. But Neugebauer also spoke frankly about structural inequities in the academy and how institutional privileges prevent diversification in the academy, something she found "troubling, problematic, and reflective of broader systematic inequalities."[13]

What happens if you land at an institution for graduate training without privilege and unrecognized as a center of excellence? Is your fate sealed as a second-rate academic? Not at all. Consider John Glover.[14] You might not know of him because he died more than thirty years ago at the age of forty, struck by a fallen tree. But before his untimely death, he was probably on his way to becoming one of the most productive educational psychologists on the planet. Over a sixteen-year career, he had published about a hundred articles and twenty-three books on topics pertaining to reading, memory, and creativity. His productivity was not about pedigree. His bachelors was in chemistry and education from Memphis State University. His master's in educational psychology was from Tennessee Technological University. Glover did not earn a Ph.D. research degree, instead earning an Ed.D. in educational psychology from the University of Tennessee. His first academic position spanned four years at Tennessee State University. None of Glover's academic landings would credential him to ride a fast track to academic success. So, what did? He did. As a professor at University of Nebraska–Lincoln, following his stint at Tennessee State, Glover worked smart and was relentless in his work ethic. It was rumored that Glover was at his desk typing before his coat stopped swinging on the coatrack and that he willed himself to write at least five pages every day. Glover embodied many of the qualities of successful scholars found throughout this book. For instance, he was inquisitive, a deep thinker, a voracious reader, a rigorous methodologist, an efficient worker, and one who could marshal and motivate colleagues and students to work with him. He also loved his work.

Let me add one more thing about centers of excellence. They can be fluid. They can be created. When Michael Pressley was a graduate student at the University of Minnesota, he gravitated to the University of Wisconsin for a time to work with Joel Levin who was exploring topics of learning and memory of interest to Pressley, who said: "I did seek out Joel Levin because Joel was particularly interested in some problems of children's memory that were attracting my attention. He was gracious enough to allow me to come to Wisconsin and we hit it off. There was a very healthy intellectual tension."[15] There was also a healthy collaboration as the pair went on to publish numerous articles on keyword mnemonic learning strategies. According to Levin, it was Pressley who put their collaborative exploration in motion:

The final part of my answer [as to what prompted me to conduct research on keyword mnemonics] begins and ends with my former student, long-time friend, and creatively tense collaborator, Mike Pressley, who never lets me (or anyone else who will listen!) forget whence sprang my mnemonic research efforts ... [At first], I tried to discourage him, being absolutely convinced that it was neither a scientifically nor educationally worthwhile extension of the associative-learning strategy work that we and others had been engaged in for years. As is his wont, however, Mike persevered and allowed me to come along for the ride. And the ride has been a fascinating one for the past 25 years of my career, even after Mike jumped off to pursue other interests.[16]

My own graduate students over the years have been savvy about expanding their centers of excellence by contacting other scholars inside and outside the university and inviting them to collaborate. Most of the senior scholars contacted are flattered and consent. As mentioned earlier, one of my recent advisees published seventeen articles upon graduation, most of those with outside collaborators. Creating or extending one's center of excellence can occur at any career point. Productive scholar Sabina Neugebauer routinely expands her circle of collaboration. She said:

I really enjoy working with other people. I really enjoy rich intellectual collaborations where we are co-constructing knowledge together. So I reach out to other scholars I don't know personally who are doing work in related disciplines ... someone I see presenting at a conference or someone whose article I read and loved. I see and admire their work and explore what could be a wonderful opportunity.[17]

Choose a Graduate School Providing Strong Financial Support

As mentioned, if you're choosing a graduate school, consider choosing an academic hotbed, where the best faculty and students congregate. There you'll build a cascade of multiplying advantages likely to get you well published, well connected with productive scholars near and far, and well on your way to a strong position postgraduation. But top schools and programs offer something else of prime importance: money. You can't get a good education anywhere if you can't afford it. When applying to graduate schools, you should try to locate and select ones that guarantee funding throughout your program in return for you working on research. All four of the graduate student award winners I investigated received guaranteed funding. Carly Robinson said: "When I was deciding among graduate schools, it largely came down to the funding package. Ultimately, my decision to attend Harvard was influenced by the fact that funding was unconstrained for the first two years, allowing me to focus solely on my research

without having to worry about securing funding through lab work."
In those two years, Robinson published, applied for external grants,
and used her time to advance her research agenda. She argued that
"those resources were indispensable in enabling me to efficiently
manage time and pursue my research interests."[1]

Sirui Wan stressed the importance of having funding lined up for the
entirety of one's graduate school program, as he did at the University
of California, Irvine, a school that guarantees all graduate students at
least five years of funding, with a possibility for a sixth and seventh year.
Wan said: "I think that [long-term funding] is super important because
once you have that kind of financial security, you can focus on your own
research and development. The funding allowed me a lot of time to
pursue my own research interests and work on my own projects. It's
definitely an important factor for graduate school success."[2]

Align Yourself with a Strong Mentor ... or Two

Remember Howard Gardner[1] found that extraordinary creators gravitated to centers of excellence. They also sought out and learned from
influential mentors. Psychoanalyst Sigmund Freud was mentored by
several scholars including Ernst Brücke at the University of Vienna
who guided Freud in his research on brain anatomy and histology.
Another mentor was Wilhelm Fliess who joined Freud in controversial
speculation about sexual disorders. Rimsky-Korsakov mentored composer Igor Stravinsky. He helped his pupil with orchestration and used
his influence to get Stravinsky's compositions performed.
Choreographer and dancer Martha Graham was mentored by Louis
Horst, a pianist and composer, who was one of the first to teach
choreography as a distinct discipline.

Productive scholars credited their mentors for teaching, directing,
and supporting them. And recent data verify the importance of having
a productive mentor. Productivity lists reveal that productive early-
career scholars were mentored by productive scholars.[2]

One of those early-career scholars was Logan Fiorella who called his
advisor, Richard Mayer, "the single biggest influence on my professional life" and said that Mayer "laid the foundation for how to
develop a solid system of research." Most importantly, Mayer taught
him his "systematic approach for generating specific research questions
and for designing simple experiments to address those questions."

Just like Mayer, Fiorella wants the whole of his research output to "tell a coherent and flowing story." He also credits Mayer with influencing his "big picture" view of research outcomes, saying that both he and Mayer seek to uncover "general principles and themes rather than specific details," and that they are, therefore, more "lumpers than splitters." Toward this integrative end, Fiorella said that Mayer also stressed "imposing your own structure on the literature." For instance, rather than reporting on studies individually, Mayer advised "finding key themes and principles across studies and synthesizing those in your own way." Fiorella also credits Mayer with teaching him how to write "clearly and concisely" thereby making him a "stickler for writing, always spending a lot of time trying to make sure that my writing is clear and makes sense." Fiorella also said that Mayer modeled a "machinelike work ethic" that gets things accomplished and results in a lot of publications. Finally, Mayer also provided Fiorella with opportunities many graduate students would not normally have such as coauthoring a book on generative learning strategies and opening doors to collaborations with other well-known scholars because Mayer is "someone everyone knows." Fiorella has done enough independent work to get out from under Mayer's long shadow, but as for future collaborations, he said: "We work really well together. I love working with Rich and have no plans to stop."[3]

Richard Mayer, meanwhile, credited his own advisor:

I've been extremely fortunate to work with a lot of talented people who've gotten me interested in a lot of good research questions. I was really fortunate to work with Jim Greeno, my advisor, at the University of Michigan. That was a life transforming experience. Without that, I'm sure that my career would be completely different. I owe a lot to Jim and the University of Michigan.[4]

Another early-career scholar who benefited from having a productive mentor was Erika Patall.[5] Patall's mentor, Harris Cooper, navigated her through several career-altering moments. Early in Patall's program, Cooper laid out various directions for motivation research and encouraged Patall to choose one. According to Patall, "[Cooper] was like, 'Pick your identity today.' Then he laid out five topics that he thought were important directions motivation research would go and said, 'I think you can make one of these broad areas your thing. Get started finding a topic.'" Patall ironically chose to explore the effect of choice on intrinsic motivation and still explores that topic today. Cooper also trained and advised Patall to conduct a meta-analysis on her newfound topic. It was the first of several meta-analyses Patall conducted. In fact, Patall credits much of her success to her meta-analysis work. Patall said: "Let me be honest. Just because I've won these early career awards doesn't necessarily mean that I've produced the most. I don't think that's true. I think I've produced work that people have somehow noticed." Patall explained that meta-analyses "get noticed, get cited a lot, and will almost always be published." This early foray into meta-analyses introduced Patall to the research method for which she is best known and most cited. Finally, Cooper convinced Patall to broaden her eventual job search beyond local positions of convenience to the best national jobs available. Patall was considering limiting her job search to local universities. Cooper resisted and encouraged Patall to apply for jobs across the country – about sixty in total – and was adamant that she should pursue any offers that came from prominent universities. Ultimately, Patall followed this advice and accepted the prestigious assistant professor offer from the University of Texas at Austin. If Patall had not followed Cooper's advice to pursue opportunities outside her geographic area, then perhaps she never would have become the prominent researcher she is today.

Barry Zimmerman credits his advisor for much of his success. He said:

A key influence on my thinking and development was my mentor at the University of Arizona, John Bergan. Jack was an ideal scholar – a thoughtful man who impressed me with his awareness of the latest research literature and the rigor of scientific analysis. He showed me how to develop psychometric scales, apply statistics, and build conceptual models. Jack stood out because of his great respect for our discipline and the scholarship on which it rested.[6]

Patricia Alexander, speaking about her mentor, Ruth Garner, said: "When I met Ruth at the University of Maryland, where I got my Ph.D., it set my life on a trajectory that I still pursue. She was a superb role model for what it means to be a scholar, and I took those lessons to heart."[7] She pointed out: "Ours was a special bond that I still treasure today. Ruth revealed the power of mentoring to this young academic – a power I try to emulate with each of my doctoral students ... Ruth

Garner opened the universe of educational research to me, and I will be forever in her debt."[8] Speaking about the role of mentors in general, Alexander commented: "No one gets to the point of any of us [productive scholars], senior members of the community, without others supporting, guiding, and mentoring us. Everyone who is successful had a successful mentor, advisor, or guide somewhere in their life."[9]

Why not have two advisors, or more? Early-career scholar Ming-Te Wang had two synergistic advisors during his Harvard doctoral program. One was Robert Selman who pushed Wang to "think like a theorist"[10] and encouraged him to develop a researcher identity. Wang's other doctoral advisor was John Willett, a renowned statistician, who taught him advanced statistical methods, which allowed Wang to conduct complex quantitative research such as longitudinal data analysis. Wang had a third mentor during his postdoctoral position at Michigan. Postdoctoral advisor Jacquelynne Eccles guided Wang in how to think like a principal investigator and in how to write proposals for multimillion-dollar grants.

All four award-winning graduate student scholars had multiple mentors – all of them. Hyun Ji Lee had two mentors with unique strengths, Sung-Il Kim and Mimi Bong. Lee said: "During my doctoral program, Dr. Kim taught me how to approach new research topics and develop interesting research ideas. Dr. Kim had a talent for generating creative ideas and designing rigorous experiments. Meanwhile, Dr. Bong was skilled in statistical analysis and writing. Therefore, I learned a great deal from both of them and became a complete researcher."[11]

Sirui Wan also had two mentors with unique strengths. Mentor Drew Bailey stressed research fundamentals such as research design, coding and programming, manuscript writing, and responding to reviewers. On the other hand, mentor Jacquelynne Eccles provided expertise on the pair's shared motivation research topic and on attaining graduate school and career success. In addition, Wan's program "encouraged students to work with multiple faculty members in other research areas, to be a floater."[12] This latitude spurred Wan to also collaborate with others doing cognitive experimental research.

Apparently, sometimes two mentors are just not enough. Carly Robinson had three. While pursuing a doctoral degree at Harvard University, Robinson continued to work unofficially with her master's advisor, Todd Rogers, while also working with her assigned doctoral advisor Hunter Gehlback. When Gehlback left Harvard for another institution, Robinson worked with a new advisor, Monica Higgins. Gehlback, though, continued to advise Robinson unofficially from afar, meeting with her weekly via Zoom and providing detailed feedback on her work. Robinson said: "I had excellent mentorship and advice that was coming from all these different angles."[13]

Hyewon Lee also had three mentors who provided excellent academic training but who also helped her envision her future self. All three junior faculty mentors were like her: Asian females who transitioned to the United States for their Ph.D.s, had English as a second language, and had families of their own. Lee said: "A great thing was looking at their personal lives: How they handle their family roles and their roles as faculty members. Seeing them, I could more clearly imagine myself with the same future."[14]

I too had a rich and career-altering mentorship experience at Florida State University under the advisement of Dr. Harold Fletcher. Here is a sample of his support and influence. I fell in love with educational psychology in college and felt called to the profession. I applied to about a dozen educational psychology doctoral programs throughout the USA and was accepted by most. I whittled the list of acceptances down to about four and called a faculty member at each institution asking if they would give me an assistantship teaching educational psychology. One offered a research assistantship, two promised to find a funding source when I enrolled, and Fletcher said: "Give me a couple hours." An hour later, he called back and offered me a teaching assistantship.

When I arrived in Tallahassee, I had no place to stay. Fletcher and his wife graciously invited me to stay with them in their home until I secured lodging. Fletcher seemed especially motivated to help me secure housing after a few days and many meals, circling prospective rentals in the morning newspaper.

A few weeks into my graduate studies, I had doubts about pursuing a doctorate in educational psychology. Perhaps the program in instructional design was a better fit. Fletcher sat me in his office, lit his pipe, puffed it several times, filling the room with smoke, looked me square in the eyes, and smugly said these nerve-seeking words: "If you switch programs, you'll never be able to call yourself an educational psychologist." Gulp. Message received.

It was Fletcher who taught me how to write. When I wrote something, I was summoned to his home to review it. We sat in Fletcher's study, his pipe ablaze. "Okay, read it to me," he'd say. What, I have an advisor who can't read, I thought. As I read, Fletcher was a rapid-fire writing error detector and corrector. "Stop, your sentence is not parallel, say it this way ... Stop, move the subject up front in the sentence ... Stop, use the active voice ... Stop, anxious is the wrong word, you mean eager ... Stop, choose a more active verb like consult or confer ..."

Fletcher offered sage advice on other matters. Regarding failure, he advised: "Learn to live with failure, just don't live with it too long." Regarding my graduate school tenure, Fletcher said: "No sense sticking around here too long, you might as well get paid for doing what you are doing anyway." Under Fletcher's tutelage, I dashed from B.A. to Ph.D. in just three years. Fletcher's parting advice each time we met was this: "Stay with it now." What wonderful advice. No matter how daunting something might appear, stick with it and success will follow.

Perhaps Fletcher's most pointed advice was offered as I approached my first job interview. Naturally, I was summoned to his home to plan and practice. "Would you like a cup of coffee?" Fletcher offered upon my arrival. "No thanks," I casually replied. "What do you mean you don't want coffee?" Fletcher bellowed. "You're offered coffee at your interview, you take it, even if you don't like coffee. It's a social and bonding gesture. Of course, you accept the coffee." And on it went. What I should wear, what I should ask them, the importance of connecting with students, what I should say if someone asks about my research during a casual two-minute encounter, whether I should drink beer at dinner (yes, if others do, but just one!). He had me practice my job talk, critiquing my slides, my words, my body language. No one was ever so prepared for their inaugural interview. Result: Job offer!

Of course, Fletcher guided me through my research on note taking, six empirical studies and a literature review, all published following graduation. And Fletcher's mentorship continued postgraduation. As I set out for my first academic position, Fletcher cautioned: "Don't let them take you for granted. Keep them thinking you might leave if not appreciated. Rent, don't buy. Keep a couple unpacked boxes in your office. Walk around with a toothbrush in your pocket." Got it! Message received and followed.

Don't Forget about Peer Mentors

Some graduate programs set new students up with peer mentors, well-established graduate students who can teach the newbies the ropes. If as a graduate student you are not assigned a peer mentor, request one or seek one out on your own. Peers know a lot of things advisors don't know. When graduate students ask me about program requirements, departmental assistantships, online offerings, how to get to Varner Hall, or the best place to grab an espresso on campus, I'm clueless. I refer them to an experienced student who's been around the block – or at least campus – a few times.

Peers, though, can do more than teach new students the ropes. They can be gateways to scholarly activities and products. Carol Dweck said: "My peer group was amazing. We mentored each other completely. We talked research all the time. That was incredibly valuable."[1] Tamara van Gog also credited her doctoral cohort: "There was a whole group of motivating and productive fellow Ph.D. candidates who are now also prominent educational researchers. It was a very good group that attracted a lot of international scholars and helped me be productive and expand my network."[2] As a graduate student at the University of California, Los Angeles, Jacquelynne Eccles was part of a cohort of female graduate students who mentored one another. Eccles noted that she and the other female students had minimal access to faculty mentors because all the faculty were men and "none of the male faculty particularly wanted to mentor a female student."[3] Although Alexander Renkl, Hans Gruber, and Frank Fischer were dutifully and wonderfully mentored by Heinz Mandl at Ludwig Maximillian University of Munich, the three proteges relied on one another for peer mentorship and collaboration, which continues today, well after they moved on to academic positions.[4]

A peer mentor might even be a graduate. In addition to linking new graduate students with advanced graduate students, I also link them with successful program graduates. Doing so provides new students with an experienced and successful advice source, a well-known collaborator, and especially with a role model of their "possible selves." I tell them: "Look what so-and-so accomplished when they passed through these halls. You can do that too."

Strike a Balance: Be a Self-Starter but Open to Advice

German scholar Hans Gruber advises graduate students to strike a balance between independence from and dependence on one's advisors:

There are some students who have very independent ideas and insist on their ideas [and work independently on them]. My experience tells me that, in most cases, that doesn't work well because they insist on being so independent that they don't ask for advice. Some students are too dependent and ask for help every step. They always run to us and ask if it's okay to do this and that.[1]

I concur. I've had advisees work independently on research projects, even dissertations, and only share their work after spending a lot of time reviewing literature, planning a study, and creating materials. This is too late to seek guidance. The feedback I give at that point might throw cold water on project conception, theory, application, and tractability, necessitating sweeping changes or a complete restart.

Graduate students should not only seek guidance and feedback from their advisors throughout the research process but also from committee members. As a dissertation committee member, I sometimes see the completed proposal or dissertation for the first time just prior to formal defense meetings rather than in preliminary stages. Many a dissertation has been shot down at the defense by committee members who are just now seeing the completed product for the first time. Graduate students should certainly keep committee members in the loop as they proceed and take advantage of their expertise.

On the flip side, some students are too dependent as Gruber suggests, seeking input at every twist and turn without first generating their own ideas. Dick Anderson advises students to "first, think, talk, discuss, search your own feelings,"[2] before seeking input from others. When students do turn to advisors or committee members for council, they should bring their ideas to them in written form. Doing so forces students to more carefully think things through and to better articulate their ideas for others to evaluate. Logan Fiorella insists on written updates. He said: "I like to have something concrete in writing that we can review together rather than just talking, so I usually require a one-page summary for which I can offer explicit feedback."[3]

Approach Coursework Strategically

Maybe you've heard this old graduate school yarn. A student brags to a professor about never having received a grade less than A throughout graduate school. The professor replies: "I guess you weren't doing enough research." Good point. When graduates go on the job market, suitors never look at transcripts or ask about grades. Their main concern is usually research productivity.

Of course, graduate students must take courses, usually a lot of them. But there is leeway in the courses chosen and what is derived from them. The award-winning graduate students I investigated pushed that leeway to their advantage. Carly Robinson chose research methods courses over other elective courses because they directly advanced her ability to conduct research. Robinson also choose content electives requiring written projects, saying: "The most useful content classes were those which had ongoing project assignments or deliverables, because I could write literature reviews that I eventually used for writing manuscripts and dissertation."[1]

Of course, graduate students should embrace learning opportunists beyond the classroom. Hyun Ji Lee certainly did. Lee said:

Beyond my required coursework, I took workshops and used online resources to learn different research methodologies and master advanced quantitative methods. I also learned a lot from my senior lab members presenting their research in the lab and my advisors' feedback of their work. By learning from senior lab members and advisors, budding scholars can develop essential skills and knowledge that will help them become more successful researchers in the future.[2]

Hyewon Lee also acquired topical information and writing skills outside the classroom through reading. She said: "I was reading lots of articles in my research area, perhaps 100 toward each publication. As I read, I would feel like I was having a conversation with the authors. Some articles I read over and over again, because I was so impressed by the authors' writing, their tone of voice, or the way they made a story out of their studies. These journal articles would raise the standards of my research design and writing."[3]

Don't Rush through Graduate Training

Securing an academic position is highly competitive. As a freshly minted graduate you'll be competing with other recent graduates for postdoc positions or assistant professor positions. Your graduate student publication record matters.

Among the four graduate student award winners, the average time spent completing graduate school was seven years.[1] While in graduate school, the quartet had nine publications on average. All of them secured postdoc positions upon graduation at elite institutions: Brown University, Ohio State University, Texas A&M University, and the University of Wisconsin.

Among the six early-career award winners investigated,[2] time in graduate school ranged from four to six years, and graduate school publication totals ranged from two to eleven, with a median of five. Three of the six secured assistant professor positions immediately out of graduate school at Research 1 institutions, while the other three took postdoctoral fellowships, which kept them focused on scholarly training for another two to three years. All of them also secured faculty positions at Research 1 institutions upon postdoctoral completion.

The point is that none of the graduate student award winners or early-career award-winning scholars was in a hurry to complete graduate school, understanding that more graduate training would produce more valuable experience, a fuller CV, and greater chances securing postdoc or research-based faculty positions. There are many strong candidates on the job market and you want to amass a record that distinguishes you.

But Don't Dawdle

Although most Ph.D. programs are designed to complete in four or five years once a master's degree is in hand, the average time to completion in 2020 was between six and twelve years, with physical sciences degrees taking about six years, humanities and arts about ten years, and education about twelve years.[1] Certainly there is a lot of heavy lifting in completing a doctoral degree. There is advanced coursework, comprehensive exams, dissertation proposal, and dissertation. Students might also have teaching, research, or fellowship responsibilities. On top of that, some students have family obligations and employment outside their graduate training. Still … twelve years?

When I entered my doctoral program at Florida State University with only a bachelor's degree in hand, my advisor told me: "Don't dawdle. Get in and get out. You might as well get paid as an assistant professor for doing what you'll be doing here." I followed my advisor's dictum. I graduated in three years. During that span, I also spent two years fulfilling a teaching assistantship, one year fulfilling a research assistantship, and conducted six unique experiments pertaining to note taking, my dissertation topic. It was likely helpful that I was single, lived alone in a garage without heat, and was a thousand miles removed from New York family and friends.

Productive scholar Patricia Alexander raced through her doctoral program too, completing her Ph.D. just two years after securing her master's. Alexander was motivated to complete her doctoral degree before she died. No kidding. She had been diagnosed with a terminal illness and told she had one year to live. Despite the news, Alexander entered graduate school at the University of Maryland, near to where her parents lived so that her one-year-old son could have stability. Why graduate school? Alexander said: "I went to graduate school because I wanted to use my mind to the utmost before I lost it." Racing against the clock, she doubled her coursework, studied day and night, and earned her degree in two years. Alexander said: "I lived every day as if I was dying, and I still do. I never take any day for granted."[2]

Completing your graduate degree in just a few years can certainly be accomplished.

Consider Doing a Postdoc at a Center of Excellence

To postdoc or not to postdoc? That is the question. Among the award-winning graduate students I investigated, all four took postdoc positions following graduation, and all in top-tier universities: Texas A&M University, Ohio State University, Brown University, and the University of Wisconsin.[1] Among productive scholars I investigated, some did postdocs rather than enter the academy immediately following graduate training. This was especially true for more recent scholars.

After completing her doctoral degree, Sabina Neugebauer pondered whether to pursue a faculty position or accept a two-year postdoctoral fellowship with the Institute of Education Sciences (IES) at the University of Connecticut. Her inclination was to "rush toward getting tenure." Neugebauer's advisor, Catherine Snow, advised her to accept the postdoctoral fellowship, aware of the advantages this opportunity would bring to Neugebauer. Neugebauer accepted the postdoctoral fellowship and credits it for "jumpstarting" her career and allowing her to "solve problems of interest." Neugebauer said that "most post-doc fellowships tie a scholar to another scholar's research agenda. You're a resource for an existing project and not able to explore your own intellectual ideas." Such was not the case with the IES fellowship. Neugebauer was free to pursue her own interests while receiving "mentoring and guidance from eminent scholars," which allowed her "to observe from beginning to end how productive scholars carry out the lifecycle of a project, to see how an idea comes to be, and how that project is brought to fruition." Neugebauer continued: "So, while I was concentrating on my own work, I also had this really wonderful opportunity to watch these eminent scholars engage in that process." The postdoc benefits did not end there for Neugebauer but continued on into her eventual assistant professor position. She said: "From a time efficiency standpoint, my postdoc really set me up for success so that I could spend the time I had as a new faculty member in a school of education, with heavy service and teaching demands, mining that data and turning it into papers, as opposed to the more onerous process of data collection."[2]

Ming-Te Wang also pursued a postdoc fellowship after receiving his doctorate from Harvard. Interestingly, he had postdoc offers from Stanford, Yale, and Michigan. Wang chose Michigan even though Stanford and Yale offered a higher salary. Wang chose to work with Jacquelynne Eccles at Michigan because Eccles had access to a large, longitudinal data set that Wang could mine. Eccles told Wang: "We can't give you more money, but we can give you plenty of data to work with."[3]

Rebecca Collie chose the postdoctoral route too, securing a three-year postdoctoral position at the University of New South Wales where she worked with Andrew Martin who offered untold advice about research, writing, and academia. Collie said:

If you start out as an assistant professor, you must navigate the hidden curriculum in academia on your own. You might wonder, "Do I do it this way or that way? I guess I have to try this way." Then if it doesn't work, you must go back and do it the other way. But at the time [starting as a postdoctoral fellow], I could just go across the hallway, knock on Andrew's door, and say, "Hey, Andrew, do you have any advice about how I should approach this?" Or "should I use this theory?" There were countless times where I asked Andrew questions about how things worked in publishing or how to best navigate a reviewer's comment. Having the ability to ask questions and have them answered quickly was fantastic.[4]

Mareike Kunter also credits her time doing a postdoc at the Max Plank Institute in Germany as her most influential period. "It was really a unique atmosphere there. Everyone worked very hard, was very dedicated, and was very interested in the work."[5]

Speaking of Germany, newly minted Ph.D.s must complete an habilitation experience, similar to a postdoc experience in other countries, before attaining professor status in the German system. After receiving their Ph.D.s, German scholars Hans Gruber and Alexander Renkl gravitated to the Ludwig Maximilian University of Munich in 1991 to work under the mentorship of Heinz Mandl. In the ensuing years, the trio authored an astounding 143 collaborative works, completing projects that emphasized or combined the scholars' professional identities.[6] The habilitation pair also gleaned important lessons from their experience with Mandl that they brought to their eventual professor positions. Renkl credits his habilitation experience for making scholarly productivity a priority:

I grew up in a very rich academic environment where it was clear that you had to be productive ... I think it's important for young students to go to a productive group because I think you adapt to what others do. If you're in the Mandl group and all the others are publishing, then you want to do the same. If you're in a group with people who are only publishing once a year, then you do the same thing.[7]

Gruber attributed his tireless work ethic to his habilitation work with Mandl: "Heinz would arrive at the office sometime between 5:00 and 7:00 a.m. Heinz was certainly a workaholic. He never asked us to be similar, but we certainly learned that from him."[8]

Gravitate to Centers of Career Excellence

Productive scholars also recognize the importance of landing jobs in academic centers of excellence. For example, Carol Dweck has had professorships at Illinois, Harvard, Columbia, and Stanford. Here is what Dweck said about the support she has received along the way:

My first job was at the University of Illinois in developmental psychology. Everyone in the program shared their resources with me, invited me to join symposia, took me under their wing, and introduced me to school principals who opened their schools to me for research. It just could not have been a more supportive environment. And now at Stanford, people are so supportive of each other in untold ways. I've been fortunate to be at the institutions I've been at.[1]

Rebecca Collie and Barry Zimmerman are among the other scholars who credited their academic institutions for their resources and support. Collie holds a four-year research fellowship offered by her university, University of New South Wales Sydney, that has been central to her productivity.[2] Zimmerman said: "I have spent most of my career at the Graduate School of the City University of New York. It has been an ideal setting because of its singular focus on doctoral education. I have had the opportunity to mentor [and publish with] wonderfully dedicated students."[3]

And don't think that only a few big-name schools can boost career trajectory. Career boosting can happen most anywhere when dedicated and supportive people supply the footholds. Such was the case for me when I joined the psychology department at Utah State University. I was paid to conduct research in the summer session preceding my fall appointment, although I was a thousand miles away. Upon my arrival they had built me a new double-roomed office. I was assigned two graduate assistants who worked with me on teaching and research. Every travel or professional request I made was met. And I was encouraged to seek tenure and promotion following my first year.

Seek Mentors as a Junior Faculty Member

Finally earning your doctorate does not mean that you can no longer benefit from having a mentor. Most recent graduates in higher education find council among the professoriate. At my institution, all junior faculty are assigned a mentor to guide and support them. Mentors can also be sought outside one's university. Consider Marilla Svinicki. As a newly minted assistant professor at the University of Texas at Austin, Svinicki became a follower of Bill McKeachie, a renowned University of Michigan professor who specialized in learning and motivation and who authored the world's most-read book on teaching, *McKeachie's Teaching Tips*. Svinicki was enamored with McKeachie's ideas from afar. She said: "I never had a class with him, never researched with him. Nevertheless, I read his work and said, this is what I believe. This is what I want to do. I wanted to study how learning and motivation play out in the real world."[1]

Her University of Texas at Austin colleague, Claire Weinstein, was a close friend of McKeachie's and she arranged for the two to meet at a conference. Svinicki said: "Once I met Bill face-to-face, I think we both knew that the other was someone with similar motivations and models of learning. Bill was the kind of person I wanted to be, both personally and professionally. I used to ask myself, 'What would Bill do in this situation?'"[2]

Their like interests led to McKeachie serving as an informal mentor. Svinicki said: "Bill was my mentor from a distance. Like me, he was the kind of person who wanted to pull ideas together to make education more effective. I admired him as a scientist, a pragmatist, a creator, a stimulating thinker, and one of the kindest, most generous, most modest persons I had ever met."[3]

McKeachie's mentorship helped Svinicki grow as a scholar and opened professional doors. McKeachie read Svinicki's work and offered unsolicited feedback. He recommended her for speaking engagements at campuses where he had been invited to speak. He introduced her to other influential scholars, which led to more self-growth opportunities and visibility. Most importantly, McKeachie eventually invited Svinicki to coedit *Teaching Tips*, his long-running bestseller, in 2014. The pair worked together on two editions before McKeachie retired and handed his beloved project over to Svinicki.[4]

How different Svinicki's career might have been if she had not met McKeachie and benefited from his distant mentorship. Let this be a lesson to reach out to those whose work you admire. Perhaps you'll find a collaborator or even a mentor to help guide and support you.

Gravitate to Centers of Excellence for Collaborations

Productive scholars also seek stimulation outside their institutions by gravitating temporarily to other intellectual hotbeds for sabbaticals or less formal meetings. Barry Zimmerman said:

I am especially indebted to Al Bandura whose influence on me was profound. I was introduced to Al early in my career and came to know him personally as well as professionally. I found him to be a warm and encouraging person with a wonderful sense of humor. He invited me to contribute to books he edited. Later, I spent a sabbatical leave conducting research with Al, and we jointly published several studies that focused on links between self-efficacy- and self-regulation.[1]

Michael Pressley was seemingly always on the go visiting colleagues at various institutions like Notre Dame, Kansas, and Nebraska. Three times in the mid-1980s he visited the Max Planck Institute for Psychology and Education in Munich, Germany.[2]

Some collaborations naturally mix business and pleasure. Richard Anderson talked about the informal trips he took at the dawn of the cognitive revolution to meet with like-minded colleagues who formed the Epistemic Society to understand what the mind knows and how it knows it. "We met a couple of times a year and you know this wasn't the sort of thing where you got your department chair to approve the plane fare. Hell, we simply piled in our cars and drove down there … Our favorite place was Nashville where there was also Bluegrass to be heard."[3]

For me, annual conferences, both national and regional, have served as centers of excellence for meeting colleagues near and far, familiar and new. Many an evening was spent at conference receptions and hotel lounges plotting research studies and sketching out what we thought were innovative research questions and designs on cocktail napkins. Come morning, some of those ideas were legible and even feasible.

References

Get Solid Training

1 *skyprep.* https://skyprep.com/2013/07/29/15-inspiration-learning-and-training-quotes/.

Gravitate to Centers of Graduate School Excellence

2 Gardner, H. (1993). *Creating minds.* New York: Basic Books.
3 Kiewra, K. A., & Creswell, J. W. (2000). Conversations with three highly productive educational psychologists: Richard Anderson, Richard Mayer, and Michael Pressley. *Educational Psychology Review, 12,* 135–161.

4   Kiewra, K. A., Luo, L., & Flanigan, A. (2021). Educational psychology early career award winners: How did they do it? *Educational Psychology Review*, *33*, 1981–2018 (p. 2004).

5   Ibid. (no page numbers designated).

6   Ibid., p. 1991.

7   Patterson-Hazley, M., & Kiewra, K. A. (2013). Conversations with four highly productive educational psychologists: Patricia Alexander, Richard Mayer, Dale Schunk, and Barry Zimmerman. *Educational Psychology Review*, *25*, 19–45 (p. 29).

8   Prinz, A., Zeeb, H., Flanigan, A., Renkl, A., & Kiewra, K. A. (2020). Conversations with five highly successful female educational psychologists: Patricia Alexander, Carol Dweck, Jacquelynne Eccles, Mareike Kunter, and Tamara van Gog. *Educational Psychology Review*, *33*, 763–795 (p. 777).

9   Kiewra, K. A., Luo, L., & Flanigan, A. (2021). Educational psychology early career award winners: How did they do it? *Educational Psychology Review*, *33*, 1981–2018 (p. 2005).

10 Ibid.

11 Ibid., p. 1990.

12 Fong, C. J., Flanigan, A. E., Hogan, E., et al. (2022). Individual and institutional productivity in educational psychology journals from 2015 to 2021. *Educational Psychology Review*, *34*, 2379–2403.

13 Kiewra, K. A., Luo, L., & Flanigan, A. (2021). Educational psychology early career award winners: How did they do it? *Educational Psychology Review*, *33*, 1981–2018. (p. 1994).

14 Kiewra, K. A., & Kauffman, D. (2023). John Glover: A long overdue account of his productive scholarship methods. *Educational Psychology Review*, *35*, Article 56.

15 Kiewra, K. A., & Creswell, J. W. (2000). Conversations with three highly productive educational psychologists: Richard Anderson, Richard Mayer, and Michael Pressley. *Educational Psychology Review*, *12*, 135–161 (p. 148).

16 Levin, J. R., & Shaughnessy, M. F. (2003). An interview with Joel Levin. *Educational Psychology Review*, *15*, 297–309 (p. 300).

17 Kiewra, K. A., Luo, L., & Flanigan, A. (2021). Educational psychology early career award winners: How did they do it? *Educational Psychology Review*, *33*, 1981–2018 (p. 1996).

Choose a Graduate School Providing Strong Financial Support

1   Kiewra, K. A., Hasnin, S., Soundy, J., Premkumar, P. K., & Labenz, C. (2023). Graduate student award winners in educational psychology:

What made them successful? *Educational Psychology Review*, *35*, Article 90.

2 Ibid.

Align Yourself with a Strong Mentor ... or Two

1 Gardner, H. (1993). *Creating minds*. New York: Basic Books.

2 Fong, C. J., Flanigan, A. E., Hogan, E., et al. (2022). Individual and institutional productivity in educational psychology journals from 2015 to 2021. *Educational Psychology Review*, *34*, 2379–2403.

3 Kiewra, K. A., Luo, L., & Flanigan, A. (2021). Educational psychology early career award winners: How did they do it? *Educational Psychology Review*, *33*, 1981–2018 (pp. 1998–1999).

4 Patterson-Hazley, M., & Kiewra, K. A. (2013). Conversations with four highly productive educational psychologists: Patricia Alexander, Richard Mayer, Dale Schunk, and Barry Zimmerman. *Educational Psychology Review*, *25*, 19–45 (p. 29).

5 Kiewra, K. A., Luo, L., & Flanigan, A. (2021). Educational psychology early career award winners: How did they do it? *Educational Psychology Review*, *33*, 1981–2018 (p. 2005).

6 Patterson-Hazley, M., & Kiewra, K. A. (2013). Conversations with four highly productive educational psychologists: Patricia Alexander, Richard Mayer, Dale Schunk, and Barry Zimmerman. *Educational Psychology Review*, *25*, 19–45 (p. 29).

7 Ibid., pp. 29–30.

8 Bembenutty, H. (2022). *Contemporary pioneers in teaching and learning*, Vol. 2. Charlotte, NC: Information Age Publishing, Inc. (pp. 88–89).

9 Patterson-Hazley, M., & Kiewra, K. A. (2013). Conversations with four highly productive educational psychologists: Patricia Alexander, Richard Mayer, Dale Schunk, and Barry Zimmerman. *Educational Psychology Review*, *25*, 19–45 (p. 30).

10 Kiewra, K. A., Luo, L., & Flanigan, A. (2021). Educational psychology early career award winners: How did they do it? *Educational Psychology Review*, *33*, 1981–2018 (p. 2009).

11 Kiewra, K. A., Hasnin, S., Soundy, J., Premkumar, P. K., & Labenz, C. (2023). Graduate student award winners in educational psychology: What made them successful? *Educational Psychology Review*, *35*, Article 90.

12 Ibid.

13 Ibid.

14 Ibid.

Don't Forget about Peer Mentors

1 Prinz, A., Zeeb, H., Flanigan, A., Renkl, A., & Kiewra, K. A. (2020). Conversations with five highly successful female educational psychologists: Patricia Alexander, Carol Dweck, Jacquelynne Eccles, Mareike Kunter, and Tamara van Gog. *Educational Psychology Review*, *33*, 763–795 (p. 775).
2 Ibid.
3 Ibid.
4 Flanigan, A., Kiewra, K. A., & Luo, L. (2018). Conversations with four highly productive German educational psychologists: Frank Fischer, Hans Gruber, Heinz Mandl, and Alexander Renkl. *Educational Psychology Review*, *30*, 303–330.

Strike a Balance: Be a Self-Starter but Open to Advice

1 Flanigan, A., Kiewra, K. A., & Luo, L. (2018). Conversations with four highly productive German educational psychologists: Frank Fischer, Hans Gruber, Heinz Mandl, and Alexander Renkl. *Educational Psychology Review*, *30*, 303–330 (p. 322).
2 Kiewra, K. A., & Creswell, J. W. (2000). Conversations with three highly productive educational psychologists: Richard Anderson, Richard Mayer, and Michael Pressley. *Educational Psychology Review*, *12*, 135–161 (p. 142).
3 Kiewra, K. A., Luo, L., & Flanigan, A. (2021). Educational psychology early career award winners: How did they do it? *Educational Psychology Review*, *33*, 1981–2018 (p. 1990).

Approach Coursework Strategically

1 Kiewra, K. A., Hasnin, S., Soundy, J., Premkumar, P. K., & Labenz, C. (2023). Graduate student award winners in educational psychology: What made them successful? *Educational Psychology Review*, *35*, Article 90.
2 Ibid.
3 Ibid.

Don't Rush through Graduate Training

1 Kiewra, K. A., Hasnin, S., Soundy, J., Premkumar, P. K., & Labenz, C. (2023). Graduate student award winners in educational psychology:

What made them successful? *Educational Psychology Review, 35,* Article 90.

2 Kiewra, K. A., Luo, L., & Flanigan, A. (2021). Educational psychology early career award winners: How did they do it? *Educational Psychology Review, 33,* 1981–2018.

But Don't Dawdle

1 How long does it take to get a PhD? (May 4, 2022). *Coursera.* www .coursera.org/articles/how-long-does-it-take-to-get-a-phd.

2 Patterson-Hazley, M., & Kiewra, K. A. (2013). Conversations with four highly productive educational psychologists: Patricia Alexander, Richard Mayer, Dale Schunk, and Barry Zimmerman. *Educational Psychology Review, 25,* 19–45 (p. 30).

Consider Doing a Postdoc at a Center of Excellence

1 Kiewra, K. A., Hasnin, S., Soundy, J., Premkumar, P. K., & Labenz, C. (2023). Graduate student award winners in educational psychology: What made them successful? *Educational Psychology Review, 35,* Article 90.

2 Kiewra, K. A., Luo, L., & Flanigan, A. (2021). Educational psychology early career award winners: How did they do it? *Educational Psychology Review, 33,* 1981–2018 (p. 1995).

3 Ibid., p. 1993.

4 Ibid., p. 1998.

5 Prinz, A., Zeeb, H., Flanigan, A., Renkl, A., & Kiewra, K. A. (2020). Conversations with five highly successful female educational psychologists: Patricia Alexander, Carol Dweck, Jacquelynne Eccles, Mareike Kunter, and Tamara van Gog. *Educational Psychology Review, 33,* 763–795 (p. 777).

6 Flanigan, A., Kiewra, K. A., & Luo, L. (2018). Conversations with four highly productive German educational psychologists: Frank Fischer, Hans Gruber, Heinz Mandl, and Alexander Renkl. *Educational Psychology Review, 30,* 303–330.

7 Ibid., p. 316.

8 Ibid., p. 317.

Gravitate to Centers of Career Excellence

1 Prinz, A., Zeeb, H., Flanigan, A., Renkl, A., & Kiewra, K. A. (2020). Conversations with five highly successful female educational

psychologists: Patricia Alexander, Carol Dweck, Jacquelynne Eccles, Mareike Kunter, and Tamara van Gog. *Educational Psychology Review*, *33*, 763–795 (p. 777)

2 Kiewra, K. A., Luo, L., & Flanigan, A. (2021). Educational psychology early career award winners: How did they do it? *Educational Psychology Review*, *33*, 1981–2018.

3 Patterson-Hazley, M., & Kiewra, K. A. (2013). Conversations with four highly productive educational psychologists: Patricia Alexander, Richard Mayer, Dale Schunk, and Barry Zimmerman. *Educational Psychology Review*. *25*, 19–45 (p. 29).

Seek Mentors as a Junior Faculty Member

1 Bembenutty, H. (2022). *Contemporary pioneers in teaching and learning*, Vol. 2. Charlotte, NC: Information Age Publishing, Inc. (p. 189).

2 Ibid., p. 190.

3 Ibid., p. 189.

4 Svinicki, M., & McKeachie, W. (2014). *McKeachie's teaching tips: Strategies, research, and theory for college and university teachers*. Boston, MA: Cengage Learning.

Gravitate to Centers of Excellence for Collaborations

1 Patterson-Hazley, M., & Kiewra, K. A. (2013). Conversations with four highly productive educational psychologists: Patricia Alexander, Richard Mayer, Dale Schunk, and Barry Zimmerman. *Educational Psychology Review*, *25*, 19–45 (p. 29).

2 Kiewra, K. A., & Creswell, J. W. (2000). Conversations with three highly productive educational psychologists: Richard Anderson, Richard Mayer, and Michael Pressley. *Educational Psychology Review*, *12*, 135–161.

3 Ibid., p. 148.

3 | *Find Your Path*

The path from dreams to success does exist. May you have the vision to find it, the courage to get on to it, and the perseverance to follow it.

Kalpana Chawla[1]

There is no one clear path to scholarly success. As you'll see throughout this book, a productive scholar might be raised by academic parents, or not; might have previously been an educator, or not; might have had a postdoctoral experience, or not; might be in a writing group, or not; might work extreme hours, or not; might be married to another academic, or not ... Still, there are clearly common factors associated with scholarly success, such as: influential mentors; collaborations with colleagues and students; support from institutions, colleagues, and family; dedicated and effective work routines; an emphasis on writing processes and outcomes; willingness to embrace and learn from failure; and a passion for and commitment to producing important and impactful work.

Take a Risk

There is, however, one consistent path that successful people seem to take: risk taking. Psychologist Howard Gardner, who has put forth a theory of creativity, believes that risk taking is an essential factor that can help move somebody from expert to creative. Among creators that Gardner studied, risk taking abounded.[1,2] Wolfgang Mozart and Pablo Picasso, for example, risked their prodigious success by breaking away from the early teachings of their fathers to pursue new mentors and styles. Igor Stravinsky's risk taking was evident in one of his now best-known works, *The Rite of Spring*, a musical composition so pulsating, arhythmic, and dissonant that the audience booed, honked horns, and nearly rioted. (And I'm distracted when theatergoers chew popcorn too loudly.) Mahatma Gandhi faced the ultimate risk – his freedom and even his life – in leading Indian people in peaceful resistance movements, such as the 1930 salt march to protest British taxes on salt. Gandhi's risks led to beatings, arrests, and years spent in jail.

Former NFL football coach Bruce Arians summed up the importance of risk taking succinctly: "No risk it, no biscuit."[3]

The early-career scholars I investigated took risks. Rebecca Collie was invited to write a review article on a topic outside her area. She accepted the challenge, wrote the paper, and made this new area the defining branch of her research going forward. Collie said that she has chosen the harder, riskier path throughout her career because the harder path can be "like a rolling snowball ... leading to more diverse opportunities that extend one's self."[4]

Ming-Te Wang took a risk when he chose to do a postdoc at Michigan instead of Stanford and Yale, even though the Michigan position paid substantially less. He chose Michigan because there he would have access to a large data set he could mine and hopefully jumpstart his career.[5]

Erika Patall wanted to play it safe upon graduation by applying solely to higher education institutions in her geographic area. Her advisor pushed her to take the risk of applying nationally and leaving the comforts of home. Patall did and landed an assistant professor position at a prestigious Research 1 university.[6]

My own career is marked by risk taking. It was a risk to reduce my scholarly duties to direct my university's Academic Success Center for five years. Similarly, it was a risk to assume the editor-in-chief position for a major journal for another five years. It was also a risk to move away from my primary research area of teaching and learning to begin investigating a new area: talent development. In each case, the risk was well worth the reward. I was able to help students learn, help scholars shape their work, pioneer new talent-related research directions, and inject life and joy into my career.

William Faulkner said: "You cannot swim for new horizons until you have courage to lose sight of the shore."[7]

Be Curious

Curiosity might have killed the cat, but it's a driving force in the scholarly work of productive scholars. Sabina Neugebauer said:

Uncovering patterns and making meaning of them has always been some-thing invigorating and truly pleasurable. I get really curious about things and hooked on solving them. I become laser focused. I love what I do and become immersed in it. All my projects have sent me down roads connected by the same kernel of curiosity and the same passion for promoting educational equity.[1]

Neugebauer credits her curious nature to her childhood upbringing. She said:

I was encouraged to be curious about my environment and surroundings. Our family games often involved honing observation skills. On a train, a family member might raise the question, "Did you notice anything unusual about the person sitting across from us?" Another time, we might speculate if a relative was acting differently than usual and what this might mean. I was inducted into this inquisitive way of thinking about the world: You have to observe carefully and see patterns. I grew up in a space where there were stories to be told from everyday experiences that often went unexamined.[2]

Richard Mayer also credits curiosity for his educational psychology passion and longevity. He said: "The thing that really keeps me going is my curiosity to pursue burning questions I really want to answer and to potentially discover something new and worthwhile."[3]

Richard Anderson also trumpets curiosity as he points budding scholars away from tired research topics toward finding new or understudied topics to explore. Anderson said: "Don't take the most popular problem of the day. Think, talk, discuss, search your own feelings. Ask what is important in the general area I'm working in that is poorly understood, important, but understudied, and do an analysis of that."[4]

My own career-long note-taking investigations were prompted by curiosity. In my first-ever graduate class the professor outlawed note taking, saying that note taking distracts students from really listening to and processing the lesson. He insisted that we listen and think about the material rather than record notes. So that we had written material to review, he provided students with notes following each lesson. I was curious if more is learned by note taking or listening and if instructor notes are superior to the students' own notes. I conducted six experi-ments in graduate school and many more since to tame my curiosity.

Discover Your Element

There is a wonderful book by Sir Ken Robinson called *The Element: How Finding Your Passion Changes Everything.*[1] The book contains a wide range of stories about how certain people, or groups like the Beatles, first came to recognize their unique talents and how that recognition led them to successful careers doing what they loved. Your element is the place where the thing you love and the thing you're good at come together.

Here I retell one of Robinson's stories.[2] An eight-year-old girl's academic future was at risk. She turned assignments in late, tested poorly, fidgeted in class, and stared out the window absentmindedly. Administrators wanted her moved to a school for children with special needs. Her mother sought a psychologist's opinion. During the visit, the psychologist spoke to the mother but kept a watchful eye on the daughter. After a while, he invited the mother into the hall to speak privately. He switched on the radio as the pair left the room. Once in the hall, where the child could not see them, the psychologist told the mother to watch her daughter. Nearly immediately, the child was on her feet moving gracefully with the music, a smile of delight on her face. The psychologist turned to the mother and said: "You know, Mrs. Lynn, Gillian is not sick. She's a dancer. Take her to a dance school." And Mrs. Lynn did just that. Eventually, Gillian Lynn, the girl with the high-risk future, became one of the most accomplished dancers and choreographers of our time. Gillian Lynn had found her element.

For some productive scholars, their element was revealed early. You could almost say they were born into their eventual talent fields. Such was the case for Rich Mayer, Erika Patall, Sabina Neugebauer, Barry Zimmerman, and Dale Schunk.

Rich Mayer credits his upbringing, particularly the core values his parents instilled, for his success. He said:

As a kid I was brought up in the Midwest in a Jewish home. There was a lot of emphasis on social justice, ethical behavior, the value of hard work, and love of learning. All those core values influenced me. An interest in social justice is reflected in my trying to address practical problems in education, and an interest in the value of hard work and love of learning are reflected in my enjoyment of academic life.[3]

Mayer was directly influenced by his father's occupation – industrial psychologist. In fact, Mayer experienced psychology firsthand by working in his father's office during high school and college, often scoring tests.

Patall too got an early taste of psychology. Her father was a community college psychology professor. He paid Patall to help review quiz questions. Patall said: "I went through hundreds of questions for each chapter of an introductory psychology class. This raised an early interest in psychology."[4] Moreover, her early conversations with her father about equity issues shaped her desire to affect educational practice.

Sabina Neugebauer was also raised in an academic home. Her mother was a therapist and her father was an academic and historian. Much like Mayer and Patall, Neugebauer's father involved her in his work by having her respond to visual assessments. Neugebauer said: "I grew up surrounded by ideas about how to explore and measure what's happening in the world."[5]

Barry Zimmerman's roots to the study of self-regulation can be traced to his early environment. Zimmerman said: "I have been fascinated by the topic of learning as long as I can remember. My father was a teacher in a small town in Wisconsin, and he taught me strategies for learning long before I encountered them in class. My father was a wonderful model. He also stressed that personal dedication and practice pay dividends."[6]

Dale Schunk also credited his parents for establishing his general drive for success and his specific interest in self-efficacy. He said: "They were wonderful role models who demonstrated how effort, persistence, and self-efficacy promote success." His parents also stressed the value of education. Early in Schunk's career, his father wrote to him: "You can take satisfaction in the work you are doing in education because education helps make the world a better place to live."[7]

An early element find can lead one into an element-fitting graduate program. Such was the case for award-winning graduate students Sirui Wan and Hyewon Lee. When Wan was a student in China, he became fascinated with the choices students make regarding their educational path and decided to pursue graduate degrees to study motivation and choice. This pursuit led him to the foremost expert on the topic, Jacquelynne Eccles, a University of California-Irvine professor. Wan said:

It is important to know what research direction you want to pursue during graduate school. Recognizing that direction helps focus your energy and helps you seek people along that path who you can reach out to for advice and direction … I think my own takeaway would be to explore yourself and find things that you are really interested in, and then pursue those interests because that will really motivate you to keep going when you confront difficulty and trials, and it will also help you to find the people that can truly support you.[8]

Hyewon Lee discovered her element while teaching elementary school for seven years. She said: "I was really intrigued by what made my students have different outcomes, although they were instructed in the same environment. This intrigued me to learn more about the psychological processes and mechanisms leading to achievement differences."[9] Wanting to address this problem led Lee to pursue a master's degree at Seoul National University and to work with an advisor who studied achievement motivation.

In other cases, productive scholars discovered their elements later in life. Doug Lombardi credits his previous career stops as an engineer conducting scientific research in a federal laboratory and as a classroom teacher for his discovering his educational psychology element. Lombardi said: "This notion of scientific research and education just merged in a wonderful way. Those experiences led me to the study of educational psychology, which was my perfect home."[10]

Ming-Te Wang uncovered his education element while on a mission trip as a young adult. Wang said: "Before the trip, I wanted to be a businessman and make money. That's how I defined success. But, when I saw people with few material resources and limited educational opportunities, I wanted to help. I changed my perspective and decided I wanted to be a teacher." Wang's five-year experience teaching indigenous youth in a remote area of Taiwan led to a second element uncovering. Wang wanted to study psychology and apply it to real-world issues, such as how to build environments to help children, like those he was teaching, thrive. Wang said: "Family issues like poverty and substance abuse made it an uphill battle just to get these kids to come to school each day, let alone engage them. I left teaching and attended graduate school in order to become a professor and leverage psychological science to address real-world issues like those I saw each day in the classroom."[11]

"Rumblin', bumblin', and a stumblin'." That was how iconic broad-caster Keith Jackson described a ball carrier's less-than-smooth gallop on the football gridiron. He might have announced Rebecca Collie's and David Berliner's circuitous and eventually fortuitous career paths in the same way. Rebecca Collie stumbled before finding her psychology element. Her initial college major was engineering. It was not a good fit, and Collie dropped out of college. She returned a few years later, with a desire to help kids, and majored in education. In her final year of study, Collie completed a research assistantship that she found fascinating and inspiring. Collie knew then that she was destined for graduate school to become an educational psycholo-gist. She had found her element. Collie taught for three years before attending graduate school and studying educational psychology. Collie said: "I honestly think this zigzag path helped me find my way. Going in another direction first helped me find and really appreciate my passion."[12]

David Berliner really stumbled. He dropped out of college, actually flunked out. But while in college he had two influential instructors who helped him eventually chart his academic course. Here's Berliner:

A psychologist, John Bauer, and a historian, Joan Gadol, changed my life. The former taught a course that intrigued me, and psychology eventually became my field of study. The latter gave me feedback on a paper I wrote and on my contributions in class. She told me I was very talented and should do more with my life.[13]

Speaking about teachers' element-discovering impact, Berliner added:

Teachers are powerful forces in the lives of their students, even when they do not know that ... A respected teacher's encouragement is a bit like Dumbo's feather. It is magical. She [Joan Gadol] had no idea how her words influ-enced the rest of my life. Teachers do touch eternity, and many never know that's what they did![14]

The takeaway message is that family background might reveal your element early and start you along your path. But maybe not. One's element might shift or only come into focus later in life, perhaps because of a teacher's influence. That's fine too. Motivational speaker Zig Zigler said: "It's not where you start but where you finish that counts."[15] Keep on the lookout for your eventual or shifting element.

Accumulate Advantages

Imagine this. Two healthy boys are born in Canada in the same year. One is born January 1, the other December 31. They join a recreational hockey league as soon as they are age-eligible and are placed on the same team, where they receive the same training. Or do they? January-born is essentially a full year older than December-born and is naturally bigger and more coordinated. Because of this natural physical advantage, the coach positions January-born in prime positions and gives him more ice time in games than his slightly younger teammate. The prime positioning and extra ice time advantage widen the talent gap between the players. January-born makes the rookie all-star team; December-born does not. Now an all-star, January-born plays in a select league his second year, while December-born remains in the less-competitive recreational league. In the select league, practices are longer, coaches are better, and more games are played. These advantages widen the talent gap between the boys further still. On it goes. January-born accumulates more and more hockey-playing advantages over the ensuing seasons until he makes a national team and eventually skates for the Montreal Canadians. December-born remains a third-line player, eventually loses interest, and quits hockey. Advantages accumulate. This story is far from far-fetched, as reported by Malcom Gladwell.[1] Advantages accumulate.

Sociologist Robert Merton called this cascade of increasing advantages, wherein the rich get richer, the Matthew Effect, from the biblical Book of Matthew: "For unto every one that hath shall be given, and he shall have abundance: but from him that hath not shall be taken away even that which he hath."[2]

The early-career award-winning scholars I investigated[3] were a showcase of accumulated advantages. They attended reputation-rich graduate schools where they were guided by influential mentors who taught them the scholarly ropes and helped them secure postdocs or academic positions at research-rich institutions that, in turn, housed productive colleagues and dedicated students. In addition, the scholars received grants that funded research, reduced teaching responsibilities, and ignited collaborations with leading scholars. Their resulting productivity and visibility led to leadership positions on editorial boards and in national organizations and eventually to their early-career awards, which opened more doors still.

Much like the hockey players, some scholars benefited from their early home life advantages. Both Erika Patall[4] and Rich Mayer,[5] for example, had fathers who were psychologists and who involved their children in their work. Unlike the hockey players, though, other scholars were not handed their initial advantages, such as Logan Fiorella[6] as described earlier. Fiorella stumbled onto his career path with few advantages, some deterrents, and without much forethought or privilege. Once on the path and under Mayer's wing, however, Fiorella's advantages multiplied making him a leading, award-winning scholar.

Earlier, I described how my own academic journey was also one without privilege or early advantages. My parents were high school educated and my college days began a bit like Animal House. But, I eventually secured some advantages that propelled me. I found my educational psychology element sophomore year when I took a class from Professor Nelson DuBois who was a model of effective instruction. I wanted to do what he was doing. I stopped skipping classes and began auditing every educational psychology class on the books ... Advantage One. Still, I had no idea about how to become an educational psychologist or about graduate schools. Fortunately, Dr. DuBois counselled me on the best graduate schools for educational psychology and steered me toward Florida State University and Dr. Robert Gagné, the father of instructional psychology. Attending Florida State was Advantage Two. From there I worked hard to create my own advantages.

My department chair recently delivered a graduation address where the theme was "Say Yes!" Say yes to advantageous opportunities, even when they appear difficult or even impossible. I've tried to do that throughout my career, saying yes and seizing opportunities, invited and self-initiated alike, like authoring a book, carving a new research area, editing a journal, or accepting a speaking invitation – opportunities rewarding in their own right but also likely to yield a cascade of accumulating advantages.

Offset Structural Disadvantages

Remember those two hockey players in the preceding section born at opposite ends of the calendar? Now imagine two people born on the same date but one is white and one is black or one is male and one is female. And this time, we won't consider their hockey futures but their scholarly futures. Do all have the same opportunities for success? No, not really. Our culture unfairly favors some inborn characteristics over others, which leads to inequities even at the highest levels of education. For some, there is no accumulation of advantages but a distension of disadvantages. As an example, consider these male-female inequities in higher education:

- Although there have been dramatic increases in the number of women in academia, they are still underrepresented in the professoriate.[1]
- Regarding workplace behavior, female scientists reported that male networks often dominate daily working practices such as inclusion on research projects, publications, and other research activities and outputs, which made female scientists feel marginalized.[2]
- When women have children or plan to have them, they are more likely to drop out of the academic pipeline, work part-time, or assume nontenure teaching positions than their male counterparts.[3]
- Married women with children are less likely to enter a tenure-track position and to achieve tenure than married men with children.[4,5]
- Women spend twice as much time caring for family and household than do men, and the more children a woman has, the fewer hours she spends on professional work, whereas the opposite is true for men.[6,7]

The female scholars interviewed also reported incidents of microaggressions. Patricia Alexander reported not being listened to during meetings early in her career. She said: "It was so apparent that they had learned not to value what I said, and it was because it was me as a woman."[8]

Jacquelynne Eccles said:

What I think is hard to deal with is what is now being called "microaggressions." Women deal with them regularly – regularly being interrupted in meetings, regularly not being asked to participate in things when you should've been asked. It's those kinds of things, dismissals that I think end up grinding women down. It impacts their productivity, and it impacts their wellbeing in a way that can make them just tired.[9]

Eccles offered two personal accounts.[10] In one case, she was paid less than a man who held a similar position. She appealed her case to the university administration, which confirmed that she was underpaid given her qualifications. However, when the university offered her department money to raise her salary, the department chair refused, believing that her male colleague was worth more. In another case, a university dean denied her a sabbatical leave, saying he was not confident that she would use the time to generate new ideas. Meanwhile, a male colleague at that time was granted a leave without question, even though the male colleague had not published in ten years, whereas Eccles had multiple yearly publications and millions of grant dollars.

How might such structural disadvantages be offset? Female scholars interviewed offered this advice for hurtling the discriminatory structural barriers present in higher education:

1. **Recognize that the news is not all bad.** A generation effect has blunted the gender gap, meaning that gender gaps have narrowed over time in Western regions including Europe and the USA.[11] For example, women today are well represented among productive scholars and in scholarly activities. In my study of productive female scholars,[12] annual publication rates ranged from 4.4 to 12.9. These figures are comparable with productive male scholars whose figures ranged from 4.4 to 11.2.[13–15] Regarding scholarly activities, women now outnumber men in organizational memberships, conference presentations, journal authorship, and editorships.[16,17] Some of these positive numbers might be traced to recent policies that support gender equality in hiring, payment, and promotion.[18]

2. **Move outside the gender schema.** Carol Dweck cautions against assigning blame to gender alone: "I think when you are in a stereotyped group, there is often a tendency to say, 'That happened because I'm a woman,' or 'I didn't get that because I'm a woman,' or 'He said that because I'm a woman.' I did not tend to use that gender schema to interpret things, but I did not hesitate to act when [gender inequities] were clear."[19]

3. **Enlist powerful female role models to guide you.** Because the majority of professors are men, many female graduate students and academics perceive a lack of female role models and its negative impact on their careers. In such cases, women should seek role models, outside their institutions if necessary. When Mareike Kunter was a doctoral student at Free University, Petra Stanat, a

postdoctoral researcher at the Max Planck Institute for Human Development in Berlin, emerged as a role model for her. Kunter reported that the institute was male-dominated and that Stanat showed her it is possible to be successful in the academic world as a woman.[20] Similarly, Patricia Alexander was inspired by Maxine Greene who was one of the first female scholars in the philosophy of education field and the first woman president of the American Educational Research Association and the Philosophy of Education Society. Alexander said: "She was brilliant, and her mind was so fascinating ... She was a distant role model."[21]

4. **Form or join female support groups.** Sabina Neugebauer belongs to two female writing groups for support, collegiality, and inspiration. One comprises qualitative researchers who share a commitment to social justice research in education and the other contains pretenure scholars who discuss cutting-edge research methods. Patricia Alexander, meanwhile, was a member of a Status of Women Committee that raised and addressed campus gender equality issues. Alexander said: "I was on the front line with regard to safeguarding and promoting young women. I also taught courses for women leaders and have worked to ensure that issues of gender and racial equality are addressed."[22]

5. **Arrange for family support at home.** Academics who remain in science feel more supported by their partner than those who leave science.[23] Female scholars Mareike Kunter, Carol Dweck, Tamara van Gog, Rebecca Collie, Sabina Neugebauer, and Erika Patall all reported having supportive partners in the home, which allowed them to be successful in the home and at work.[24,25] For example, Kunter said: "My husband is very supportive. I couldn't handle both the children and my work without the support he brings into our family."[26]

6. **Succeed regardless.** Productive female scholars succeeded despite heavy family obligations.[27] Jacquelynne Eccles struggled with shared support in her home, was divorced, and raised two children on her own. Patricia Alexander raised a child as a single mother throughout much of her career. Mareike Kunter took a year off from work and then worked reduced hours to parent. All succeeded despite the gender obstacles they faced. In all cases, their success stemmed from will, a relentless desire to be successful, and from skill, how they went about their careers and their daily work, the

kinds of skills revealed throughout this book. Mareike Kunter said: "People have often underestimated me because I'm female and also look quite young. So, I could surprise people. They didn't expect me to be as tough or as well-informed."[28] Eccles said: "When injustices do arise, don't be quiet about it. Talk to those in your support network and those who can help."[29]

7. **Help enact change.** Learn about and support the growing Open Science movement calling for greater emphases on diversity and inclusion in scientific policy, funding, and publishing, so that all scientists can collaborate better and innovate faster.[30]

Hopefully, changes in policy, attitudes, and behaviors will enact more changes so that structural disadvantages are a thing of the past.

Keep Scholarly Activities on Your Mind

Country singers will tell you. Willie Nelson warbled: "You were always on my mind. You were always on my mind." Glenn Campbell crooned: "That keeps you in the backroads, by the rivers of my memory, that keeps you ever gentle on my mind."

Productive scholars will tell you too. Keep scholarship on your mind. Jacquelynne Eccles was summoning her inner Willie Nelson when she said: "I'm always thinking about my research. I dream grants. I dream articles. I dream talks. That's essentially what's always on my mind."[1] Sabina Neugebauer remarked: "I love what I do and become immersed in it."[2]

Michael Pressley said:

Ideas are constantly on my mind. And the people I'm working with, I'm always talking to them about it. Sometimes, we'll just sit around for a day and a half and brainstorm, and those are interesting sessions ... I seek out literature in the bookstores or library or I sit in my office and think about possibilities. I'm sort of always turning stuff over in my head, and then I'll run into things that sort of set off associations in my head and "click." I make sure I get those down.[3]

John Glover's colleague, Barbara Plake, reported that Glover had a deep commitment to scholarship:

John had a non-stop commitment to scholarship. If you wanted to play on John's team, you had to be willing to be here and be part of it all the time.

When there was work to be done, you were expected to be just as enthusiastic as John was. So, he cultured a mentality that this is fun, this is what we do, and it's your life ... He would come early and stay late; we were in research production around the clock.[4]

Colleague Bob Brown told a humorous story about how research was always on Glover's mind. When a tornado drill sent Glover and Brown to a tornado shelter, Glover looked around at the dozens of others with them and half-jokingly said: "If I had only thought to bring a survey with me, look at the data I could collect."[5]

Doug Lombardi remarked: "I work all the time. But is that a bad thing? I don't think so. It's energizing. It's wonderful. I love it. I love what I do."[6] Lombardi commented specifically on his writing contemplation. He said: "A lot of my writing is done when I'm taking a shower, washing my hair, or brushing my teeth. A lot of my writing is done on walks because I think about this stuff all the time."[7]

Of course I think about work when I'm working, but I also think a lot about work when I'm on a long run or walk, especially on nature's thought-releasing trails. There my mind might contemplate the design for my latest study, a clever means for introducing a topic in my teaching or writing, or spin out the words for an important correspondence.

Productive scholars' thoughts are rarely far from their work.

References

Find Your Path

1 Chawla, K. *BrainyQuotes*. www.brainyquote.com/topics/path-quotes.

Take a Risk

1 Gardner, H. (1993). *Creating minds*. New York: Basic Books.
2 Gardner, H. (1997). *Extraordinary minds*. New York: Basic Books.
3 Laine, J. (October 22, 2019). 'No risk it, no biscuit': What Bruce Arians' coaching lingo teaches us. *ESPN*. www.espn.com/blog/tampa-bay-buccan eers/post/_/id/22930/no-risk-it-no-biscuit-what-bruce-arians-coaching-lingo-teaches-us.
4 Kiewra, K. A., Luo, L., & Flanigan, A. (2021). Educational psychology early career award winners: How did they do it? *Educational Psychology Review*, *33*, 1981–2018 (p. 1999).

5 Ibid. (no page numbers designated).
6 Ibid. (no page numbers designated).
7 Faulkner, W. *Goodreads.* www.goodreads.com/quotes/132400-you-cannot-swim-for-new-horizons-until-you-have-courage.

Be Curious

1 Kiewra, K. A., Luo, L., & Flanigan, A. (2021). Educational psychology early career award winners: How did they do it? *Educational Psychology Review, 33,* 1981–2018 (p. 1997).
2 Ibid., p. 1994.
3 Kiewra, K. A., Walsh, J., & Labenz, C. (2023). Moving beyond fulfillment: Wisdom years stories of passion, perseverance, and productivity. *Educational Psychology Review, 35,* Article 20, p. 10.
4 Kiewra, K. A., & Creswell, J. W. (2000). Conversations with three highly productive educational psychologists: Richard Anderson, Richard Mayer, and Michael Pressley. *Educational Psychology Review, 12,* 135–161 (p. 142).

Discover Your Element

1 Robinson, K. (2009). *The element: How finding your passion changes everything.* New York: Viking.
2 Ibid., pp. 2–3.
3 Patterson-Hazley, M., & Kiewra, K. A. (2013). Conversations with four highly productive educational psychologists: Patricia Alexander, Richard Mayer, Dale Schunk, and Barry Zimmerman. *Educational Psychology Review, 25,* 19–45 (p. 28).
4 Kiewra, K. A., Luo, L., & Flanigan, A. (2021). Educational psychology early career award winners: How did they do it? *Educational Psychology Review, 33,* 1981–2018 (p. 2004).
5 Ibid., p. 1994.
6 Patterson-Hazley, M., & Kiewra, K. A. (2013). Conversations with four highly productive educational psychologists: Patricia Alexander, Richard Mayer, Dale Schunk, and Barry Zimmerman. *Educational Psychology Review, 25,* 19–45 (p. 28).
7 Ibid.
8 Kiewra, K. A., Hasnin, S., Soundy, J., Premkumar, P. K., & Labenz, C. (2023). Graduate student award winners in educational psychology: What made them successful? *Educational Psychology Review, 35,* Article 90.

9 Ibid.

10 Kiewra, K. A., Luo, L., & Flanigan, A. (2021). Educational psychology early career award winners: How did they do it? *Educational Psychology Review*, *33*, 1981–2018 (p. 2001).

11 Ibid., p. 1991.

12 Ibid., p. 1998.

13 Bembenutty, H. (2022). *Contemporary pioneers in teaching and learning*, Vol. 2. Charlotte, NC: Information Age Publishing, Inc. (p. 5).

14 Ibid.

15 Zigler, Z. *quotefancy*. https://quotefancy.com/quote/943772/Zig-Ziglar-It-s-not-where-you-start-but-where-you-finish-that-counts.

Accumulate Advantages

1 Gladwell, M. (2008). *Outliers: The story of success*. Boston, MA: Little, Brown and Company.

2 Merton, R. K. (1968). The Matthew Effect in science. *Science*, *159*, 56–63.

3 Kiewra, K. A., Luo, L., & Flanigan, A. (2021). Educational psychology early career award winners: How did they do it? *Educational Psychology Review*, *33*, 1981–2018.

4 Ibid.

5 Patterson-Hazley, M., & Kiewra, K. A. (2013). Conversations with four highly productive educational psychologists: Patricia Alexander, Richard Mayer, Dale Schunk, and Barry Zimmerman. *Educational Psychology Review*, *25*, 19–45.

6 Kiewra, K. A., Luo, L., & Flanigan, A. (2021). Educational psychology early career award winners: How did they do it? *Educational Psychology Review*, *33*, 1981–2018.

Offset Structural Disadvantages

1 Yousaf, R., & Schmiede, R. (2017). Barriers to women's representation in academic excellence and positions of power. *Asian Journal of German and European Studies*, *2*, 1–13.

2 Howe-Walsh, L., & Turnbull, S. (2016). Barriers to women in academia: Tales from science and technology. https://core.ac.uk/download/pdf/52401414.pdf.

3 Williams, W. & Ceci, S. (2012). When scientists choose motherhood. *American Scientist*, *100*, 138–145.

4 Ibid.

5 Mason, M., Goulden, M., & Frasch, K. (2010). Keeping women in the science pipeline. Alfred Sloan Foundation. www.usna.edu/CTL/Faculty_Resources/Recommended_Reads_Content/mason.pdf.

6 Elbers, F., & Grigore, A. (2018). The gender gap: Past, present and perspectives. *Revista de Management Comparat International,* *19,* 504–515.

7 Ecklund, E., & Lincoln, A. (2011). Scientists want more children. *PLoS* *ONE, 6,* e22590.

8 Prinz, A., Zeeb, H., Flanigan, A., Renkl, A., & Kiewra, K. A. (2020). Conversations with five highly successful female educational psychologists: Patricia Alexander, Carol Dweck, Jacquelynne Eccles, Mareike Kunter, and Tamara van Gog. *Educational Psychology Review, 33,* 763–795 (p. 781).

9 Ibid.

10 Ibid. (no page numbers designated).

11 *The global gender gap report* (2018). World Economic Forum. www3 .weforum.org/docs/WEF_GGGR_2018.pdf.

12 Prinz, A., Zeeb, H., Flanigan, A., Renkl, A., & Kiewra, K. A. (2020). Conversations with five highly successful female educational psychologists: Patricia Alexander, Carol Dweck, Jacquelynne Eccles, Mareike Kunter, and Tamara van Gog. *Educational Psychology Review, 33,* 763–795.

13 Kiewra, K. A., & Creswell, J. W. (2000). Conversations with three highly productive educational psychologists: Richard Anderson, Richard Mayer, and Michael Pressley. *Educational Psychology Review,* *12,* 135–161.

14 Patterson-Hazley, M., & Kiewra, K. A. (2013). Conversations with four highly productive educational psychologists: Patricia Alexander, Richard Mayer, Dale Schunk, and Barry Zimmerman. *Educational Psychology* *Review, 25,* 19–45.

15 Flanigan, A., Kiewra, K. A., & Luo, L. (2018). Conversations with four highly productive German educational psychologists: Frank Fischer, Hans Gruber, Heinz Mandl, and Alexander Renkl. *Educational* *Psychology Review, 30,* 303–330.

16 Griffin, M. M., Hogan, E., Fong, C. J., Gonzales, C., Fathi, Z., & Robinson, D. H. (2023). Women as top-producing authors, editors, and editorial board members in educational psychology journals from 2017 to 2021. *Educational Psychology Review, 35,* Article 10.

17 Greenbaum, H. K., Goodsir, H. L., Smith, C. M., & Robinson, D. H. (2018). Female participation as top-producing authors, editors, and editorial board members in educational psychology journals from 2009 to 2016. *Educational Psychology Review, 30,* 1283–1289.

18 Nagele-Piazza, L. (October 28, 2021). White House releases plan to promote gender equality. *SHRM.* www.shrm.org/resourcesandtools/ legal-and-compliance/employment-law/pages/white-house-releases-plan-to-promote-gender-equality.aspx.

19 Prinz, A., Zeeb, H., Flanigan, A., Renkl, A., & Kiewra, K. A. (2020). Conversations with five highly successful female educational psychologists: Patricia Alexander, Carol Dweck, Jacquelynne Eccles, Mareike Kunter, and Tamara van Gog. *Educational Psychology Review*, *33*, 763–795 (p. 782).

20 Ibid. (no page numbers designated).

21 Ibid., pp. 775–776.

22 Ibid., p. 782.

23 Van Balen, B., van Arensbergen, P., van der Weijden, I., & Van den Bessler, P. (2012). Determinants of success in academic careers. *Higher Education Policy*, *25*, 313–334.

24 Kiewra, K. A., Luo, L., & Flanigan, A. (2021). Educational psychology early career award winners: How did they do it? *Educational Psychology Review*, *33*, 1981–2018.

25 Prinz, A., Zeeb, H., Flanigan, A., Renkl, A., & Kiewra, K. A. (2020). Conversations with five highly successful female educational psychologists: Patricia Alexander, Carol Dweck, Jacquelynne Eccles, Mareike Kunter, and Tamara van Gog. *Educational Psychology Review*, *33*, 763–795.

26 Ibid., p. 781.

27 Ibid. (no page numbers designated).

28 Ibid., p. 780.

29 Ibid., p. 783.

30 Beck, A. (February 2, 2023). Writing the future: The aspirations of early career researchers. *frontiers.* https://blog.frontiersin.org/2023/02/02/ writing-the-future-the-aspirations-of-early-career-researchers/?id_mc= 360024020&utm_source=sfmc&utm_medium=email&utm_campaign= NL+02+2023&utm_id=2033517.

Keep Scholarly Activities on Your Mind

1 Prinz, A., Zeeb, H., Flanigan, A., Renkl, A., & Kiewra, K. A. (2020). Conversations with five highly successful female educational psychologists: Patricia Alexander, Carol Dweck, Jacquelynne Eccles, Mareike Kunter, and Tamara van Gog. *Educational Psychology Review*, *33*, 763–795 (p. 778).

2 Kiewra, K. A., Luo, L., & Flanigan, A. (2021). Educational psychology early career award winners: How did they do it? *Educational Psychology Review*, *33*, 1981–2018 (p. 1997).

3 Kiewra, K. A., & Creswell, J. W. (2000). Conversations with three highly productive educational psychologists: Richard Anderson, Richard Mayer,

and Michael Pressley. *Educational Psychology Review*, 12, 135–161 (p. 146).

4 Kiewra, K. A., & Kauffman, D. (2023). John Glover: A long overdue account of his productive scholarship methods. *Educational Psychology Review*, 35, Article 56.

5 Ibid.

6 Kiewra, K. A., Luo, L., & Flanigan, A. (2021). Educational psychology early career award winners: How did they do it? *Educational Psychology Review*, 33, 1981–2018 (p. 2002).

7 Ibid., p. 2004.

4 | *Forge an Identifiable Research Program*

Each man is capable of doing one thing well. If he attempts several, he will fail to achieve distinction in any.

Plato[1]

Establish a Professional Identity

Paraphrasing Shakespeare: To thine's own work be true. Find, pursue, and establish your professional identity.

Do you know who Michael Connelly is? He is the best-selling author of thirty-six crime novels that revolve around a few main characters, namely Harry Bosch, Mickey Haller, Terry McCaleb, and Renee Ballard. This simple consistency of theme and character make Connelly's books both identifiable and enticing. Connelly has established a professional identity. He developed a working formula and stuck with it.

Not so much for Coca-Cola. In 1985, the Coca-Cola company shockingly changed their Coke soft drink formula that had stood for ninety-nine years, which spawned consumer angst like never seen before or since. The change brought a firestorm of calls, complaints, and protests as well as some desperation stockpiling of the original soft drink. To their credit, the company realized and reversed their mistake less than three months later. Moral of the story: Don't change your identity. Don't mess with success.

A professional identity is also important in the scholarly world. It is better to establish your expertise in one area than to be a jack of all trades and master of none. Scholar Alexander Renkl encourages aspiring scholars to focus research investigations on a specific topic such that one's name becomes attached with that topic. Renkl described the benefits: "What you should achieve is to have a topic connected to your name ... It helps to get you cited." Renkl went on to advise:

"Don't run after the newest or most in-vogue topic."[1] Renkl's advice stems from his own international notoriety as the worked-examples expert – the practice of providing students with detailed examples that show the solution process and product. Renkl's curriculum vitae lists dozens of publications, conference presentations, and invited talks related to worked examples. By establishing himself as an expert in the design and use of worked examples, Renkl has forever attached his name to this research agenda.

The other scholars I investigated have well-established and recognizable identities too. Carol Dweck's is mindset,[2] Barry Zimmerman's and Dale Schunk's[3] is self-regulation, Richard Anderson's[4] is reading. Want to know about the expectancy-value theory of motivation, that's Jacquelynne Eccles'[5] identity. Search the literature for information on design elements of multimedia learning, and you'll find Logan Fiorella.[6] Want to know about reading strategies, check the work of Michael Pressley.[7] Productive scholars recommend focusing on one (or possibly two) main themes that characterize your research rather than spreading yourself across too many areas.

Professionally, I hitched my wagon to a couple stars, first note taking and later talent development. Doing so has led to numerous invitations to write and speak about these topics and even an invitation to go to court. Here's that story. I was sitting in my campus office one day (prepandemic when professors frequented their offices) and the phone rang (before budget cuts snipped our office landlines). It was an attorney for a major energy company. She asked if this was Professor Kiewra of note-taking fame. "Well, that and I eclipsed 200,000 points in the game of Tetris while on sabbatical," I replied. "How can I help you?" She said that the energy company she represented was being indicted by the Securities and Exchange Commission for misleading investors. The Commission's primary evidence being investors' notes from meetings with the company's CEO. She asked if I could provide expert testimony about the inaccuracy of notes and offered a fee. "For that I can make notes disappear," I said. In truth, I did review the evidentiary notes for the defense and prepare an affidavit that helped the energy company avoid prosecution. For the first and only time, note taking went on trial.[8] When it comes to establishing a professional identity, the verdict is in: Link your name to topic. Distinguish yourself.

Do Pioneering Science

Let's begin with a couple important and inspiring quotations from one of the most creative scientists all time – Albert Einstein.

The one who follows the crowd will usually get no further than the crowd. The one who walks alone is likely to find themselves in places no one has ever been before.[1]

I have little patience for scientists who take a board of wood, look for its thinnest part, and drill a great many holes when drilling is easy.[2]

Productive scholar Richard Anderson cautions budding scholars not to become normal scientists who simply follow the crowd doing easy and familiar work. Anderson warns against simply replicating the work of others or following the hot topics of the day. He prompts scientists to be pioneering scholars who discover and tackle new problems using the powers of observation and original thinking. Here's Anderson:

I feel that too many people are contributing footnotes to other people's history rather than making some substantial and unique – at least distinctive – contribution on their own. We do a fairly good job of training normal scientists – people who run the 101st adjunct question study, the 500th feedback study, the 600th study on maps, the incremental improvement, or the additional control. We've gotten to the point of paint-by-number science ... Don't take the most popular problem of the day. Ask what is important in the general area I'm working in that is poorly understood, important, but understudied, and do an analysis of that ... First, think, talk, discuss, search your own feelings. If there is something you can watch or do, do that before you go out and read everything written on the subject. All graduate training pushes you in the other direction. We have become experts at reading the ideas and research of others.[3]

Other scholars agreed. Patricia Alexander said: "Find out what ideas truly matter to you and fuel your passion. Then, pursue those ideas with vigor and commitment."[4] Carol Dweck said: "Don't go for the hot topic, don't go in for things that seem prestigious. Go in for something you really, really care about and think is important because that will sustain you."[5] Jacquelynne Eccles believes that scholars are most productive when doing work that is intrinsically meaningful to them.[6]

All of these scholars conducted pioneering science. After conducting research in well-worn areas such as problem-solving and programmed learning, Anderson blazed new trails into topics related to reading, such as the role of schema in text learning, independent reading, and vocabulary acquisition.[7] Alexander too first investigated familiar topics – text comprehension and learner strategies – before going off-road with her pioneering investigations of how the interplay among knowledge, strategies, and motivation impacts domain learning.[8] Dweck's pioneering work revolves around mindset, how the beliefs one holds about ability being biologically fixed or environmentally malleable shape learning and motivation. Dweck's mindset work has explored several new trails including mindset origins, interventions, and links to personality, motivation, and development.[9] Eccles pioneered research on the expectancy-value theory of motivation and applied that to understudied areas such as secondary school transitions and after-school activities.[10]

I fortunately stumbled onto some pioneering science paths in my career.[11] One involves note taking. As a first-year doctoral student at Florida State University, I took a course in statistics taught by my advisor Harold Fletcher. The first day of class, Dr. Fletcher shockingly outlawed note taking, saying that note taking pulled students' attention away from lecture engagement. Note taking, he believed, made students passive learners in the classroom. Knowing that notes are needed for review, however, Dr. Fletcher provided students with a complete set of notes following each lesson. Most in the class loved the idea of kicking back during lectures yet receiving notes for review. Not me. I was a voracious note taker who had twice been named Note Taker of the Year Runner-Up in college. So, given Dr. Fletcher's no-note-taking dictum, I retreated to the back of the room and became a clandestine note taker, taking notes on a small pad perched on my lap, thereby making me the world's first laptop note taker. On one occasion, however, Dr. Fletcher crept behind me surreptitiously while I was consumed by my illicit note-taking activity. As he stood over me, Dr. Fletcher bellowed, "Mr. Kiewra, are you taking notes in my class?" Caught pen-handed, I lied: "Ah, no, I'm writing a note to a buddy back home." Dr. Fletcher chortled and wryly replied: "How nice of you to tell him about omnibus testing." That experience piqued my interest in note taking and led to my conducting six note-taking studies while in graduate school under Dr. Fletcher's advisement. At the time, only a handful of studies had investigated note taking. Over the years, I have carved new note-taking paths investigating instructor- or student-employed strategies such as provided notes, borrowed notes, matrix notes, organizational cueing, lecture repetition, and note revision.

Another pioneering pathway came to light when my first child took a keen interest in chess and was becoming increasingly talented. I wondered how parents cultivate children's talents. Finding little on the topic, I pioneered a research program to find out how to parent talent. Since that time, I have interviewed the parents of dozens of supremely talented children in diverse domains such as chess, baton twirling, rodeo, swimming and diving, figure skating and speed skating, music, and academics to understand parents' roles in talent development.[12]

Remember: "Those who follow the crowd usually get lost in it" (Anonymous).

Be a Systematizer

Ideally, one's research agenda should not be scattered like wind-carried seeds but systematic like farmer-planted crops. Scholar Logan Fiorella[1] reported that his research program revolves around a single question: How do we help students learn for understanding? That remains the central question whether the helping-aids Fiorella investigates are visualizations or explanations or whether they are instructor-generated or student-generated.

Richard Mayer, who was Fiorella's advisor, is the king of scholarship systematizing.[2] As shown in Figure 4.1, Mayer's research examines (a) the role of instructional variables in terms of delivery systems, such as lecture, text, and multimedia; content such as math and science; and methods such as questions, signals, organizers, and illustrations; (b) the role of learner activities such as note taking and elaboration; and (c) the role of learner characteristics such as prior knowledge and spatial ability. Each study examines how one or more of these variables promotes meaningful as opposed to nonmeaningful learning outcomes.

For example, Mayer's article "Systematic Thinking Fostered by Illustrations in Scientific Text"[3] assessed whether students with low knowledge (learner characteristic) about science (content) could transfer ideas (meaningful learning) or recognize verbatim facts (nonmeaningful learning) from text (delivery system) containing varying types

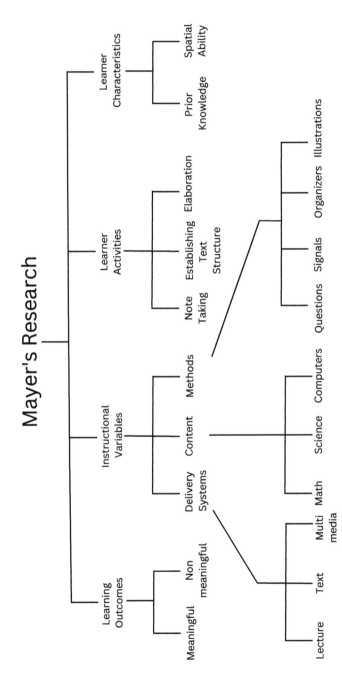

Figure 4.1 Mayer's systematic research agenda

of illustrations (instructional methods). Mayer's systematic approach is also evident in review articles. In the review article "Multimedia Learning: Are We Asking the Right Questions?,"[4] Mayer demonstrates that (a) multimedia delivery systems are better than verbal explanations, (b) instructional methods involving coordinated verbal and visual explanations are better than either alone, and (c) effects are strongest for students with the learner characteristics of low prior knowledge and high spatial ability.

John Glover was visibly systematic within his studies as most of them contained multiple experiments seeking to answer a series or subset of research questions. For example, one study included five experiments (Palmere et al., 1983),[5] another included seven (Glover et al., 1988),[6] and a third included Experiments 1, 2, 3, 4a, 4b, and 4c (Glover, 1989).[7] Colleague Barbara Plake said:

> John's work was a series of related studies, each one adding to the argument that he was trying to make. He saw research as building an argument, and you couldn't build an argument with a single study because it would be too complex and have too many confounds. Also, all experiments leave questions, leave voids, and John was intent on answering those questions and filling those voids, assembling the completed puzzle.[8]

I have tried to mimic Mayer's systematic style in my research on a teaching and learning system I developed called SOAR,[9] an acronym that stands for the four learning and instruction components: Select, Organize, Associate, and Regulate. Table 4.1 shows my systematic research agenda over four experiments, which includes variations in (a) experimental design (SOAR versus Preferred methods or SQ3R methods), (b) instructional support (SOAR materials fully provided, partially provided, or not provided), (c) the presence or absence of training, (d) material content (wildcats, apes, or reinforcement schedules), (e) material medium (printed or computer text), (f) material length (varied but all chapter length), and (g) results across three learning outcomes (facts, relationships, and concepts).

This systematic investigation of SOAR allows me to draw these conclusions: Using SOAR study methods leads to higher achievement than one's preferred methods or the SQ3R method whether or not students are trained in SOAR, use SOAR independently, or are given SOAR support materials. Results hold for chapter-length single-text learning, via print or computer, or chapter-length multitext learning

Table 4.1 *Systematic SOAR research*

	Experiment 1	Experiment 2	Experiment 3	Experiment 4
Design	SOAR v. Preferred	SOAR v. Preferred	SOAR v. Preferred	SOAR v. SQ3R
Support	SOAR Provided	SOAR Assisted	None	SOAR Provided
Training	None	None	30 min	30 min
Content	Wildcats	Wildcats	Apes	Reinforcement
Medium	Printed Text	Computer Text	5 Computer Texts	Printed Text
Length (Words)	1500	1500	1400	2100
Results	SOAR>Preferred	SOAR>Preferred	SOAR>Preferred	SOAR>SQ3R
Facts	80 76	71 42	74 66	70 56
Relationships	94 46	84 21	70 39	72 51
Concepts	– –	– –	57 46	71 57

via computer. SOAR's greatest achievement impact occurs for relationship learning.

And an Extender

Mayer has also extended his research path throughout his career. His early work involved traditional instructional mediums like lecture and text. Next Mayer added the study of illustrations, which was, in turn, extended to animations (moving illustrations). This path led to investigating the broader medium of multimedia learning and a resulting host of famous principles for designing multimedia instruction.[10] The most recent extension involves the value and design of educational games.[11]

Even Mayer's research method for investigating educational games is extended one variable at a time. Mayer said:

I'm taking the value-added approach to studying games. This means that you take an existing game and add one instructional feature at a time to see if that helps or hurts learning. This approach pinpoints what features actually improve learning. Some of the things that we have found to be effective include: self-explanations, asking people to explain their moves, giving detailed feedback about why a move was successful or unsuccessful, and providing worksheets that get players to focus on the underlying principles of successful play.

Mayer summed up his extender approach when he said: "The same underlying theories and research methodologies (I've used to explore other mediums) are involved in studying educational games. What I'm doing is seeing how far these theoretical ideas will travel."[12]

And a Straddler

Alexander Renkl's primary research area is worked examples.[1] His research confirms that providing problems, solution steps, and final solution aid student problem-solving. Like most scholars, he has delved systematically into the nuances of worked examples. For instance, he has explored worked examples variables such as self-explanations, incentives, and the use of nonexamples. Renkl, though, credits his productivity and influence to straddling multiple domains. He does this by taking his well-established worked examples research to new areas and problems such as how worked examples can

influence educational journaling. Renkl contends that domain straddling allows him to investigate multiple things in familiar ways.

Ivar Braten is a straddler.[2] His initial research domain was epistemic
cognition, which concerns thinking and beliefs about the nature of
knowledge and the process of knowing. He later developed a second
research interest, that of multiple document literacy, which examines
how readers integrate information across multiple texts about a subject. Now, Braten straddles these two research areas by studying
epistemic cognition in relation to multiple document literacy and by
creating the integrated model of epistemic beliefs and multiple-
text comprehension.

Barry Zimmerman is a straddler.[3] His work on self-regulation spans
several domains, such as dart throwing, free-throw shooting, volleyball
serving, health issues such as asthma, and school learning.

Most researchers straddle, and I have too. I have used my qualitative
interviewing techniques to examine talent among child prodigies, then
productive scholars, and then those still productive in their
wisdom years.

And an Assembler, a Lumper

It is said we should try to see the forest through the trees. Too often, we
see individual pieces rather than how those pieces form some overrid-
ing pattern, integrated whole, or assembled puzzle. Patricia Alexander
is all about seeing the forest. She considers herself an assembler, one
who assembles individual ideas or findings trying to understand the
whole. Alexander said:

My biggest contribution to the field is not any one thing. What I am
is an assembler. I am about bringing ideas together. One thing that
irritates me is that people fragment things; they pull them apart.
I always want to put them back together. Someone might be interested
in goal orientation, but I want to know how goal orientation fits with
something else.[1]

Alexander also assembles theory and practice. She said: "I would never
look at theory and practice as separate constructs. Whatever I put forth
theoretically has practical implications as well. So, my work in stra-
tegic behavior, epistemic beliefs, and interest all come together and
serve practice."[2]

Logan Fiorella, much like Alexander, seeks the forest, the big picture. Fiorella said:

I look for the big picture, general principles, and themes. I avoid getting bogged down on the specific details. In that way, I'm more a lumper than a splitter. For example, in my field, researchers have tested dozens of different learning strategies and instructional methods. They all have different names and are implemented in different ways. I tend to look for the similarities across these studies. What do effective learning strategies and instructional methods have in common? Some activate prior knowledge or reduce cognitive load; others encourage elaboration, organization, or retrieval. There is so much research out there – what can we confidently take away from all of it? What is the smallest set of research-based principles that explain the most about how students learn and how to help students learn?[3]

Assembly was required in my own scholarly work. My initial research on note taking led to research on graphic organizers, a spatial form of notes. Wanting to understand how best to learn from notes led to my developing and investigating the SOAR teaching and learning method. SOAR is an acronym for the method's four components: Select (via note taking), Organize (via graphic organizers), Associate, and Regulate. Assembling these four components provided an integrated method for effective instruction and learning.[4]

And an Applicator

Two scientists scan a whiteboard filled with mathematical formulae. One turns proudly to the other and says: "The beauty of this is that there is no way it can be applied." Hogwash. Research should both advance science and influence practice. Productive scholar Dale Schunk is among the many scholars whose research focus is the application of scientific findings. Schunk's scholarly career has focused on "establishing the relevance of self-efficacy theory to education." This career focus was born when Schunk was a graduate student at Stanford in the 1970s. Schunk took a class from Albert Bandura, the guru of social cognitive theory, who had just published a book that described self-efficacy in clinical settings. Schunk said: "I thought that the idea of self-efficacy would be very appropriate to education. At that point, it had not been applied in education." Schunk invited Bandura to work with him on this new line of applied research and to be his advisor. Schunk said: "My dissertation was really the first project that applied self-efficacy theory directly to education."[1]

Since that time, Schunk has investigated self-efficacy in a range of applied settings from elementary-aged children with learning disabilities[2] to its role in mentoring.[3] By working with diverse learners, Schunk has uncovered similar patterns of results (for example, showing students that they are making progress builds self-efficacy and improves learning) that widen the scope of educational applicability. Schunk said: "A lot of the ideas that I helped develop have been very well received by practitioners who were able to see their importance in their own classrooms."[4]

In order to formulate educational applications, Schunk often abandons the precision of laboratory research environments for the disorder of classroom research environments. Speaking of classroom-based research, Schunk said: "My research studies have been almost exclusively in schools. I have worked with curriculum directors, teachers, and counselors. Many have been collaborators with me on projects and co-authors of articles. They have taught me a lot about life in school and how learning occurs in school." Schunk's own motivation to apply his work to student learning was evident when he said: "I want to come into schools. I want to work with children. I want to help them learn. I want to help them believe they are capable of learning and to try to get them motivated to learn."[5]

And a Me-Searcher

Pursue your personal research interests. Be a me-searcher.

Carol Dweck grounds her research program in personal experiences. Dweck began her investigations into mindset because of her own weak mindset. She said: "Although I did really well in school, I didn't like challenges, and I really didn't like setbacks. So, there's a way in which this is not just research but what I call me-search." Dweck has always pursued her interests. She said: "I've always done work I thought was important, not what I thought the field thought was important. I always followed my instincts – and my students' instincts – to the next topic."[1]

Logan Fiorella also delved into a research topic of personal interest.[2] Considering the pros and cons of his own work habits prompted Fiorella to explore productive habits scientifically. This exploration led to his publishing a review article on the topic and to teaching a productive habits seminar.

Carol D. Lee, professor emerita of learning sciences at Northwestern University, received the Distinguished Contributions to Research in Education Award from the American Educational Research Association in 2021. Lee is a me-searcher. As an eleventh grader in Chicago, Lee asked a question about the ACT (American College Testing) application process. The response, "it doesn't matter because you won't pass anyway," was representative of the wall of disrespect many African Americans experienced then and now. That dismissive comment and other racially born slights led Lee to earn her doctoral degree, publish extensively, garner numerous national awards, and pursue a decades-long career establishing African-centered schools called New Concept intended to right such wrongs. Lee said: "All of my [scholarly] work is built on the foundation of the work that we did with New Concept School. There has always been a direct relation between the nature of my scholarship as an education researcher and the work we have done in the community building these institutions."[3]

Much like Lee, Jacquelynne Eccles became a me-searcher because of the sexist discrimination she faced as a graduate student and as an early-career professor. That discrimination led Eccles to investigate gender and motivation.[4] Add Patricia Alexander to the list of me-searchers. Alexander struggled with reading as a child and still struggles with reading today, which led to her research focus on reading. Alexander said: "I have dedicated my professional life to the study of reading so that others need not struggle with print, as I did."[5]

Much of my own research has been me-directed. I began studying note taking in graduate school when my statistics professor outlawed student note taking in class and provided notes for students to review. I just had to see if provided notes were superior to students recording and reviewing their own notes. When my children were in school and being inundated with homework, robbing them and family from pursuing better things, I conducted a study to learn about parents' homework perceptions and behaviors.[6] When my first child became interested in chess and I did not know how to grow his chess talent, I began a series of studies investigating the roles parents play in talent development.[7] When I wanted to know how to boost my own research productivity, I began the line of productive scholar research that is the subject of this book. And as I neared retirement, I investigated people who produce at a high level in their wisdom years to understand what drives them and how they accomplish what they do.[8]

Don't hesitate to pursue the research questions most interesting and valuable to you.

And an Essayist

Another way to be productive and to move the field is being an essayist, one who comments on matters of interest and importance. Although this type of writing might be best suited for those with long experience and well-earned academic capital, the forum is open to anyone with something valuable to say. Here is what David Berliner said about his late-career essay writing: "I like to write essays now. Interpretations of the world, as I see it, but with a research grounding. I think I have attained a bit of wisdom as I aged, and I like to share it and see if anyone finds it useful."[1] Essay or commentaries are published in some journals, but authors need not restrict their ideas to journal forums. Blog posts represent a modern and visible outlet for essays bound to generate reader interest and comments. Here are the titles of some recent Berliner essays.[2]

- Kids missing school? Don't worry
- The "required" curriculum versus "the not required" curriculum
- This is your homework: Berliner on education and inequality

References

Forge an Identifiable Research Program

1 Plato. *AZ Quotes*. www.azquotes.com/quote/670216.

Establish a Professional Identity

1 Flanigan, A., Kiewra, K. A., & Luo, L. (2018). Conversations with four highly productive German educational psychologists: Frank Fischer, Hans Gruber, Heinz Mandl, and Alexander Renkl. *Educational Psychology Review*, 30, 303–330 (p. 323).
2 Prinz, A., Zeeb, H., Flanigan, A., Renkl, A., & Kiewra, K. A. (2020). Conversations with five highly successful female educational psychologists: Patricia Alexander, Carol Dweck, Jacquelynne Eccles, Mareike

Kunter, and Tamara van Gog. *Educational Psychology Review*, *33*, 763–795.

3 Patterson-Hazley, M., & Kiewra, K. A. (2013). Conversations with four highly productive educational psychologists: Patricia Alexander, Richard Mayer, Dale Schunk, and Barry Zimmerman. *Educational Psychology Review*, *25*, 19–45.

4 Kiewra, K. A., & Creswell, J. W. (2000). Conversations with three highly productive educational psychologists: Richard Anderson, Richard Mayer, and Michael Pressley. *Educational Psychology Review*, *12*, 135–161.

5 Prinz, A., Zeeb, H., Flanigan, A., Renkl, A., & Kiewra, K. A. (2020). Conversations with five highly successful female educational psychologists: Patricia Alexander, Carol Dweck, Jacquelynne Eccles, Mareike Kunter, and Tamara van Gog. *Educational Psychology Review*, *33*, 763–795.

6 Kiewra, K. A., Luo, L., & Flanigan, A. (2021). Educational psychology early career award winners: How did they do it? *Educational Psychology Review*, *33*, 1981–2018.

7 Kiewra, K. A., & Creswell, J. W. (2000). Conversations with three highly productive educational psychologists: Richard Anderson, Richard Mayer, and Michael Pressley. *Educational Psychology Review*, *12*, 135–161.

8 Kiewra, K. A. (2016). Note taking on trial: A legal application of note-taking research. *Educational Psychology Review*, *28*, 377–384.

Do Pioneering Science

1 Einstein, A. *Goodreads*. www.goodreads.com/quotes/1286532-the-person-who-follows-the-crowd-will-usually-go-no.

2 Einstein, A. *Goodreads*. www.goodreads.com/quotes/7472713-i-have-little-patience-with-scientists-who-take-a-board.

3 Kiewra, K. A., & Creswell, J. W. (2000). Conversations with three highly productive educational psychologists: Richard Anderson, Richard Mayer, and Michael Pressley. *Educational Psychology Review*, *12*, 135–161 (p. 142).

4 Prinz, A., Zeeb, H., Flanigan, A., Renkl, A., & Kiewra, K. A. (2020). Conversations with five highly successful female educational psychologists: Patricia Alexander, Carol Dweck, Jacquelynne Eccles, Mareike Kunter, and Tamara van Gog. *Educational Psychology Review*, *33*, 763–795 (p. 783).

5 Ibid.

6 Ibid. (no page numbers designated).

7 Kiewra, K. A., & Creswell, J. W. (2000). Conversations with three highly productive educational psychologists: Richard Anderson, Richard Mayer, and Michael Pressley. *Educational Psychology Review*, *12*, 135–161.

8 Patterson-Hazley, M., & Kiewra, K. A. (2013). Conversations with four highly productive educational psychologists: Patricia Alexander, Richard Mayer, Dale Schunk, and Barry Zimmerman. *Educational Psychology Review, 25,* 19–45.
9 Prinz, A., Zeeb, H., Flanigan, A., Renkl, A., & Kiewra, K. A. (2020). Conversations with five highly successful female educational psychologists: Patricia Alexander, Carol Dweck, Jacquelynne Eccles, Mareike Kunter, and Tamara van Gog. *Educational Psychology Review, 33,* 763–795.
10 Ibid.
11 Bembenutty, H. (2022). *Contemporary pioneers in teaching and learning,* Vol. 2. Charlotte, NC: Information Age Publishing, Inc.
12 Kiewra, K. A. (2019). *Nurturing children's talents: A guide for parents.* Santa Barbara, CA: Praeger.

Be a Systematizer

1 Kiewra, K. A., Luo, L., & Flanigan, A. (2021). Educational psychology early career award winners: How did they do it? *Educational Psychology Review, 33,* 1981–2018.
2 Kiewra, K. A., & Creswell, J. W. (2000). Conversations with three highly productive educational psychologists: Richard Anderson, Richard Mayer, and Michael Pressley. *Educational Psychology Review, 12,* 135–161 (p. 143).
3 Mayer, R. E. (1989). Systematic thinking fostered by illustrations in scientific text. *Journal of Educational Psychology, 81,* 240–246.
4 Mayer, R. E. (1997). Multimedia learning: Are we asking the right questions? *Educational Psychologist, 32,* 1–19.
5 Palmere, M., Benton, S. L., Glover, J. A., & Ronning, R. R. (1983). Elaboration and recall of main ideas in prose. *Journal of Educational Psychology, 75,* 898–907.
6 Glover, J. A., Dinnel, D. L., Halpain, D. R., McKee, T. K., Corkill, A. J., & Wise, S. L. (1988). Effects of across-chapter signals on recall of text. *Journal of Educational Psychology, 80,* 3–15.
7 Glover, J. A. (1989). The "testing" phenomenon: Not gone but nearly forgotten. *Journal of Educational Psychology, 81,* 392–399.
8 Kiewra, K. A., & Kauffman, D. (2023). John Glover: A long overdue account of his productive scholarship methods. *Educational Psychology Review, 35,* Article 56.
9 Daher, T., & Kiewra, K. A. (2016). An investigation of SOAR study strategies for learning from multiple online resources. *Contemporary Educational Psychology, 46,* 10–21.

And an Extender

10 Mayer, R. E. (2021). *Multimedia learning* (3rd ed.). New York: Cambridge University Press.
11 Mayer, R. E. (2022). Multimedia learning with computer games. In R. E. Mayer & L. Fiorella (eds.), *The Cambridge handbook of multimedia learning* (3rd ed.; pp. 474–488). New York: Cambridge University Press.
12 Patterson-Hazley, M., & Kiewra, K. A. (2013). Conversations with four highly productive educational psychologists: Patricia Alexander, Richard Mayer, Dale Schunk, and Barry Zimmerman. *Educational Psychology Review*, 25, 19–45 (p. 28).

And a Straddler

1 Flanigan, A., Kiewra, K. A., & Luo, L. (2018). Conversations with four highly productive German educational psychologists: Frank Fischer, Hans Gruber, Heinz Mandl, and Alexander Renkl. *Educational Psychology Review*, 30, 303–330.
2 Bembenutty, H. (2022). *Contemporary pioneers in teaching and learning*, Vol. 2. Charlotte, NC: Information Age Publishing, Inc.
3 Patterson-Hazley, M., & Kiewra, K. A. (2013). Conversations with four highly productive educational psychologists: Patricia Alexander, Richard Mayer, Dale Schunk, and Barry Zimmerman. *Educational Psychology Review*, 25, 19–45.

And an Assembler, a Lumper

1 Patterson-Hazley, M., & Kiewra, K. A. (2013). Conversations with four highly productive educational psychologists: Patricia Alexander, Richard Mayer, Dale Schunk, and Barry Zimmerman. *Educational Psychology Review*, 25, 19–45 (p. 27).
2 Ibid.
3 Kiewra, K. A., Luo, L., & Flanigan, A. (2021). Educational psychology early career award winners: How did they do it? *Educational Psychology Review*, 33, 1981–2018 (pp. 1988–1989 and personal communication, January 13, 2021).
4 Kiewra, K., Luo, L., Colliot, T., & Lu, J. (2021). Learning strategies that help students SOAR to success. In L. Zhang (ed.), *Oxford research encyclopedia of education* (pp. 670–700). Oxford: Oxford University Press, Vol. 2. doi.org/10.1093/acrefore/9780190264093.013.868.

And an Applicator

1 Patterson-Hazley, M., & Kiewra, K. A. (2013). Conversations with four highly productive educational psychologists: Patricia Alexander, Richard Mayer, Dale Schunk, and Barry Zimmerman. *Educational Psychology Review*, 25, 19–45 (p. 26).
2 Schunk, D. H., & Rice, J. M. (1992). Influence of reading comprehension strategy information on children's achievement outcomes. *Learning Disability Quarterly*, 15, 51–64.
3 Schunk, D. H., & Mullen, C. A. (2013). Toward a conceptual model of mentoring research: Integration with self-regulated learning. *Educational Psychology Review*, 25, 361–389.
4 Patterson-Hazley, M., & Kiewra, K. A. (2013). Conversations with four highly productive educational psychologists: Patricia Alexander, Richard Mayer, Dale Schunk, and Barry Zimmerman. *Educational Psychology Review*, 25, 19–45 (p. 26).
5 Ibid., p. 27.

And a Me-Searcher

1 Prinz, A., Zeeb, H., Flanigan, A., Renkl, A., & Kiewra, K. A. (2020). Conversations with five highly successful female educational psychologists: Patricia Alexander, Carol Dweck, Jacquelynne Eccles, Mareike Kunter, and Tamara van Gog. *Educational Psychology Review*, 33, 763–795 (p. 774).
2 Kiewra, K. A., Luo, L., & Flanigan, A. (2021). Educational psychology early career award winners: How did they do it? *Educational Psychology Review*, 33, 1981–2018.
3 Stewart, P. (October 22, 2021). Dr. Carol D. Lee: Picking up the pieces. *Diverse Issues in Higher Education*. www.diverseeducation.com/home/article/15280341/dr-carol-d-lee-picking-up-the-baton.
4 Prinz, A., Zeeb, H., Flanigan, A., Renkl, A., & Kiewra, K. A. (2020). Conversations with five highly successful female educational psychologists: Patricia Alexander, Carol Dweck, Jacquelynne Eccles, Mareike Kunter, and Tamara van Gog. *Educational Psychology Review*, 33, 763–795.
5 Bembenutty, H. (2022). *Contemporary pioneers in teaching and learning*, Vol. 2. Charlotte, NC: Information Age Publishing, Inc. (p. 86).
6 Kiewra, K. A., Kauffman, D. F., Hart, K., et al. (2009). What parents, researchers, and the popular press have to say about homework. *Scholarlypartnerships.edu*, 4, 93–109.

7 Kiewra, K. A., & Witte, A. (2013). How to parent chess talent: Classic and modern stories. In M. Shaughnessy (ed.), *The nurturing of talent, skills, and abilities* (pp. 139–162). Hauppauge, NY: NOVA Science Publishers.
8 Kiewra, K. A., Walsh, J., & Labenz, C. (2023). Moving beyond fulfillment: Wisdom years stories of passion, perseverance, and productivity. *Educational Psychology Review, 35,* Article 20.

And an Essayist

1 Bembenutty, H. (2022). *Contemporary pioneers in teaching and learning,* Vol. 2. Charlotte, NC: Information Age Publishing, Inc. (p. 28).
2 *Diane Ravitch's blog.* https://dianeravitch.net/.

5 | *Use Productive Research Approaches*

Great acts are made up of small deeds.

Lao Tzu[1]

How are some scholars so productive? How can you join the ranks of the highly productive? Here are some hidden-curriculum tips from those who know what it takes to be productive.

Prioritize Research

It almost goes without saying that productive scholars prioritize research. How else could some produce ten or more research publications per year and perhaps hundreds over their career?

Productive scholar Erika Patall was clear about prioritizing research: "You can't be a jack of all trades. To be a successful researcher, you must prioritize research over all else. You have to accept that you'll be less good at other things. I don't ever want to be bad at anything, especially teaching, but once I meet a threshold of good enough, I accept that."[1]

John Glover certainly prioritized research over other academic duties. Colleague Barbara Plake said: "I don't think John was the least bit interested in service. He ducked committees as hard and fast as he possibly could, because they took away from the important [scholarly] work that he wanted to do. If he was on a committee, he gave it minimal attention because that's not what he was here to do."[2]

In order to be productive, scholars usually spend about half their work days focused on research activities, usually preserving the morning hours for these tasks because research is their top priority and they want to be sure it gets their full attention before other duties or interruptions surface. Some like Tamara van Gog preserve entire days to work solely on research activities.[3] Some contend that research is such a priority that it is always on their mind. Doug Lombardi said: "I think about this stuff [research and writing] all the time."[4] Jacquelynne Eccles said: "I'm always thinking about research. I dream grants, I dream articles, I dream talks. That's essentially what's always on my mind."[5]

When it comes to teaching, productive scholars have found ways to minimize their teaching commitment. First, most are at research-focused universities that tend to assign a small course load in order to support research productivity. Logan Fiorella, University of Georgia, said: "My university has been highly supportive of my research. They've assigned me a manageable course load and few service obligations that allow me to be productive."[6] Second, most push classes to the afternoon, preserving the morning hours for scholarly activities when they feel freshest. Third, several teach the same courses from semester to semester, making preparation time minimal. Fiorella teaches the same two graduate courses, and one of them is a doctoral seminar wherein he and doctoral students collaborate on research projects.[7] Former Glover student Alice Corkill said this about Glover's streamlined teaching approach and research priority:

John taught the typical two and two load. The rest of the time he devoted to graduate students and to research. I don't think he needed to spend much time preparing to teach because he was teaching the same courses over and over again, and once you've taught a course many times, you don't have to spend much time preparing the instructional materials and writing tests, so you can streamline teaching. That way you have more time to spend on your research.[8]

Christine McCormick and Benita Barnes[9] also found that productive scholars limit classroom preparation time and course modifications once the course is established and spend that time on scholarly activities. Last, some scholars secure grants or fellowships that buy them out of teaching responsibilities altogether. Rebecca Collie, for example, has had university and national fellowships that reduce or eliminate teaching duties.[10]

In my view, research prioritization is also the pathway to tenure and promotion for faculty with research apportionments. I have served on my college's Tenure and Promotion Committee for eight years, five as committee chair, and have reviewed and voted on more than a hundred candidate files in that capacity. Here is what I learned: Publication record, and not much else, matters. In only one case was someone's teaching record deemed unsatisfactory, but that was combined with low research productivity, leading to a negative vote. In every other case, one's teaching and service records were not challenged. In every case, decisions were made solely upon the candidate's publication record. This occurred despite there being clearly articulated standards, about four of each, for research, teaching, and service. Like it or not, the "publish or perish" dictum is still alive and kicking today.

Collaborate

Productive scholars rarely publish alone. The early-career scholars, for example, collaborated on about 95 percent of their works.[1] More seasoned scholars also collaborate a lot. About half the time for Rich Mayer and Dale Schunk,[2] about three-quarters of the time for Patricia Alexander and Barry Zimmerman,[3] and about 90 percent of the time for Jacquelynne Eccles[4] throughout their long careers. A recent study about productivity in educational psychology[5] found that the top scholars had collaborated on 88 percent of their publications in the past five years. Collaboration is on the upswing among scholars. In 2008, the mean number of authors per article over the previous five-year period was 2.6. That figure rose to 3.3 in the five-year period ending in 2015 and rose again to 3.6 during the next five-year period. The increasing collaboration trend is evident in Rich Mayer's most recent CV. Just one of Mayer's last twenty-four empirical publications was sole authored.

Ivar Braten, an educational psychologist who studies multiple document literacy, is a poster scholar for collaboration. Among his three hundred–plus publications and conference presentations, only two have been sole authored in the past ten years. Most impressively, Braten has collaborated on his published work with eighty different scholars from thirteen different countries. Many of Braten's collaborators are drawn from the eighty-plus students or postdoctoral fellows he has advised throughout his career. Braten's collaborative style is immersive and intense. Braten said:

These collaborations are the *sine qua non* of my research, and I gain at least as much as I give by them. We usually plan all aspects of the studies, including designing and creating materials, in close collaboration [and] I'm nearly always taking part in data collection. Typically, we decide who will be the main person responsible for writing a particular paper or we will split up the writing, but sometimes I have also been sitting together with doctoral students co-writing a manuscript from the first to the last word, trying to externalize all my thinking and reflection during the writing process. This way of authoring a manuscript may be more time consuming but has been among the writing experiences I have enjoyed the most.[6]

Scholars Dale Schunk and Barry Zimmerman both advised budding scholars to connect with seasoned scholars because they can help you develop your thinking, help you get work done, and become your friends.[7] Zimmerman offered these suggestions to all scholars for connecting with potential collaborators:

Associate with other prolific scholars. Identify a burning topic, locate other researchers who are doing research on the topic or related topic, and set up a symposium at a professional conference where this group can meet to discuss common issues and points of agreement and contention. Organize an edited book to summarize research from the various perspectives on the topic.[8]

When productive scholars collaborate, they most often lead the way by assuming first authorship on most of their collaborative work (50–75 percent of the time) with the exception of Mayer (36 percent of the time).[9] Mayer's relatively lower first-authorship status is likely a function of his mentoring style wherein he allows graduate collaborators to claim first authorship while he drives the research project and its writing from the back seat, as many seasoned scholars – no longer hurdling tenure and promotion barriers – are apt to do. Mayer's research and writing signatures are evident regardless of his authorship status. In summary, productive scholars collaborate a lot but often lead the way and presumably do the lion's share of the work. They are not scooping up publications as third and fourth authors.

The benefits of collaboration are obvious. The division of labor and the inclusion of multiple viewpoints can lead to higher output and greater quality. Regarding output, many hands make light work. Collaboration allows scholars to complete projects more quickly and to work on several projects simultaneously. Regarding quality, two or more heads are better than one. Collaboration produces work that combines the best ideas and work of coinvestigators. Michael Pressley said: "Throughout my career, every time I have done something important, it's been with somebody else. The breadth and depth of your thoughts and certainly your personal fulfillment is going to be a lot greater if you spend your life doing important things with other people."[10] Rebecca Collie said much the same: "I can't speak highly enough of my collaborators. They've been fantastic in helping me be productive. I learn so much from them."[11] Sabina Neugebauer added: "I really enjoy the rich intellectual collaborations where we are co-constructing knowledge together."[12]

Collaboration also helps build professional networks that can pay later dividends. Hans Gruber said: "Those who are inspired to join different groups and develop contacts have an easier time moving forward with their own research. Having a system of knowledgeable and experienced contacts is especially helpful for graduate students and junior faculty who can turn to these contacts for guidance while conducting research."[13]

As to how to choose collaborators, David Berliner offers this insight: "I choose my [collaborators] for two reasons. Number 1: I like them. Number 2: They have ideas and skills that may well be better than mine. They are quite likely to make me look good!"[14]

John Glover followed Berliner's second collaborator-choosing rationale. Glover chose collaborators who offered unique contributions and who covered his weaknesses. Former colleague Barbra Plake half-joked:

I don't think John had ever run a statistical test in his life. He just knew that he needed to run them. So, like most of us, John was dependent on the expertise of others ... John had an antennae for finding the right collaborators. He was clever in his associations. He didn't randomly pick people to work with; he picked people that could contribute unique and important things to the project. For example, I think he sought to work with me because he knew that I was skilled in measurement and statistics and that was something that would aid him. Moreover, he made you feel like your contribution was imperative. John would say, "You are absolutely the best person to do this. I couldn't do it without you. This is so important. The field will suffer if you don't help." He would make you feel like you'd be ending science if you didn't participate.[15]

One collaboration caution: Although Ming-Te Wang collaborates on 99 percent of his published work, he cautioned young scholars about the pitfalls of exploring too many new collaborations, especially with those outside one's area, early in one's career. Regarding his own experience, Wang said: "I was highly cautious about what collaborations I accepted or pursued .... In general, I chose to avoid multiple

collaborations during my pre-tenure years to raise productivity."[16]
Using a cooking analogy: Being involved with too many cooks, especially those preparing foods tangential to one's own tastes, can overfill
one's plate.

Get Grants but Don't Chase Grants Too Early

When I began my academic career in 1982, grant getting was not the
priority it is today. My recollection is that faculty largely sought grants
to support their research if need be. It was not necessarily an expectation for advancing in the academy. My research largely involved
collecting simple note-taking and achievement data from college students in my own backyard, so grants were not a priority for me
personally. My, how things have changed. Over the years, I've watched
my department, college, and university make grant getting a top priority and expectation and also offer resources for grant attainment,
things like specialized training, in-house starter grants, funding
announcements, grant recognitions and awards, and staff assistance.
I have also witnessed how annual evaluation, tenure, and promotion
standards have shifted to include the potential to generate or actually
obtain external support.

In addition to meeting administrative expectations, grant getting can
certainly aid scholarly productivity. Grant funding can be used to
reduce teaching load, allowing more time to focus on research, and
to hire research assistants who can share the workload to accelerate
and raise productivity.

Productive scholars are certainly grant getters. Consider German
scholars Heinz Mandl and Frank Fischer.[1] Throughout his career,
Mandl's research has been fueled by special priority programs (SPPs).
SPPs are research initiatives funded by the German Science Foundation
involving small groups of researchers who independently conduct
related studies on a single topic. Throughout his career, Mandl has
initiated three SPPs with colleagues. Frank Fischer, Mandl's former
student, directs a research center that has amassed seven million dollars
in funding and brought together interdisciplinary scholars to conduct
the research.

A glance at Patricia Alexander's CV reveals twenty-five funded
grants, most in the tens of thousands of dollars and a few in the
millions of dollars. Rich Mayer's CV reveals more than forty funded

grants with Mayer as principal or co-principal investigator. Most of these were awarded by the National Science Foundation, National Institute of Education, Pacific Rim Research Program, US Department of Education, and Office of Naval Research, with funding usually in the tens of thousands of dollars with some exceeding a million dollars.

Although grant getting can help faculty meet administrative expectations and can bolster productivity, scholar Ming-Te Wang sounded a warning. Wang cautioned junior scholars not to chase external grants too vigorously early in their careers because obtaining external funding is a bit of a longshot. Wang suggested that a young scholar's time is better spent trying to publish articles than pursuing grants: "Don't chase grants early on. You can always find a home for a paper in a second-tier journal but grant writing can easily go nowhere because the acceptance rate might be just 10%. Solely focusing on writing grant proposals or chasing money is not a wise use of time for junior scholars."[2]

Self-Regulate

In laymen's terms, self-regulation is the process of monitoring and evaluating one's thinking and behaviors. It is an ongoing, inner conversation of reflection. For example, as you converse with a friend, your inner conversation at times might sound like this:

- Did what I just say make sense? Doesn't seem so. Maybe I should try another angle . . .
- She seems annoyed. I should not have asked about her situation . . .
- Is she suggesting this is my fault? Seems so. Stay calm and listen . . .
- Okay, that hurts. Don't retaliate. Find out why she feels that way . . .

Self-regulation is vital in any domain. Consider chess, where players internally converse about their position (my knight in this closed position is an advantage over her dark squared bishop) and their move options (if I play Queen h7+, she is likely to block check with her bishop, which I can pin with my rook). Consider rock climbing, where an alpinist internally converses about the climbing holds (this crack is shallow and will only allow my first knuckles) and the conditions (looks like a storm is rolling through the canyon).

In psychology terms, self-regulated learning is a cyclical process that aids learning, wherein the learner uses (a) forethought to set goals and make plans, (b) cognitive strategies when executing the plan, and (c) self-reflection to monitor progress and performance. I interviewed two self-regulation kingpins, Barry Zimmerman and Dale Schunk, who use and advocate self-regulation as a means for being a more productive scholar.[1]

Zimmerman uses the cyclical phase model of self-regulation he developed. First, he uses forethought to maximize his work time. For example, he knows that morning is his most productive time, so he writes then and schedules student meetings or leisure activities in the afternoon. He also sets goals and poses questions to guide his research and writing activities. Second, Zimmerman uses cognitive strategies to enhance performance. For example, he uses templates for planning and describing research because they have proven helpful throughout his career. One such template, he said, "involved a series of research questions, psychological dimensions underlying these questions, self-regulation attributes associated with each dimension, and self-regulatory processes designed to influence each attribute." Last, Zimmerman uses self-reflection for evaluating his work. When reflecting on his writing, Zimmerman raises and answers a series of questions for each manuscript section as shown:[2]

Front Matter

___ Is the title compelling?
___ Does the abstract give a succinct overview of the sample, variables, research questions, and results?

Introduction

___ Does the introduction present key constructs, prior research, unanswered questions, and the rationale for additional research?

Method

___ Are the operational definitions accurate and clear?
___ Are there confounding variables?

Results

___ Are the data examined and interpreted appropriately?
___ Are follow-up analyses needed to clarify unclear issues?

Discussion

___ Do the data support the research narrative?
___ What findings were unexpected and how should they be interpreted
___ What are the implications for researchers and practitioners?

Dale Schunk said: "I try to practice self-regulation strategies in my own work: setting goals, assessing progress, monitoring performance, choosing strategies, and seeking help when needed."[3] Schunk sets yearly goals each August as a new academic term begins. He lists five or six projects along with timelines for completing them. Monthly, he monitors his work progress and revisits and modifies his goals as needed. Schunk sets weekly goals every Sunday and makes fairly detailed plans for meeting them. He also sets daily goals. Every night he lists the main things he wants to accomplish the next day. When Schunk writes, he sets specific time goals for completing the manuscript (such as completing it in three weeks) and for each of its sections (such as completing Section 2 in four days).

Ming-Te Wang and Mareike Kunter also employ self-regulation techniques. Wang said: "I set goals, lay out a very specific timeframe for achieving them, and stick with that timeframe."[4] Kunter[5] sets goals and creates detailed to-do lists for meeting them. She monitors her performance by documenting things such as writing time and words written and whether plans are followed and goals are met.

Rich Mayer self-regulates more now in his wisdom years than in his younger years by using "workarounds" to bolster his occasionally failing memory. Mayer said: "I can't trust myself to remember things, so I write everything down and have different systems for noting and remembering things." Mayer uses a monthly calendar to record appointments, a yellow pad to list weekly goals and plans, and Post-it notes to record daily tasks to complete. Mayer said: "This system keeps me focused on what I'm trying to accomplish long term, medium term, and short term."[6]

Psychological support for self-regulation activities can be traced to the 1920s and psychologist Bluma Zeigarnik,[7] who demonstrated that to-do list planning reduced cognitive brain strain by freeing the brain from worrying about unfinished tasks by externalizing them to a written list. Today, conventional wisdom supports having a written plan for accomplishing one's goals and crossing off to-do-list items to improve task completion.[8] In Stephen Covey's *The 7 Habits of Highly Effective People*,[9] he recommends making to-do lists specific by breaking larger tasks like "write paper" into more specific tasks, such as "write introduction" and "create tables."

In my scholarly work, I like to think about self-regulation as a three-phase process: before, during, and after a particular task. Suppose I'm conducting an interview study to learn how some scholars are so productive. Here is a bit of my self-regulatory inner conversation.

Before

- Are these questions sufficient for understanding the sacrifices made?
- Should I explore the role that family played?
- I'm going to tape a card to my computer that says "Record" so I don't forget to start the recording.

During

- This response is too general. I need to prompt him for details.
- This response is about her work, not her methods. I need to jump in and redirect.
- Oh my, that's a surprise. I'll want to retell that story.

After

- I need to follow up with two of them and find out more about sacrifices they might have made.
- Seems surprising that three of them had conflicts with their advisor. I need to handle that delicately.
- The second interview did not add much. Maybe I leave that out.

However you self-regulate, keep that inner voice talking.

Mine Large Data Sets

Cambridge University Press has a third-edition book titled *Mining of Massive Datasets*,[1] so you know that mining large data sets must be a valuable thing. Some productive scholars certainly think so. It relieves them from the burdensome and time-consuming demands of data collection.

Ming-Te Wang chose to do a postdoc at Michigan over Stanford and Yale, even though Michigan offered less money than the others. Wang chose Michigan for one reason: Jacquelynne Eccles had a large data set that Wang could mine. Wang said:

As a junior scholar, it is difficult and time consuming to attain grants to collect your own data, especially for longitudinal studies. With that in mind, the best option is to work with someone who already has a large data set. I took advantage of the opportunity of working with Dr. Eccles at Michigan and was able to publish a lot of important papers in top journals using her data set in the first three years of my career.[2]

Sabina Neugebauer said much the same about the data-mining potential of her postdoc experience at the Institute of Education Sciences at the University of Connecticut: "From a time efficiency standpoint, my postdoc really set me up for success so that I could spend the time I had as a new faculty member in a school of education, with heavy service and teaching demands, mining that [postdoc] data and turning it into papers, as opposed to the more onerous process of data collection."[3]

Of course, existing data sets need not be massive to be of value to you. The real point is to seek, find, and use convenient data sets that fit your goals and needs. Although a quick Google search can reveal dozens of free data repositories, such as Data.Gov and Harvard Dataverse, in various domains, your search might best be accomplished by reviewing literature in your area, finding those working with germane data sets, and contacting them to see if you might have access to the data or even collaborate on a joint study.

Consider Conducting Meta-analyses

Meta-analysis is a statistical technique used to analyze results from multiple scientific studies addressing the same research question. For example, a scholar might conduct a meta-analysis on the effect of note taking on lecture learning, as did William Henk and Norman Stahl.[1] They addressed these questions: (a) Does the process of note taking aid recall? (b) Does reviewing notes aid recall? When conducting meta-analysis, researchers pool data from several previously conducted studies to derive a pooled estimate of the unknown effect size of a given variable, such as note taking. In the note-taking meta-analysis, Henk and Stahl found that the process of recording notes had a 0.34 effect size and that the review of notes had a 1.56 effect size. This meant that note taking is likely to raise recall by one-third of a standard deviation above the mean (a move from the fiftieth to the sixty-second percentile), whereas review is likely to raise recall about one and a half standard deviations above the mean (a move from the fiftieth to the ninety-second percentile). Both effects are considered large and statistically significant.

Ming-Te Wang is an early-career award-winning scholar who conducts meta-analysis research.[2] One recent study investigates how parental ethnic-racial socialization practices impact children of color's psychosocial and behavioral adjustment and academic success. Another recent meta-analysis investigated how classroom climate impacts children's academic and social well-being.

Early-career award-winner Erika Patall learned how to conduct meta-analysis from her graduate school mentor Harris Cooper. This training had a profound impact on Patall's eventual productivity and national reputation. In fact, Patall credits much of her success to her meta-analysis work. Patall explained that meta-analyses "get noticed, get cited a lot, and will almost always be published."[3] This early foray into meta-analyses introduced Patall to the research method for which she is best known and most cited. Among her publications are ten meta-analyses on topics such as prosocial modeling, academic underachievement, negative feedback's effect on intrinsic motivation, effect of choice on intrinsic motivation, and juvenile delinquency interventions.

Do Some Conceptual Writing

In our publish or perish academic world, what you publish often matters too. Some institutions favor peer-reviewed publications over those that are not peer-reviewed when making tenure decisions. Operationally, this often means empirical journal articles in the peer-reviewed corner and chapters and books in the non-peer-reviewed corner. Empirical articles advance new scientific discoveries. Chapters and books advance conceptual ideas.

How much conceptual writing do scholars do? In Germany, apparently quite a bit.[1] Among Heinz Mandl's nearly five hundred publications, about 73 percent are conceptual. Among Hans Gruber's two hundred–plus publications, about 66 percent are conceptual. In the United States, apparently far less. Over Patricia Alexander's forty-plus-year career, her CV shows that about 39 percent of her publications are conceptual. Things are similar for Jacquelynne Eccles. Conceptual works make up about 35% of her CV publications over her nearly fifty-year career.

What about scholars earlier in their careers, how much conceptual writing do they do? Apparently far less. Early-career award-winning scholars Erika Patall and Sabina Neugebauer have about 19 percent and 17 percent conceptual writings among their total CV-listed publications, respectively. This makes sense given that some conceptual writing might not be considered peer-reviewed against the peer-reviewed emphases involved in tenure decisions.

It might be that scholars do more conceptual writing as they advance up the professorial ranks for a couple reasons. One, they have passed through the heavily peer-reviewed-guarded tenure gates, allowing them greater freedom over what they publish. Two, being more senior and more visible in their post-tenure careers, more invitations to write conceptual pieces likely follow. Scholar Rich Mayer is a case in point. Examining Mayer's CV, early-career publications were about 20 percent conceptual. Examining his publications over the past few years, about 40 percent are conceptual.

As to why scholars would want to write conceptual pieces, four reasons stand out. One, it is a wonderful opportunity to formulate and express your ideas. Two, it is a means for making your ideas and yourself more visible. Edited volumes are often well read as they contain the ideas of experts. Three, writing a conceptual piece is easier than doing empirical research. There is no Institutional Review Board looking over your shoulder, no data collection, and no statistical analyses. When Dale Schunk was an administrator, his scholarship turned largely from empirical to conceptual because the latter was less time-consuming. It was a way for him to continue being productive while being an administrator.[2] Last, with conceptual writing, you are likely to avoid rejection and endless rounds of revision so common in the peer-review publishing world.

Write a Literature Review

A first-semester doctoral student recently asked the faculty at a program meeting what she should do during the upcoming summer term. My colleagues' suggestions included "load up on coursework," "get a teaching assistantship," and the unhelpfully vague "do some research." That's when I told her about the most important and most productive summer of my academic career.

It was the summer of 1980, and I had just completed my first year in the doctoral program at Florida State University. I decided to leave school for the summer. I didn't want to endure Florida's stifling heat, and the Long Island beaches and Mom's cooking were calling me home. After a couple weeks of sleeping in, hitting the surf, and reestablishing my pre-graduate school body weight, I grew antsy and decided to start reading up on my potential dissertation topic: note taking.

As this was the pre-internet old days, this meant driving to a local college library, riffling through the card catalogue for note-taking articles, pulling dusty journal volumes from shelves, and dropping untold nickels into a Xerox machine as I vainly photocopied page after page shielded by unyielding book bindings.

I read a few articles and then a few more, scribbling margin notes on each as I read. I soon established a note-taking framework for recording notes about each article, chronicling things about literature review, participants, design, methods, and findings. Gradually that framework expanded to include specific variables appearing in the literature such as lecture rate, note-taking cues, review placement, type of test, and many others. Weeks rolled by, each day spent at the library, as my tanned skin turned pale. But I loved this. I loved the reading and the note taking and the learning. I loved discovering and scrutinizing what was done previously. I especially loved piecing it all together, finding patterns never reported before. I began to write. I wrote about specific variables like lecture rate and review placement, and I wrote across variables, such as how certain types of notes were best for certain types of tests. By summer's end, I had read nearly a hundred note-taking articles, completed framework notes for each, and wrote dozens of pages for what would become my dissertation literature review.

How valuable was that summer experience? It was career altering. It was not only the impetus for conducting six dissertation-related note-taking experiments at Florida State but for conducting dozens more in subsequent years. It was the backbone for my dissertation literature review but also for publishing several review articles thereafter as a junior professor.[1–3] It led to my eventual recognition as an authority on note taking. Even the Beach Boys didn't have summers this good.

Writing a literature review is not easy, but it is perhaps the most important writing a scholar can do. It identifies, organizes, scrutinizes, and chronicles a wide body of literature on a topic. It records a scientific history and offers new avenues for exploration. It cements the writer as an expert on that topic. Consider just a few of Rich Mayer's early-career literature reviews that helped establish his expertise and national visibility:

- Information processing variables in learning to solve problems. *Review of Educational Research.*[4]
- Can advance organizers influence meaningful learning? *Review of Educational Research.*[5]
- Twenty years of research on advance organizers: Assimilation theory is still the best predictor of results. *Instructional Science.*[6]
- Aids to prose comprehension. *Educational Psychologist.*[7]

Do Some Champions League Research

If you're a true fan of football, what Americans call soccer, you're well aware of the Union of European Football Association's Champions League. The Champions League includes the top thirty-two clubs from various European leagues. It is the creme de la creme of European football. That's a bit of context for understanding German scholar Alexander Renkl when he offers this publishing advice: "You have to show that you can play in the Champions League. So, publish a few papers in top journals while also publishing in well-respected journals with higher acceptance rates. You want to have a good balance between the number of papers that you publish while also showing that you can play Champions League."[1]

Renkl might have learned the value of publishing high-impact articles from his mentor Heinz Mandl. Mandl[2] pushed his proteges against the German tradition of writing long books toward the American tradition of publishing research articles bound for international journals. Hans Gruber, another Mandl protegee, noted how the first important lesson Mandl taught him was the importance of publishing high-quality research in internationally read journals. By emphasizing this valuable lesson, Mandl positioned Gruber, Renkl, and other mentees to resist German scholarship practices and, instead, adopt more American-oriented practices of publishing impactful scientific studies.

American scholar Ming-Te Wang also stressed the importance of playing with the big boys and girls. Wang advised: "Have a few really impactful publications rather than many less impactful publications in not-so-good journals. It's important to do groundbreaking work that moves the field forward and for people to know your work."[3]

How do you know, though, if a journal is Champions League material? One way is to check its published impact factor, which is an index reflecting the journal's yearly mean number of citations for articles published in the past two years. It's calculated this way: The ratio between the number of citations received for publications in a journal in a given year that were published in the two preceding years divided by the total number of citable items published in that journal during the two preceding years. Whew ... got that?

The scientific community takes impact factors seriously. Erin McKiernan and colleagues[4] noted that impact factor data have a strong influence on the scientific community, affecting decisions on where to publish, whom to promote or hire, the success of grant applications, and even salary bonuses and that 40 percent of universities in the USA and Canada specifically mentioned impact factor as part of the tenure and promotion processes. This viewpoint was echoed in a recent article saying that "the pressure to publish in high-impact journals is becoming a serious problem in scholarly communication. Scientific success is often measured by the number of high-impact articles a researcher has co-authored, and this can even affect his/her academic career and influence job or grant applications."[5]

If you're keeping score, in most fields an impact factor of ten or greater is considered an excellent score. But less than 2 percent of journals earn a score of ten or greater. Three is considered good, and about 23 percent of journals score three or higher. The average score among all journals is actually less than one. Here are a few psychology journal impact factors that were easily found on the journal websites:

- *American Psychologist*, 16.40
- *Developmental Psychology*, 4.50
- *Health Psychology*, 5.56
- *Journal of Applied Psychology*, 11.80
- *Journal of Educational Psychology*, 6.86
- *Journal of Experimental Psychology: Learning, Memory, and Cognition*, 3.14
- *Psychology Bulletin*, 23.03
- *Psychology of Popular Media*, 2.90

Impact factors pertain to journals, but what about the direct impact of your published work? To gauge personal impact or influence, determine how many times your article is cited. There are websites that simply report this such as Web of Science and Google Scholar. And, there are even studies showing which scholars are most cited.[6]

So, what's a good citation rate? Five to ten times cited is great, real Champions League material. Here's why. Almost 44 percent of all published articles are never cited. Therefore, even one citation for an article and you are nearly in the top half. With ten or more citations, your work is in the top 24 percent of the most cited work worldwide. This increases to the top 1.8 percent as you reach a hundred or more citations.[7]

Although it seems right to follow Renkl's advice and at least occasionally play in the Champions League, it is also important to find an appropriate landing spot for your work where it is likely to be read by those most interested in your topic. Although Rich Mayer publishes most of his scientific work in *Journal of Educational Psychology* (impact factor 6.86), he also publishes in other journals with lower impact factors that are especially well suited for his subject. For example, an article about individual differences in gender-role beliefs[8] was published in *Learning and Individual Differences* (impact factor 3.14).

Meanwhile, David Berliner offers an alternative view to Renkl's emphasis on publishing Champions League research. Berliner said: "I regard it as a scholar's obligation to share what they know. Moreover, with open access journals and free online publications in this age, a high-quality journal is not the only way to promote one's research."[9]

Work on Multiple Projects

All the productive graduate students and scholars I investigated work on multiple projects at any given time. Award-winning graduate student scholar Sirui Wan worked on several projects simultaneously while often taking the lead on three projects at any given time.[1]

Among German scholars,[2] Heinz Mandl and Hans Gruber report that they work on three to seven projects at a time. Alexander Renkl often handles ten projects at a time, while Frank Fischer juggles fifteen. Renkl and his co-investigators stagger projects so that they are at different points of completion. Renkl said: "We're working on two projects where we are writing the proposal. We have six to seven projects that are running and two more that we are trying to get accepted for publication."[3] By staggering project timing, Renkl and his team always have a variety of tasks (such as study design, material development, data collection, and manuscript writing and revising) to keep them busy. American scholars Logan Fiorella and Sabina Neugebauer do much the same.[4] Fiorella reports working on five to seven different projects at various stages of completion. Neugebauer typically has "many projects going on in different phases within the lifecycle of a project."[5]

A key element to working on multiple projects is marshalling and directing collaborators. This way, a scholar can work with various collaborators (students, postdocs, or colleagues) on an assortment of projects or with a team of collaborators on one or more projects. Scholar Richard Anderson credits the graduate student research teams he forms and trains for his productivity: "If you're going to be a productive researcher, you need to get your new people enculturated, get them motivated, and get them to understand what they're supposed to do. It's good for them; it keeps up the productivity of the whole group and the senior professor."[6] Frank Fischer also credits his ability to marshal and direct student collaborators for his productivity. Fischer said: "My student collaborators are really doing the research in terms of data collection, data analysis, and typically writing the draft of the paper."[7] Meanwhile, Fischer positions himself behind the scenes – monitoring the progress of manuscripts, providing feedback, and helping maintain accountability within the group. Fischer also holds weekly meetings with his team and provides up to fifteen rounds of feedback on written products.

When marshalling collaborators, it is important to delegate responsibilities according to strengths. For example, conducting and interpreting statistical analyses is not my strength, so I delegate this task to someone with these skills. My forte comes in designing studies, creating experimental materials, and manuscript writing, so the bulk of my efforts goes there.

There are several obvious advantages to working on multiple projects simultaneously, including:

- Boosting productivity. Many hands make light work. The more people working together on more things, the more and faster things get done.
- Spreading your bets. Not every project is a winner, not every article is Champions League material. With multiple projects going, the failure of one is less traumatic or impactful.
- Gap filling. In the life cycle of a project, there are gaps when not much can be done, such as when waiting for IRB approval or waiting eight months while your manuscript is under review. These and other gaps are easily filled by working on other projects in varying phases of completion.
- Avoiding burnout. Working for a long time on a single project can send you down a fiery rabbit hole. It's good to keep fresh by spreading your attention over various projects.

Here are a few more tips for working on multiple projects, in addition to the marshalling-and-directing-collaborators advice offered earlier:

- Don't try to captain every ship. That requires too much effort, time, and responsibility. Take the helm on some projects; add some power from the stern on others.
- Mix in some conceptual projects. Work on both empirical studies and conceptual pieces. Both are important. Conceptual pieces, though, do not ordinarily require as many resources or as much work. For instance, there are no materials to create, subjects to run, or data to analyze.
- Don't leave things sitting too long as you move among projects. Ming-Te Wang warned that when you put something aside for too long, "it's really difficult to find the thread and pick back up."[8]

Table 5.1 *The Eisenhower Matrix*

	Urgent	Not Urgent
Important	Do It	Schedule It
Not Important	Delegate It	Delete It

- Keep good records. Have a paper or electronic folder for each research project. Each time you work on a project, note what was accomplished and what you plan to do next. That will save a lot of "Where was I?" time wasting.
- Be guided by the Eisenhower matrix. In a 1954 speech, President Eisenhower quoted an unnamed university president who said: "I have two kinds of problems, the urgent and the important. The urgent are not important, and the important are not urgent."[9] Good point. Our problem-solving tendency, though, is to give our primary attention to the urgent present rather than the important future. A *Journal of Consumer Research* study[10] found that our attention is drawn to time-sensitive tasks over tasks that are less urgent, even when the less urgent tasks offer greater rewards. Enter Stephen Covey, author of *The 7 Habits of Highly Effective People*,[11] who repackaged Eisenhower's insights into the Eisenhower Matrix in Table 5.1 that helps in prioritizing multiple tasks or projects.

According to the matrix, here's what you should do. When things are both urgent and important, meaning there is a clear deadline and consequences for not taking immediate action, like completing a grant proposal before a hard deadline, then do it. When things are not urgent but important, meaning there are activities to complete that bring you closer to your goals but there is no set deadline, like writing the introduction for a research study, then don't simply procrastinate, schedule it. When things are urgent but not important, meaning things need to be done but don't require your specific skills, like formatting a manuscript, delegate the task to others. And, when things are neither urgent nor important, meaning they need not get done and certainly not now, like checking social media, delete it or do in moderation so as not to steal time from other urgent and/or important tasks. Hopefully, this matrix can help you move across your multiple projects while also handling, or not handling, other nonscholarly tasks.

Be Selective

A scholarly career is only so long, and each day is but twenty-four hours. So, be selective about the projects on which you choose to work. Scholar Tamara van Gog is guided by this question: "What do I have to get involved in, what do I want to get involved in, and what do I not want to get involved in?"[1] In the same vein, Alexander Renkl recommends that scholars establish a professional identity, have a primary topic connected to their name, and not run after the newest or most vogue topic.[2]

Logan Fiorella has a research program that keeps him focused and selective. All his projects address one broad research question: How do we help students learn for understanding? Fiorella turns down most collaborative invitations not central to that question.[3] Ming-Te Wang advises scholars, especially junior ones, to say no to project invitations that lead them outside their professional identities. Wang said: "Early on, I focused on my own work rather than getting lost exploring different collaborations with different people. I was highly cautious about what collaborations I accepted or pursued, only choosing those I found promising and doable."[4]

I recall one colleague, a methodologist, who had a long publication list. The problem was that the list stretched over dozens of research topics because the methodologist was invariably playing second, third, or fourth fiddle to someone else's work, supplying methodological know-how but never carving a personal identity.

Scholars also mentioned the need to say "no" to competing tasks that can pull them off their scholarly track. Fiorella finds that making too many commitments, even small ones, distracts him.[5] Wang said: "I needed to learn to say 'no' to people and stay true to the goals I wanted to accomplish."[6]

So, is it ever okay to move outside one's selected topic and join the work of others? Yes, so long as you are focusing first and foremost on your personal identity and so long as one or more of these conditions apply:

- You are likely to learn something. Something about a topic, something about design and methodology, something about data analysis, something about writing that will ultimately help you in your other scholarly work.

- The work is likely to be of high quality and likely to be published. Having a strong publication record is not a be-all, end-all, but it is vital when it comes to things like annual evaluation, promotion and tenure, and grant getting. Don't join projects with low viability.
- You expand or strengthen your professional network. Having strong colleagues in your corner is invaluable. Over the years, I have been able to reach out to research collaborators for career advice, manuscript reviews, invited talks, and support letters. I've also been able to link my graduate advisees to these colleagues. The adage, "it's not what you know but who you know that counts," certainly has some validity.

Formulate Good Research Questions

I have seen it many times. A graduate student has written a proposal complete with literature review and intended design, methods, and analyses. "Nice work," I say, "but what's your research question?" "My what?" the student sheepishly replies. Proposing a study without a research question is like building a home without first drafting blueprints or like heading out on vacation without a destination in mind. The research question guides all else.

Former student Alice Corkill indicated that John Glover was a master at formulating and answering research questions:

> John was not interested in collecting bunches of data, he was interested in collecting specific pieces of data that were going to answer highly specific questions. He always had his research questions firmly in mind before he collected the data. This made it possible for him to design simple, clean, and sharp studies and to develop measures that would best answer the specific questions he had posed.[1]

Productive scholar Rich Mayer declared that the single most important thing in doing good research was raising good research questions. He said: "Good research questions are personally interesting, have educational and theoretical relevance, and are also feasible to carry out."[2]

Productive scholar Patricia Alexander echoed Mayer's feasibility sentiment. She said: "Students often try to answer the world. Their questions are too big, too unmanageable. Ask and answer manageable questions."[3]

Productive scholar Ivar Braten speaks to the origin of good research questions. He said:

Identifying essential research questions can only be done by reading widely and deeply because by doing that, interesting and relevant questions are easily identifiable. Besides, the research questions tend to grow naturally out of what we have already done within the research team because we are mostly doing programmatic research where addressing one [research question] usually highlights the need to address at least five new ones.[4]

It is important that your research questions are specific and manageable. Here are some weak and strong examples:

- Weak: What effect do behavioral objectives have?
- Strong: What effect do behavioral objectives have on the learning of objective-directed content?
- Weak: Does a graphic organizer aid learning?
- Strong: Is a graphic organizer more effective than an outline for increasing relationship learning?
- Weak: Should students test themselves?
- Strong: Is self-testing of lesson material more effective than reviewing the lesson material prior to testing?
- Weak: Do students mark their texts?
- Strong: How do students mark their texts in terms of markers of importance, organization, and elaboration?

Design Feasible Studies

Graduate students with a couple research methods courses under their belt and looking to flex their research design muscle are prone to designing overly complicated and esoteric studies. They think, "why not have a really cool 2 × 3 × 3 factorial design?" Because a much simpler design might be best for answering your research question, that's why. Rich Mayer said:

Feasibility is a big problem for most students. Sometimes they have a great research question but their plan for answering the question is not feasible. So, sometimes you might need to give up a little bit in order to actually do a study. Find a research method that allows you to answer your question, but is also as simple and as straightforward as possible. A lot of students make the methodology more complicated than it needs to be. They put in too many factors and explore unnecessary side issues. Keep things simple and clean.[1]

Mayer advocates designing studies that focus on one clear question rather than many questions. He especially recommends a simple first study that compares the most extreme versions of just two groups.[2] Following Mayer's parsimony principle, if you want to know whether pre-questions inserted in text aid comprehension, you might design a simple initial study that compares one group with pre-questions and one without pre-questions. If results show a pre-questions advantage, then you can explore more revealing research designs, such as comparing pre-questions to objectives, comparing pre-questions to post questions, or assessing the effect of pre-questions on various learning outcomes such as factual and conceptual knowledge.

Reuse Materials

I recall the work of John Glover and colleagues who conducted numerous and wonderful studies on prose processing. In several of these studies, the same reading materials were used. Participants across studies read a text about the fictitious country of Mala. I joked with the authors, asking if their findings could generalize outside Mala. Certainly this team of researchers is not alone in reusing experimental materials. Rich Mayer has reused materials on the scientific topics of brakes, radar, and lightning, to name a few. I have reused material on topics such as creativity, wildcats, educational measurement, and learning hierarchies.

Reusing materials makes sense because a lot of time and effort goes into creating a set of materials. Researchers go to great pains to create materials on the right topic, with the right length, at the right level, and with the right assessments. They might also need to analyze materials for idea units and conduct item analyses for tests. They might need to create accompanying adjunct materials too, such as advance organizers, embedded questions, and graphic organizers. They might need to create multiple versions of materials such as those presented at slow or fast rates or those delivered via text or video.

Although it is important to eventually replicate findings across different learning conditions, even leaving the friendly confines of Mala, you'd be wise to sensibly reuse previously developed materials for your research when feasible.

And not just research. Consider that when Michael Pressley wanted to write an educational psychology text, one was not enough. Pressley simultaneously coauthored three educational psychology texts, one for undergraduates, one for early-program graduate students, and one for advanced graduate students, all drawn from a common literature base.[1]

Of course the reuse of well-developed materials is also prudent when it comes to teaching or invited presentations. The degree to which you can reuse course or presentation materials, the more time you'll have available for scholarship.

Frame Failure

You win some, you lose some; some are rained out, and you can't get tickets for the rest. That's baseball ... and also scholarship. Not everything is going to go your way. Not everything is going to get published. There will be disappointments and setbacks. But when failure rears its ugly head, don't ignore it, don't be disheartened by it, and don't run from it. Frame failure instead. That's what successful people do.

Understand that everyone fails. Abraham Lincoln was a poster president for failure. Before being elected President of the United States, Lincoln failed in business, was defeated in his run for the Legislature, failed in business again, and was defeated, in succession, for Elector, Congress, Congress, Senate, Vice President, and Senate. Ty Cobb is the greatest hitter in baseball history, with a career batting average of .366. Way to go, but that means that Cobb failed to get a hit in two-thirds of his at bats. Author F. Scott Fitzgerald once had more than a hundred rejection letters pinned to his walls before penning classics like *The Great Gatsby* and *Tender Is the Night*.

Among scholars, even Rich Mayer, the most productive educational psychologist on the planet, has work rejected. Mayer said: "I've probably had more papers rejected from the *Journal of Educational Psychology* than anyone in the history of that journal. That's one thing about this field, you have to learn how to take rejection and how to take criticism."[1]

Early-career award-winning scholar Ming-Te Wang has experienced his share of rejection. Wang said: "All academics must get used to rejection, and young scholars must realize that rejection is something all scholars must live with and learn from no matter how senior." He somewhat jokingly added that young scholars would better understand that no scholars are immune from rejection "if we all published a

CV of rejections."[2] Tamara van Gog cautioned: "If you want to get into the top journals, you have to expect rejections and multiple revision rounds. Accept that failure is part of it."[3] Some scholars failed dismally almost before they started. Rebecca Collie dropped out of college,[4] and David Berliner flunked out.[5]

Dale Schunk advises budding scholars to "ride the wave." Schunk said:

Being a scholar is like riding a wave ... There were periods when I was very productive and other periods when I was not so productive. If you look at my publication record over the years, it goes up and then tapers off a little bit. Then it goes up and tapers off a little bit again and again. When I thought about this pattern, I realized that even during those periods when I was not publishing so much, I was still being productive as I thought about things and planned new projects. [My advice, then,] is to keep thinking about the future, what you're going to do next, [and keep riding that wave].[6]

Psychologist Howard Gardner, who studied highly creative people, found that all of them failed, producing more flops than hits, but that all of them framed failure in positive ways, seeing it as a learning opportunity and pathway to eventual success. Gardner went so far as designating failure framing as one of the three virtues of successful creators.[7] General Colin Powell agrees. He said: "There are no secrets to success. It is the result of preparation, hard work, and learning from failure."[8] Writer James Michener echoed that sentiment: "Character consists of what you do on the third and fourth tries."[9]

Patricia Alexander is a failure framer. She said:

No journey that culminates in academic success will be uncomplicated or straightforward. Instead, that journey will be marked by twists and turns, ups and downs, and moments of triumph and tribulation. Everyone will stumble and fall at some point – it is inevitable. Yet, as I heard my father say many times, the real measure of individuals is not how many times they stumble or fall, but how many times they pick themselves up and try again ... [When you do fall], analyze the circumstances that contributed [to the fall] before dusting off and giving it another try ... Expect your professional journey to be eventful, occasionally exhilarating, and frustrating, and learn to relish each and every step along the way ...[10]

Let failure be your catalyst and your guide.

References

Use Productive Research Approaches

1 Tzu, L. *Inc.* www.inc.com/lolly-daskal/100-powerful-quotes-that-will-boost-your-productivity.html.

Prioritize Research

1 Kiewra, K. A., Luo, L., & Flanigan, A. (2021). Educational psychology early career award winners: How did they do it? *Educational Psychology Review, 33*, 1981–2018 (p. 2007).
2 Kiewra, K. A., & Kauffman, D. (2023). John Glover: A long overdue account of his productive scholarship methods. *Educational Psychology Review, 35*, Article 56.
3 Prinz, A., Zeeb, H., Flanigan, A., Renkl, A., & Kiewra, K. A. (2020). Conversations with five highly successful female educational psychologists: Patricia Alexander, Carol Dweck, Jacquelynne Eccles, Mareike Kunter, and Tamara van Gog. *Educational Psychology Review, 33*, 763–795.
4 Kiewra, K. A., Luo, L., & Flanigan, A. (2021). Educational psychology early career award winners: How did they do it? *Educational Psychology Review, 33*, 1981–2018 (p. 2012).
5 Prinz, A., Zeeb, H., Flanigan, A., Renkl, A., & Kiewra, K. A. (2020). Conversations with five highly successful female educational psychologists: Patricia Alexander, Carol Dweck, Jacquelynne Eccles, Mareike Kunter, and Tamara van Gog. *Educational Psychology Review, 33*, 763–795 (p. 778).
6 Kiewra, K. A., Luo, L., & Flanigan, A. (2021). Educational psychology early career award winners: How did they do it? *Educational Psychology Review, 33*, 1981–2018 (p. 1989).
7 Ibid. (no page numbers designated).
8 Kiewra, K. A., & Kauffman, D. (2023). John Glover: A long overdue account of his productive scholarship methods. *Educational Psychology Review, 35*, Article 56.
9 McCormick, C. B. & Barnes, B. J. (2008). Getting started in academia: A guide for educational psychologists. *Educational Psychology Review, 20*, 5–18.
10 Kiewra, K. A., Luo, L., & Flanigan, A. (2021). Educational psychology early career award winners: How did they do it? *Educational Psychology Review, 33*, 1981–2018.

Collaborate

1 Kiewra, K. A., Luo, L., & Flanigan, A. (2021). Educational psychology early career award winners: How did they do it? *Educational Psychology Review*, *33*, 1981–2018.

2 Patterson-Hazley, M., & Kiewra, K. A. (2013). Conversations with four highly productive educational psychologists: Patricia Alexander, Richard Mayer, Dale Schunk, and Barry Zimmerman. *Educational Psychology Review*, *25*, 19–45.

3 Ibid.

4 Prinz, A., Zeeb, H., Flanigan, A., Renkl, A., & Kiewra, K. A. (2020). Conversations with five highly successful female educational psychologists: Patricia Alexander, Carol Dweck, Jacquelynne Eccles, Mareike Kunter, and Tamara van Gog. *Educational Psychology Review*, *33*, 763–795.

5 Fong, C. J., Flanigan, A. E., Hogan, E., et al. (2022). Individual and institutional productivity in educational psychology journals from 2015 to 2021. *Educational Psychology Review*, *34*, 2379–2403.

6 Bembenutty, H. (2022). *Contemporary pioneers in teaching and learning*, Vol. 2. Charlotte, NC: Information Age Publishing, Inc. (p. 252).

7 Patterson-Hazley, M., & Kiewra, K. A. (2013). Conversations with four highly productive educational psychologists: Patricia Alexander, Richard Mayer, Dale Schunk, and Barry Zimmerman. *Educational Psychology Review*, *25*, 19–45.

8 Ibid., p. 39.

9 Patterson-Hazley, M., & Kiewra, K. A. (2013). Conversations with four highly productive educational psychologists: Patricia Alexander, Richard Mayer, Dale Schunk, and Barry Zimmerman. *Educational Psychology Review*, *25*, 19–45.

10 Kiewra, K. A., & Creswell, J. W. (2000). Conversations with three highly productive educational psychologists: Richard Anderson, Richard Mayer, and Michael Pressley. *Educational Psychology Review*, *12*, 135–161 (p. 148).

11 Kiewra, K. A., Luo, L., & Flanigan, A. (2021). Educational psychology early career award winners: How did they do it? *Educational Psychology Review*, *33*, 1981–2018 (p. 1999).

12 Ibid., p. 2009.

13 Flanigan, A., Kiewra, K. A., & Luo, L. (2018). Conversations with four highly productive German educational psychologists: Frank Fischer, Hans Gruber, Heinz Mandl, and Alexander Renkl. *Educational Psychology Review*, *30*, 303–330 (p. 324).

14 Bembenutty, H. (2022). *Contemporary pioneers in teaching and learning*, Vol. 2. Charlotte, NC: Information Age Publishing, Inc. (p. 23).

15 Kiewra, K. A., & Kauffman, D. (2023). John Glover: A long overdue account of his productive scholarship methods. *Educational Psychology Review*, 35, Article 56.

16 Kiewra, K. A., Luo, L., & Flanigan, A. (2021). Educational psychology early career award winners: How did they do it? *Educational Psychology Review*, 33, 1981–2018 (p. 2010).

Get Grants but Don't Chase Grants Too Early

1 Flanigan, A., Kiewra, K. A., & Luo, L. (2018). Conversations with four highly productive German educational psychologists: Frank Fischer, Hans Gruber, Heinz Mandl, and Alexander Renkl. *Educational Psychology Review*, 30, 303–330.

2 Kiewra, K. A., Luo, L., & Flanigan, A. (2021). Educational psychology early career award winners: How did they do it? *Educational Psychology Review*, 33, 1981–2018 (p. 1993).

Self-Regulate

1 Patterson-Hazley, M., & Kiewra, K. A. (2013). Conversations with four highly productive educational psychologists: Patricia Alexander, Richard Mayer, Dale Schunk, and Barry Zimmerman. *Educational Psychology Review*, 25, 19–45.

2 Ibid., p. 26.

3 Ibid.

4 Kiewra, K. A., Luo, L., & Flanigan, A. (2021). Educational psychology early career award winners: How did they do it? *Educational Psychology Review*, 33, 1981–2018 (p. 1992).

5 Prinz, A., Zeeb, H., Flanigan, A., Renkl, A., & Kiewra, K. A. (2020). Conversations with five highly successful female educational psychologists: Patricia Alexander, Carol Dweck, Jacquelynne Eccles, Mareike Kunter, and Tamara van Gog. *Educational Psychology Review*, 33, 763–795.

6 Kiewra, K. A., Walsh, J., & Labenz, C. (2023). Moving beyond fulfillment: Wisdom years stories of passion, perseverance, and productivity. *Educational Psychology Review*, 35, Article 20, p. 20.

7 Stillman, J. (December 20, 2012). You don't understand your to-do list. *Inc.* www.inc.com/jessica-stillman/you-do-not-understand-your-to-do-list .html.

8 Varvogil, L. (March 26, 2018). The magical act of crossing items off your list. *Medium.* https://drliza.medium.com/the-magical-act-of-crossing-items-off-your-llist-1916e1fc20e8.
9 Covey, S. R. (2020). *The 7 habits of highly effective people.* New York: Simon & Schuster.

Mine Large Data Sets

1 Leskovec, J., Rajaraman, A., & Ullman, J. (2020). *Mining of massive datasets* (3rd ed.). Cambridge: Cambridge University Press.
2 Kiewra, K. A., Luo, L., & Flanigan, A. (2021). Educational psychology early career award winners: How did they do it? *Educational Psychology Review, 33,* 1981–2018 (p. 1993).
3 Ibid., p. 1995.

Consider Conducting Meta-analyses

1 Henk, W. A., & Stahl, N. A. (1985). A meta-analysis of the effect of notetaking on learning from lecture. *Journal of Reading, 34,* 614–622.
2 Kiewra, K. A., Luo, L., & Flanigan, A. (2021). Educational psychology early career award winners: How did they do it? *Educational Psychology Review, 33,* 1981–2018.
3 Ibid., p. 2005.

Do Some Conceptual Writing

1 Flanigan, A., Kiewra, K. A., & Luo, L. (2018). Conversations with four highly productive German educational psychologists: Frank Fischer, Hans Gruber, Heinz Mandl, and Alexander Renkl. *Educational Psychology Review, 30,* 303–330.
2 Patterson-Hazley, M., & Kiewra, K. A. (2013). Conversations with four highly productive educational psychologists: Patricia Alexander, Richard Mayer, Dale Schunk, and Barry Zimmerman. *Educational Psychology Review, 25,* 19–45.

Write a Literature Review

1 Kiewra, K. A. (1985). Providing the instructor's notes: An effective addition to student notetaking. *Educational Psychologist, 20,* 33–39.
2 Kiewra, K. A. (1985). Investigating notetaking and review: A depth of processing alternative. *Educational Psychologist, 20,* 23–32.

3 Kiewra, K. A. (1987). Notetaking and review: The research and its implications. *Journal of Instructional Science*, *16*, 233–249.
4 Mayer, R. E. (1975). Information processing variables in learning to solve problems. *Review of Educational Research*, *45*, 525–541.
5 Mayer, R. E. (1979). Can advance organizers influence meaningful learning? *Review of Educational Research*, *49*, 371–383.
6 Mayer, R. E. (1979). Twenty years of research on advance organizers: Assimilation theory is still the best predictor of results. *Instructional Science*, *8*, 133–167.
7 Mayer, R. E. (1984). Aids to prose comprehension. *Educational Psychologist*, *19*, 30–42.

Do Some Champions League Research

1 Flanigan, A., Kiewra, K. A., & Luo, L. (2018). Conversations with four highly productive German educational psychologists: Frank Fischer, Hans Gruber, Heinz Mandl, and Alexander Renkl. *Educational Psychology Review*, *30*, 303–330 (p. 324).
2 Ibid. (no page numbers designated).
3 Kiewra, K. A., Luo, L., & Flanigan, A. (2021). Educational psychology early career award winners: How did they do it? *Educational Psychology Review*, *33*, 1981–2018 (p. 2015).
4 McKiernan, E. C., Schimanski, L. A., Muñoz Nieves, C., Matthias, L., Niles, M. T., & Alperin, J. P. (2019). Use of the journal impact factor in academic review, promotion, and tenure evaluations. *eLife*, *8*, e47338. doi/10.7554/eLife.47338.
5 Integrity or impact: What matters in scientific publishing? (January 22, 2021). *Ego Academy*. www.enago.com/academy/integrity-or-impact-what-matters-in-scientific-publishing.
6 Baas, J., Boyack, K., & Loannidis, J. P. A. (October 8, 2020). Data for "updated science-wide author databases of standardized citation indicators." *Elsevier Data Repository*. https://elsevier.digitalcommonsdata.com/datasets/btchxktzyw/2?utm_source=miragenews&utm_medium=miragenews&utm_campaign=news.
7 Beaulieu, L. (November 19, 2015). How many citations are actually a lot of citations? *Ruminating…* https://lucbeaulieu.com/2015/11/19/how-many-citations-are-actually-a-lot-of-citations.
8 Massa, L. J., Mayer, R. E., & Bohon, L. M. (2005). Individual differences in gender role beliefs influence spatial ability test performance. *Learning and Individual Differences*, *15*, 99–111.
9 Bembenutty, H. (2022). *Contemporary pioneers in teaching and learning*, Vol. 2. Charlotte, NC: Information Age Publishing, Inc. (p. 22).

Work on Multiple Projects

1 Kiewra, K. A., Hasnin, S., Soundy, J., Premkumar, P. K., & Labenz, C. (2023). Graduate student award winners in educational psychology: What made them successful? *Educational Psychology Review*, *35*, Article 90.

2 Flanigan, A., Kiewra, K. A., & Luo, L. (2018). Conversations with four highly productive German educational psychologists: Frank Fischer, Hans Gruber, Heinz Mandl, and Alexander Renkl. *Educational Psychology Review*, *30*, 303–330.

3 Ibid., p. 321.

4 Kiewra, K. A., Luo, L., & Flanigan, A. (2021). Educational psychology early career award winners: How did they do it? *Educational Psychology Review*, *33*, 1981–2018.

5 Ibid., p. 1997.

6 Kiewra, K. A., & Creswell, J. W. (2000). Conversations with three highly productive educational psychologists: Richard Anderson, Richard Mayer, and Michael Pressley. *Educational Psychology Review*, *12*, 135–161 (p. 142).

7 Flanigan, A., Kiewra, K. A., & Luo, L. (2018). Conversations with four highly productive German educational psychologists: Frank Fischer, Hans Gruber, Heinz Mandl, and Alexander Renkl. *Educational Psychology Review*, *30*, 303–330 (p. 315).

8 Kiewra, K. A., Luo, L., & Flanigan, A. (2021). Educational psychology early career award winners: How did they do it? *Educational Psychology Review*, *33*, 1981–2018 (p. 1992).

9 The Eisenhower Matrix: The key to productivity and time management. (August 14, 2019). *Xebrio*. https://medium.com/xebrio/eisenhower-matrix-the-key-to-productivity-and-time-management-f510cbd808e1.

10 Zu, M., Yang, Y., & Hsee, C. K. (February 9, 2018). The mere urgency effect. *Journal of Consumer Science*, *45*, 673–690.

11 Covey, S. R. (2020). *The 7 habits of highly effective people*. New York: Simon & Schuster.

Be Selective

1 Prinz, A., Zeeb, H., Flanigan, A., Renkl, A., & Kiewra, K. A. (2020). Conversations with five highly successful female educational psychologists: Patricia Alexander, Carol Dweck, Jacquelynne Eccles, Mareike Kunter, and Tamara van Gog. *Educational Psychology Review*, *33*, 763–795 (p. 778).

2 Flanigan, A., Kiewra, K. A., & Luo, L. (2018). Conversations with four highly productive German educational psychologists: Frank Fischer, Hans

Gruber, Heinz Mandl, and Alexander Renkl. *Educational Psychology Review, 30,* 303–330.

3 Kiewra, K. A., Luo, L., & Flanigan, A. (2021). Educational psychology early career award winners: How did they do it? *Educational Psychology Review, 33,* 1981–2018.

4 Ibid., p. 1993.

5 Ibid. (no page numbers designated).

6 Ibid., p. 1993.

Formulate Good Research Questions

1 Kiewra, K. A., & Kauffman, D. (2023). John Glover: A long overdue account of his productive scholarship methods. *Educational Psychology Review, 35,* Article 56.

2 Patterson-Hazley, M., & Kiewra, K. A. (2013). Conversations with four highly productive educational psychologists: Patricia Alexander, Richard Mayer, Dale Schunk, and Barry Zimmerman. *Educational Psychology Review, 25,* 19–45 (p. 39).

3 Prinz, A., Zeeb, H., Flanigan, A., Renkl, A., & Kiewra, K. A. (2020). Conversations with five highly successful female educational psychologists: Patricia Alexander, Carol Dweck, Jacquelynne Eccles, Mareike Kunter, and Tamara van Gog. *Educational Psychology Review, 33,* 763–795 (p. 783).

4 Bembenutty, H. (2022). *Contemporary pioneers in teaching and learning,* Vol. 2. Charlotte, NC: Information Age Publishing, Inc. (p. 251).

Design Feasible Studies

1 Patterson-Hazley, M., & Kiewra, K. A. (2013). Conversations with four highly productive educational psychologists: Patricia Alexander, Richard Mayer, Dale Schunk, and Barry Zimmerman. *Educational Psychology Review, 25,* 19–45 (p. 39).

2 Mayer, R. E. (2008). Old advice to new researchers. *Educational Psychology Review, 20,* 19–28.

Reuse Materials

1 Kiewra, K. A., & Creswell, J. W. (2000). Conversations with three highly productive educational psychologists: Richard Anderson, Richard Mayer, and Michael Pressley. *Educational Psychology Review, 12,* 135–161.

Frame Failure

1 Kiewra, K. A., Walsh, J., & Labenz, C. (2023). Moving beyond fulfill-ment: Wisdom years stories of passion, perseverance, and productivity. *Educational Psychology Review*, *35*, Article 20, p. 12.

2 Kiewra, K. A., Luo, L., & Flanigan, A. (2021). Educational psychology early career award winners: How did they do it? *Educational Psychology Review*, *33*, 1981–2018 (p. 1993).

3 Prinz, A., Zeeb, H., Flanigan, A., Renkl, A., & Kiewra, K. A. (2020). Conversations with five highly successful female educational psycholo-gists: Patricia Alexander, Carol Dweck, Jacquelynne Eccles, Mareike Kunter, and Tamara van Gog. *Educational Psychology Review*, *33*, 763–795 (p. 783).

4 Kiewra, K. A., Luo, L., & Flanigan, A. (2021). Educational psychology early career award winners: How did they do it? *Educational Psychology Review*, *33*, 1981–2018.

5 Bembenutty, H. (2022). *Contemporary pioneers in teaching and learn-ing*, Vol. 2. Charlotte, NC: Information Age Publishing, Inc.

6 Patterson-Hazley, M., & Kiewra, K. A. (2013). Conversations with four highly productive educational psychologists: Patricia Alexander, Richard Mayer, Dale Schunk, and Barry Zimmerman. *Educational Psychology Review*, *25*, 19–45 (pp. 39–40).

7 Gardner, H. (1997). *Extraordinary minds*. New York: Basic Books.

8 Powell, C. *BrainyQuote*. www.brainyquote.com/quotes/colin_powell_121363.

9 Michener, J. A. *BrainyQuote*. www.brainyquote.com/quotes/james_a_michener_116031.

10 Bembenutty, H. (2022). *Contemporary pioneers in teaching and learn-ing*, Vol. 2. Charlotte, NC: Information Age Publishing, Inc. (p. 87).

6 | *Leverage Student Mentoring*

Michael Pressley said: "I've been able to have around me just very, very smart graduate students who were able to take me into things that I wouldn't have gotten into otherwise. We explore these things together and cut some paths that neither of us would have found on our own."[1]

Collaborate with Students

Productive scholars rarely publish alone. The early-career scholars sole authored about 5 percent of their works (ranging between 1 and 20 percent), and many of their collaborations were with students.[1] For example, 70 percent of Ming-Te Wang's publications and about 50 percent of Logan Fiorella's postgraduation publications include student authors. Erika Patall also collaborates more with students than with colleagues. She said: "I don't have a lot of collaborations with colleagues … For me, almost everything is done with students."[2] Looking at the recent CV publication data of a more established scholar, just one of Rich Mayer's last twenty-four empirical publications was sole authored. The others included sixty-one coauthors (2.5 coauthors per publication), with almost all coauthors being students. Mayer quipped: "I have wonderful students to work with who, of course, do all the work. We all know this is the secret to success in academia. They really are hardworking and inventive and a joy to be around."[3]

A quick check of my own CV revealed about 150 students – past or present – as coauthors on publications. In comparison, just a handful of coauthors were faculty.

Productive scholars offer these reasons for including graduate students in their work:

- **Multiple projects.** As mentioned earlier, scholars often oversee a team or teams of students working on multiple projects. This allows a faculty mentor and students to stagger projects so there is usually plenty of work to keep everyone busy on project tasks at various stages such as literature review, study design, material development, data collection, and manuscript writing.

- **New directions.** Just as mentors can lead students, students can lead mentors in new directions. Productive scholars credited students for steering them toward new and interesting research paths. Patricia Alexander reported that her work on epistemic beliefs and technology's influence on knowledge and truth were prompted by student interests.[4] Dale Schunk noted that some of his interests in school-based research stem from the school practitioners with whom he collaborates.[5] Jacquelynne Eccles credits one of her postdoctoral students for helping her develop expectancy-value theory.[6] Rebecca Collie credits her graduate students for pushing her "to learn more about statistics and to implement more robust ways of doing analyses."[7] Patricia Alexander added: "My students are great thinkers, and I owe them a lot for how they push me in this direction or that direction."[8] "My amazing doctoral students keep me on my toes. They make me think, and they always open new avenues of inquiry for me."[9] "My productivity is not my merit alone. It's that of many people."[10] Carol Dweck said this about her student collaborations: "Every idea was developed with them – through our constant conversations and discussions, through pouring over data."[11] Let students take you for a ride.
- **Increased energy.** Students bring energy to research projects and to their senior professors. Patricia Alexander said: "You cannot imagine the energy in these lab meetings when this many brilliant and engaged students collectively tackle one problem."[12]
- **Passing the torch.** Perhaps a scholar's most important role is training the next generation of scholars. Michael Pressley thought so. He said:

> You want to orient yourself to the students and to the people younger than you are because that really is your future ... What you're really supposed to be doing at the university is nurturing talent. I figured out you orient yourself to the young and do as much as you can to make it comfortable for them to interact with you and get a lot out of it, because the [young] ones are always grappling to find the cutting edge and are determined to define the cutting edge. The old ones, you know their ideas already. They're very public. A lot of [new faculty] I watch do it the other way.

They felt you come in here and you really orient yourself to the senior faculty and try to do things their way. I've never had that headset. And especially as you get older and more senior, it's critical to the future of the country and the discipline that you [work well] with your students. The one thing I always have to keep in mind is that most of these people will live 25 years or more longer into the next century than I will.[13]

Patricia Alexander also voiced a commitment to her students' accomplishments and legacies:

My academic family ... is what fills me with the greatest pride.[14] I would not be where I am today without my students, past and present. The most important thing to me is not what I accomplish, but what my students accomplish. I keep in touch with my graduate students, from the first to the present members. I am so proud of each of them and what they have accomplished. Long after I am gone, they will be the marks for which I will be remembered.[15]

Find Student Collaborators

In my department, when graduate students apply for admission, program faculty evaluate them, decide who to admit, and then assign newly admitted students to faculty based on faculty–student match and faculty load. The hope is that new students will be productive and raise the level of productivity among faculty as well. This is a fairly standard model for linking graduate students and professors, but it is not the only model. Consider these other methods professors use for attracting and working with students.

• **Grants.** Graduate students often apply to multiple institutions and their enrollment decision often weighs heavily on whether they are funded. Rich Mayer is among many scholars who seek extramural funding for his research and use the funding to attract and support graduate students. At any one time, Mayer's research grants support two to five graduate students who assume research assistantship positions in his research laboratory.[1] Ming-Te Wang directs a center on motivation at the University of Pittsburg. From that perch, Wang secures grants that fund graduate students conducting research Wang directs on motivation.[2]

- **Teaching assistantships.** A student need not have a research assistantship to become part of a research team. As a professor at Utah State University, I supervised three graduate teaching assistants assigned to teach educational psychology. I invited them to join me in conducting research projects on teaching and learning that was over and beyond their teaching duties. All accepted and, over a two-year period, we conducted and published four research studies.
- **Undergraduate students.** Some undergraduate students are eager research collaborators. At my own university, honors students conduct research under faculty supervision to complete an honors thesis. Students can also do a U-CARE project (Undergraduate Creative Activities and Research Experience), which is a paid opportunity to work one-on-one with a faculty member on research. I have often invited ambitious undergraduate students from my classes to join me on research projects. On one occasion, I taught a small honors section of an educational psychology class and together we conducted two studies. Sabina Neugebauer has been resourceful in transforming work study students slated to do clerical work in her department into paid research assistants. The students gain valuable research experience and even authorships.
- **Floaters.** No, not the little squiggles that sometimes cloud your vision. Erika Patall defines floaters as students who join research projects not supervised by their advisor. Student floating is an accepted practice at institutions where Patall has worked because advisors are not territorial in their graduate student collaborations.[3] Floating is accepted practice in my department too. One of my former doctoral advisees floated onto several projects while at Nebraska and graduated with seventeen publications and a wide range of valuable experiences.

Be Cautious about Your Advising Load

As for taking on advisees and chairing doctoral committees, be cautious. Although advising students is likely a doctoral program obligation, certainly an opportunity and privilege to train the next generation of scholars, and often a means to expanding one's own research interests and productivity, student advising can also prove onerous. Despite your best intentions and guidance, some students will struggle mightily. They might not show up or show interest. Even when on board, they might lack initiative or might steer off course repeatedly even in the calmest of waters. Struggling students will inordinately occupy your thoughts and time and offer little in return.

To offset such possibilities, be cautious about who is admitted to your doctoral program and who you choose to advise. Scrutinize student applications and hold interviews, even over Zoom or by phone, to best make sure that applicants are motivated, focused, and have a track record of success. Once students are on board, do your best to mentor them but ultimately recognize that they must chart a course, navigate stormy waters, and hold the tiller. I tell students: "I'm here for you, but I won't come looking for you. This is your journey."

The productive scholars I interviewed relished their mentoring roles but most limited their advising loads to three to five doctoral students at any given time. Such limitations were based, in part, on student funding resources and time availability.

On the flip side there are Patricia Alexander, who supervised twelve doctoral students at a time who worked in her laboratory.[1] There is also John Hattie. During Hattie's thirty-plus-year career, he supervised 206 graduate students to completion and considers that his proudest achievement. Hattie said: "Supervision is the fun part of being an academic as you learn so many new things. You are at the cutting edge of the discipline; you see and feel the [students'] passion [and learn about] their passion ... My proudest achievement is these 206."[2]

When asked how he wants to be remembered, Hattie replied:

I want my students to recall the fun of not knowing, discovering and making connections, bringing together seemingly unrelated ideas, and learning how to critique, write, and communicate. Yes, they will recall the pain, the blind alleys, and that I refused to do their work for them and was never satisfied until they could do all the writing, statistical analyses, and interpretations for themselves. I hope they will instill the love of research in their students [and help them] to make original and substantive contributions.[3]

Be a Talent Scout

When I was an undergraduate student at Oneonta College in New York, I took a developmental psychology course in my sophomore year from a young assistant professor named Dennis Hocevar. I performed well in the course, scoring 100 percent on all the course exams. When Professor Hocevar returned my last exam, he wrote boldly across the top: "When you are ready to apply to graduate schools, let me write a letter of recommendation for you." I was familiar with the concept of letter but had no idea what graduate school was or why I would be going there. No kidding. This was honestly the first time I had heard about graduate school, let alone considered a graduate school path. Two years and several educational psychology courses later, I realized that a doctorate in educational psychology was in my future. When it came time to apply, Professor Hocevar wrote a letter. To this day, I credit Professor Hocevar for recognizing my potential and mining a diamond in the rough.

Gale Sinatra, a former professor at the University of Nevada, Las Vegas, did much the same in recognizing that a student in her class should study educational psychology and in paving the way. The student was Doug Lombardi, who not only entered graduate school on her recommendation but who became an early-career award winner. Lombardi said: "I took a class from Gale, and she showed a lot of interest in me. She said, 'You should do this.' That's when I chose to study educational psychology. That's when it all clicked."[1]

Michael Pressley was a talent scout. He enjoyed finding and mining diamonds in the rough – students with good but unrefined ideas – through choice moments in classes, at conferences, or during consultations. He invited such students to join his research projects or to carve their own research studies with his assistance. I personally saw Pressley focused on students and junior faculty on several occasions, including visits to the University of Nebraska and while holding court at conference social hours. Pressley was sincere when he said: "You orient yourself to the young and do as much as you can to make it comfortable for them to interact with you and get a lot out of it."[2]

Enculturate Students

Richard Anderson said: "If you're going to be a productive researcher, you need to get your new people enculturated, get them motivated, and get them to understand what they're supposed to do. It's good for them; it keeps up the productivity of the whole group and the senior professor."[1] The enculturation process plays out as students meet weekly with Anderson and fellow students on multiple research projects. More senior students are assigned more leadership roles and aid in the rope-learning, mentoring process of more junior students. Experienced students also reap more of the publication rewards. Enculturating students is hardly a chore for Anderson, who said:

My sense of excitement [for my work] builds when that excitement is shared by the eager young people who together are going to do great things. It's exciting to come to work and bounce ideas around with these kids. I can now call them kids. I have been able to attract a stream of exceptional young people to work with. That keeps you young. That keeps you fresh.[2]

All the productive scholars take steps to enculturate their students, which starts with having regular, usually weekly, team and individual meetings. Logan Fiorella holds weekly meetings with students, but these are not mentor directed. Students must have completed written assignments in preparation for meetings and then share those ideas with one another. Fiorella said: "I like to have something concrete in writing that we can review together rather than just talking, so I usually require a one-page summary for which [we] can offer explicit feedback."[3]

Erika Patall said: "For each project, one graduate student is designated as the project leader. I like expectations to be clear from the get-go about what people's roles are and what kind of credit each is going to get."[4] Biweekly meetings with project leaders, project teams, and individual students keep Patall updated and involved in all project aspects.

Heinz Mandl enculturated his German students, who, in turn, are now enculturating the next generation of students. Mandle held weekly research meetings with students "where some of the strongest discussions took place, because I was very hard but also very helpful. Alexander, Hans, and the others had to speak about what they were working on and how they were going to conduct experiments."[5] One of those students, Hans Gruber, holds similar meetings that he calls whiteboard meetings. Gruber said: "I have a whiteboard in my office. The students write their plans on the whiteboard and then I go up and wipe out everything that is not clear, which often ends up being the complete board by the end of the meeting. That sounds very destructive, but it is really constructive because it tells them to make things clear."[6] Former Mandl student Frank Fischer holds weekly white box meetings. White boxes are the pizza boxes scattered about the room as students and mentor share and critique research ideas and activities over a pizza lunch. Former Mandle student Alexander Renkl spoke of the importance of group meetings and holding people accountable. He said: "You don't want to be the only one who says that you only reached 30% of your writing goal for that week while the others are at 100%. When this happens, students have discussions about why they didn't reach their goals and get stern advice from me and other students on how to reach their goals next time."[7]

Mareike Kunter said this about enculturating students: "What I really try to create is a team atmosphere where people are fearless, where everyone feels they can contribute, and where we learn and develop new things together."[8]

John Glover was an enculturator too, able to build and radiate a culture of research among students. Former colleague Bob Brown said: "John was like a shot of adrenaline among [students] he worked with,"[9] always building excitement for research. Former colleague Barbara Plake said this about Glover:

John met with a lot of students, and he met a lot. It was not unusual to see students in his office or him in the graduate student office. He spent a lot of time in there kicking around ideas. He was always kicking around ideas ... John also motivated students to think of their work as scholarship rather than just work. John always encouraged them to take an idea and turn it into a researchable question. Always encouraged them to pursue publication. He believed that no good idea should go unpublished.[10]

Former Glover student Alice Corkill added: "John's door was always open. He was always willing to interact with students, and when you'd walk through the door he would put down whatever it was he was doing and give you his full attention."[11]

Patricia Alexander works with about a dozen students in her research laboratory. Alexander finds the mentoring process intensive and time consuming but rewarding. She said: "When you have as many students as I have, you are always reading student work, meeting with them, and planning projects ... You cannot imagine the energy in these lab meetings when this many brilliant and engaged students collectively tackle one problem." Although Alexander fosters an engaged and friendly work environment that "blurs personal and professional," she has no trouble asserting her tough love authority and holding students accountable when enculturating them. She said: "I have no trouble being in charge, being the family's matriarch. There are points in time when I put my hand up and say, 'go speak to the hand because this is how it is.' At those points in time, I cause terror. When I speak, they listen."[12] Alexander added:

My doctoral students are my legacy. Their contributions and achievements will continue long after my own have ceased ... You must be willing to engage in tough love. As a mentor. You do whatever is required to ensure that your students are prepared to step out into the professional community and succeed. You never ask more of them than you ask yourself, but you hold them to the highest standard in all they do ... I want them to follow their paths and not be deterred by the barriers they will inevitably encounter. I want them to look back on their doctoral experiences with fondness, remember the good and forgive my failings. I hope that this is not too much to ask.[13]

Be a Director

Frank Fischer sees his mentoring role as that of a stage director. Fischer said: "My student collaborators are really doing the research in terms of data collection, data analysis, and typically writing the draft of the paper."[1] Meanwhile, Fischer positions himself behind the scenes – monitoring the progress of manuscripts, providing feedback, and helping maintain accountability within the group. The director role is not without a heavy workload. Fischer holds weekly meetings with student collaborators, provides up to fifteen rounds of feedback on a manuscript before submission, and oversees a research center that has amassed seven million dollars in funding to support the team's research efforts.

Being a director is much like being a back-seat driver: plotting a course, keeping things on course, but never turning the wheel. With back-seat driving often comes back-end authorship. Consider the three most productive scholars in educational psychology over the most recent five-year period: None of them had a first-author publication, but the trio of seasoned scholars had the highest number of last-author publications, a sign that they assumed director roles and generously credited students and junior faculty who could benefit most.[2]

Help Students Carve Their Own Research Areas

Although graduate students often join their advisors on advisor-conceived-and-led projects, some advisors are adamant that students develop and pursue their own research ideas. Rich Mayer said:

Students are in graduate school to become independent researchers, not to be my research assistants. I help them develop an initial research study that they can get up and running early in their program. I see my job as making sure that their study can be successful. That it is feasible and can make a contribution to the field. It is important that students work on their own ideas. People are a lot more productive when they work on something they are interested in.[1]

Similarly, Patricia Alexander said: "I do not ask students to study my model. I do not ask them to become the next generation of MDL [Model of Domain Learning] researchers."[2] Former John Glover student Alice Corkill recalled that Glover invited students onto his projects initially while eventually helping them carve their own research areas. Corkill said: "John got graduate students involved with research as quickly as possible by inviting them onto his projects. At the same time, he encouraged them to develop and pursue their own research interests. This helped students find their niche while expanding John's research agenda."[3]

Let's back up a bit and talk about admitting students to a graduate program. Some of my colleagues insist that we must only admit graduate students interested in pursuing a faculty member's research agenda. Two reasons why: (1) This best serves the faculty member in building a strong and coherent research team and program. (2) This is best and only fair for the graduate student who needs someone with topical knowledge to direct them. I say baloney.

First of all, if I waited to accept a graduate student with investigative interest in note taking or productive scholars, I might wait until icebergs reform and never have graduate advisees. Second, many prospective students are not really sure about their potential research agenda when they apply. Most probably discover that during their first year as they take classes, meet faculty, and learn what other students are doing. I certainly had no idea what area of research I would pursue when applying to graduate schools. Frankly, I had no idea that graduate school even involved doing research. Third, and most importantly, I believe that I can advise most any graduate student effectively regardless of topic. My primary role as advisor is to unveil the hidden curriculum, to pass along the type of graduate-school and career how-to-be-successful advice found throughout this book. An advisee with a research interest somewhat outside my topical expertise is not a problem. I can guide the student to master that topic by combing the literature and by consulting with me and others – both within and outside the university – about the topic. As with all dissertation research, it's the student who ultimately gains expertise through reading, consulting with others, and conducting research. The student becomes the expert informing the advisor and others.

Don't get me wrong. I'm not saying that I would invite any graduate student interested in any topic to become my advisee. Like Rich Mayer, I set the general parameter that "students have an interest in applying the science of learning to educational issues."[4] That broad parameter leaves a wide girth for accepting and advising many qualified students with varying research interests.

Help Students Network

I led a cloistered life as a graduate student. I never attended a conference or met faculty and students outside my university. I didn't even know that doing so was a thing. This omission didn't slow me down as I raced through graduate school in three years, but it limited my intellectual experiences and diminished my forming an academic network. Since graduate school, I have attended many academic conferences, which has allowed me to meet many influential scholars, several who are named throughout this book, during conference sessions and socials. Establishing a scholarly network has certainly paid off. Many of the invitations and collaborations that have come my way have stemmed from those meetings. I recall one particular meeting that was career changing. It took place in San Francisco in 1984, two years into my career. A new movement was afoot to study studying and self-regulated learning, and Bill Rohwer and John Thomas invited about a dozen influential scholars with interests in learning and motivation to talk about it ... and me. That single meeting was the springboard for my becoming an American Educational Research Association special-interest group chair and conference program chair, participating in several conference symposia, and having several publishing opportunities.

As a graduate advisor, I try to help my students form academic networks. I've done this by encouraging conference attendance and introducing them to influential scholars there, having them join regional and national organizations and nominating them for organizational positions, including them as student reviewers when I review journal manuscripts, taking them on visits to other universities, and having them join collaborative projects with scholars outside our university. My efforts have paid dividends as I've watched students and former students form networks leading them to editorial board posts, postdocs and faculty positions, and key roles in regional and national organizations.

Graduate student award winner Hyun Ji Lee's advisors helped her build a scholarly network while in graduate school by exposing her to the written work of international scholars and introducing her to them at international conferences. Lee said: "My advisors believed it was essential for me to keep up with the research of productive and influential scholars in my area and to meet those scholars firsthand. Meeting international scholars was inspirational for me because becoming an international scholar and conducting research on a global scale suddenly seemed a feasible goal for me."[1]

European scholars Hans Gruber and Tamara van Gog emphasized the research productivity value of developing a professional network. Gruber said: "Those who are inspired to join different groups and develop contacts have an easier time moving forward with their own research"[2] because they can turn to these contacts for guidance while conducting research.

Van Gog's networking began in graduate school. She had two highly influential mentors working in her cognitive load interest area, Jeroen Merriënboer and Fred Paas. They introduced her to their cognitive load network, including John Sweller and Anders Ericsson. Speaking of her graduate school experience, van Gog said:

It was a very good group that attracted a lot of international scholars and helped me be productive and expand my network ... Because I was in an environment that was highly productive, well-known, and internationally oriented, I got to do a lot of symposia at international conferences with leading researchers and research groups from around the world. We were well connected at the Open University. Those connections definitely helped my work and established visibility.[3]

Tell Students Not to Forget Their Advisor

As a decades-long member on my college's promotion and tenure committee, I have seen dozens of files submitted by those seeking tenure and promotion. As you might surmise, the ultimate decision often comes down to one thing – publication numbers – despite their being about a dozen unique standards revolving around teaching, research, and service. Determining publication numbers is not a matter of simple counting. Committee members tend to look deeper into the numbers. For one, they want to see how many publications are single or first authored, believing that such publications earmark scholars who are project leaders, not followers. Members do this despite a college guideline indicating that both independent and collaborative works are valued. They also do this despite findings that seasoned scholars often take secondary authorship positions to support graduate student coauthors.[1] Committee members are also quick to recognize if candidates have largely published with their doctoral advisor in the past and especially in the present. Their faulty reasoning is that true scholars cut their graduate school cords and pursue and lead their own research programs. Again, members do this despite guidelines offering no mention that ongoing collaborations with one's advisor are verboten or discouraged.

I find my colleagues' concerns about scholars continuing to work with their advisors unfounded, and so do scholars operating in the German system.[2] The largely American practice of separating from your advisor and proving you can stand on your own, is not a practice shared in the German system. German scholars continue to work with their advisors post graduate school if the collaboration proves fruitful for mentor and former student. Advisor Heinz Mandl, for example, published more than two hundred works with protégés Hans Gruber, Alexander Renkl, and Frank Fischer at Ludwig Maximilian University of Munich, with many of those works coming after the trio either graduated (Fischer) or left for professorships (Gruber and Renkl). American scholar Logan Fiorella is of similar mind. Speaking about his ongoing collaborations with former doctoral advisor Rich Mayer, Fiorella said: "[Rich and I] work really well together. I love working with Rich and have no plans to stop."[3]

I continue to work with a number of my former graduate students from time to time, sometimes by their invitation and sometimes by mine. In most cases, though, I insist that they take the lead and hold first authorship, as doing so just might be necessary to convince some campus evaluators that they are research leaders.

Teach Students the Hidden Curriculum

At the beginning of this book, I introduced the hidden curriculum, the behind-the-scenes insider information about academia that seasoned scholars know well, and likely take for granted, but is often shrouded from graduate students and junior faculty. Help bring students out of the dark and better prepare them for academia by shining a light on the hidden curriculum.

As previously mentioned, Rebecca Collie credits much of her scholarly success to the mentors who taught her the hidden curriculum in academia, the insider knowledge that helped her avoid dead ends and saved her "years-worth of wasted time." Collie pointed out that many assistant professors are not well versed on the workings of academia and have to navigate the hidden curriculum on their own. Collie said: "You might wonder, 'Do I do it this way or that way? I guess I have to try it this way.' Then if it doesn't work, you have to go back and do it the other way."[1]

Graduate student Carly Robinson was fortunate to take a professional development course at Harvard University that allowed her to explore the hidden curriculum for success in academia, ideas akin to those in this book. Robinson said: "I took a course designed to unearth the hidden curriculum. In this course, for example, we watched job talks and critiqued them to understand the do's and don'ts of job talks and that there is a recipe for writing literature reviews."[2]

Graduate student Sirui Wan took a similar writing course at UC Irvine aimed at helping him become a more productive scholar. Wan said:

The writing group class helped a lot. Every week, one person provided their writing sample and then others provided writing feedback. Because students hailed from different disciplines, the feedback especially helped me communicate research ideas to a wide audience. There was also a lot of good advice about other academic skills such as time management, planning, and dealing with rejection. Receiving this kind of information as a graduate student is tremendously important.[3]

In my mind, teaching students the hidden curriculum is best accomplished in the same way that academic skills, such as note taking and self-testing, are best taught, by embedding them into authentic situations, like history or science classes, rather than teaching them in a stand-alone study skills class apart from any curriculum. The skills are best understood and applied when associated with authentic learning situations.

The embedded curriculum might look like this: A history teacher covering Chinese dynasties might teach students how to construct matrix notes that visually capture associations among dynasties. This is done by modeling matrix construction, offering verbal pointers along the way, and telling students when they might create matrices in other learning situations. A science teacher might teach students how to generate fact, concept, and skill practice questions in advance of a test on molecular reactions. This is done by modeling practice question generation, offering verbal pointers along the way, and telling students when they might create practice items in other learning situations. In each case, the teaching of academic skills is seamlessly embedded within content instruction.

Turning to teaching graduate students the hidden curriculum of academia, the same embedded approach is recommended. When working on a conference presentation, the time is ripe for teaching students how to use graphics in a presentation, what to leave out of a presentation so it won't run long, and how to score free hors d'oeuvres and drinks at evening social events. When preparing your materials for annual evaluation, the time is ripe for teaching students how to record and document yearly activities and how to summarize and highlight accomplishments. When resubmitting a "revise and resubmit" manuscript, the time is ripe for teaching students how to craft a reviewer response letter. When you're serving on a search committee, the time is ripe for teaching students how to write a powerful application letter, how to best format a CV, and how to select and approach potential references.

You get the idea. You invite students to look over your academic shoulder. You welcome them to listen to your inner voice as you mull academic matters. You reveal the hidden curriculum.

Teach Students to Self-Regulate

Perhaps the ultimate hidden-curriculum skill you can teach students is how to self-regulate – how to act as their own inner-voice colleague and critic as they navigate academia. Self-regulation was previously covered more generally as part of Chapter 5.

Barry Zimmerman and Dale Schunk, bastions of self-regulation research and practice, employ mentoring styles designed to develop students' self-regulatory behaviors. Schunk said:

I try to apply self-regulation principles because the ultimate goal is for students to be self-regulating in their careers after graduate school. Thus, we set research and writing goals and sub-goals with timelines. I model research and writing skills as appropriate and gradually withdraw my guidance as students become more skillful. I provide constructive feedback to improve their skills and build self-efficacy.[1]

Zimmerman employs a similar mentoring style. He said: "I first model how a researcher plans and conducts a study, prepares a manuscript for publication, and responds to critics. Over time, my role changes: My modeling is diminished and my focus is on providing feedback."[2]

How else might teaching students to self-regulate play out during graduate school? Here's a few graduate school scenarios depicting things you might say to students to build self-regulation skills:

- "Let's anticipate some questions you might be asked at this job interview. It's best to anticipate questions and prepare responses so you're not caught off guard."
- "There might come a time that you'll want to rush through the dissertation revision process to meet a graduation deadline. That won't be happening. It will be finished when it's finished. Let's think through things together and make a realistic plan for a July completion."
- "As you construct your course syllabus, you'll need policies for handling late or missing work. Think about how you'll want to handle this. Consider how you might handle incidents where students are ill and incidents where students request extensions."

Tell Students to Pay It Forward

Faculty spend untold time and energy enculturating, directing, and supporting graduate students, and the benefits are many. As Patricia Alexander said: "My doctoral students are my legacy. Their contributions and achievements will continue long after my own have ceased."[1] This is especially true if such mentoring is passed down through one's academic family. University of Texas at Austin faculty member Claire

Ellen Weinstein did not assume that would happen naturally. Ivar Braten told this story:

I remember one of the first days that I visited [Claire Ellen's] lab during my sabbatical with her. A doctoral student of hers who had just defended her dissertation successfully came into her tiny office and thanked her warmly for all her personal and academic support during her work on the dissertation, upon which Claire Ellen just replied, "You remember this when you become a professor!"[2]

References

Leverage Student Mentoring

1 Kiewra, K. A., & Creswell, J. W. (2000). Conversations with three highly productive educational psychologists: Richard Anderson, Richard Mayer, and Michael Pressley. *Educational Psychology Review*, *12*, 135–161 (p. 153).

Collaborate with Students

1 Kiewra, K. A., Luo, L., & Flanigan, A. (2021). Educational psychology early career award winners: How did they do it? *Educational Psychology Review*, *33*, 1981–2018.
2 Ibid., p. 2007.
3 Kiewra, K. A., Walsh, J., & Labenz, C. (2023). Moving beyond fulfillment: Wisdom years stories of passion, perseverance, and productivity. *Educational Psychology Review*, *35*, Article 20, p. 11.
4 Patterson-Hazley, M., & Kiewra, K. A. (2013). Conversations with four highly productive educational psychologists: Patricia Alexander, Richard Mayer, Dale Schunk, and Barry Zimmerman. *Educational Psychology Review*, *25*, 19–45.
5 Ibid.
6 Prinz, A., Zeeb, H., Flanigan, A., Renkl, A., & Kiewra, K. A. (2020). Conversations with five highly successful female educational psychologists: Patricia Alexander, Carol Dweck, Jacquelynne Eccles, Mareike Kunter, and Tamara van Gog. *Educational Psychology Review*, *33*, 763–795.
7 Kiewra, K. A., Luo, L., & Flanigan, A. (2021). Educational psychology early career award winners: How did they do it? *Educational Psychology Review*, *33*, 1981–2018 (p. 1999).

8 Prinz, A., Zeeb, H., Flanigan, A., Renkl, A., & Kiewra, K. A. (2020). Conversations with five highly successful female educational psychologists: Patricia Alexander, Carol Dweck, Jacquelynne Eccles, Mareike Kunter, and Tamara van Gog. *Educational Psychology Review, 33,* 763–795 (p. 776).

9 Bembenutty, H. (2022). *Contemporary pioneers in teaching and learning,* Vol. 2. Charlotte, NC: Information Age Publishing, Inc. (p. 99).

10 Prinz, A., Zeeb, H., Flanigan, A., Renkl, A., & Kiewra, K. A. (2020). Conversations with five highly successful female educational psychologists: Patricia Alexander, Carol Dweck, Jacquelynne Eccles, Mareike Kunter, and Tamara van Gog. *Educational Psychology Review, 33,* 763–795 (p. 776).

11 Ibid.

12 Patterson-Hazley, M., & Kiewra, K. A. (2013). Conversations with four highly productive educational psychologists: Patricia Alexander, Richard Mayer, Dale Schunk, and Barry Zimmerman. *Educational Psychology Review, 25,* 19–45 (p. 35).

13 Kiewra, K. A., & Creswell, J. W. (2000). Conversations with three highly productive educational psychologists: Richard Anderson, Richard Mayer, and Michael Pressley. *Educational Psychology Review, 12,* 135–161 (pp. 153–154).

14 Prinz, A., Zeeb, H., Flanigan, A., Renkl, A., & Kiewra, K. A. (2020). Conversations with five highly successful female educational psychologists: Patricia Alexander, Carol Dweck, Jacquelynne Eccles, Mareike Kunter, and Tamara van Gog. *Educational Psychology Review, 33,* 763–795 (p. 773).

15 Patterson-Hazley, M., & Kiewra, K. A. (2013). Conversations with four highly productive educational psychologists: Patricia Alexander, Richard Mayer, Dale Schunk, and Barry Zimmerman. *Educational Psychology Review, 25,* 19–45 (p. 35).

Find Student Collaborators

1 Patterson-Hazley, M., & Kiewra, K. A. (2013). Conversations with four highly productive educational psychologists: Patricia Alexander, Richard Mayer, Dale Schunk, and Barry Zimmerman. *Educational Psychology Review, 25,* 19–45.

2 Kiewra, K. A., Luo, L., & Flanigan, A. (2021). Educational psychology early career award winners: How did they do it? *Educational Psychology Review, 33,* 1981–2018.

3 Ibid.

Be Cautious about Your Advising Load

1 Patterson-Hazley, M., & Kiewra, K. A. (2013). Conversations with four highly productive educational psychologists: Patricia Alexander, Richard Mayer, Dale Schunk, and Barry Zimmerman. *Educational Psychology Review, 25,* 19–45.
2 Bembenutty, H. (2022). *Contemporary pioneers in teaching and learning,* Vol. 2. Charlotte, NC: Information Age Publishing, Inc. (p. 161).
3 Ibid., p. 178.

Be a Talent Scout

1 Kiewra, K. A., Luo, L., & Flanigan, A. (2021). Educational psychology early career award winners: How did they do it? *Educational Psychology Review, 33,* 1981–2018 (p. 2003).
2 Kiewra, K. A., & Creswell, J. W. (2000). Conversations with three highly productive educational psychologists: Richard Anderson, Richard Mayer, and Michael Pressley. *Educational Psychology Review, 12,* 135–161 (p. 153).

Enculturate Students

1 Kiewra, K. A., & Creswell, J. W. (2000). Conversations with three highly productive educational psychologists: Richard Anderson, Richard Mayer, and Michael Pressley. *Educational Psychology Review, 12,* 135–161 (p. 142).
2 Ibid.
3 Kiewra, K. A., Luo, L., & Flanigan, A. (2021). Educational psychology early career award winners: How did they do it? *Educational Psychology Review, 33,* 1981–2018 (p. 1990).
4 Ibid., p. 2007.
5 Flanigan, A., Kiewra, K. A., & Luo, L. (2018). Conversations with four highly productive German educational psychologists: Frank Fischer, Hans Gruber, Heinz Mandl, and Alexander Renkl. *Educational Psychology Review, 30,* 303–330 (p. 320).
6 Ibid.
7 Ibid.
8 Prinz, A., Zeeb, H., Flanigan, A., Renkl, A., & Kiewra, K. A. (2020). Conversations with five highly successful female educational psychologists: Patricia Alexander, Carol Dweck, Jacquelynne Eccles, Mareike

Kunter, and Tamara van Gog. *Educational Psychology Review, 33,* 763–795 (p. 779).

 9 Kiewra, K. A., & Kauffman, D. (2023). John Glover: A long overdue account of his productive scholarship methods. *Educational Psychology Review, 35,* Article 56.

10 Ibid.

11 Ibid.

12 Patterson-Hazley, M., & Kiewra, K. A. (2013). Conversations with four highly productive educational psychologists: Patricia Alexander, Richard Mayer, Dale Schunk, and Barry Zimmerman. *Educational Psychology Review, 25,* 19–45 (p. 35).

13 Bembenutty, H. (2022). *Contemporary pioneers in teaching and learning,* Vol. 2. Charlotte, NC: Information Age Publishing, Inc. (p. 100).

Be a Director

1 Flanigan, A., Kiewra, K. A., & Luo, L. (2018). Conversations with four highly productive German educational psychologists: Frank Fischer, Hans Gruber, Heinz Mandl, and Alexander Renkl. *Educational Psychology Review, 30,* 303–330 (p. 315).

2 Fong, C. J., Flanigan, A. E., Hogan, E., et al. (2022). Individual and institutional productivity in educational psychology journals from 2015 to 2021. *Educational Psychology Review, 34,* 2379–2403.

Help Students Carve Their Own Research Areas

1 Patterson-Hazley, M., & Kiewra, K. A. (2013). Conversations with four highly productive educational psychologists: Patricia Alexander, Richard Mayer, Dale Schunk, and Barry Zimmerman. *Educational Psychology Review, 25,* 19–45 (p. 34).

2 Ibid., p. 35.

3 Kiewra, K. A., & Kauffman, D. (2023). John Glover: A long overdue account of his productive scholarship methods. *Educational Psychology Review, 35,* Article 56.

4 Patterson-Hazley, M., & Kiewra, K. A. (2013). Conversations with four highly productive educational psychologists: Patricia Alexander, Richard Mayer, Dale Schunk, and Barry Zimmerman. *Educational Psychology Review, 25,* 19–45 (p. 34).

Help Students Network

1 Kiewra, K. A., Hasnin, S., Soundy, J., Premkumar, P. K., & Labenz, C. (2023). Graduate student award winners in educational psychology:

What made them successful? *Educational Psychology Review, 35,* Article 90.

2 Flanigan, A., Kiewra, K. A., & Luo, L. (2018). Conversations with four highly productive German educational psychologists: Frank Fischer, Hans Gruber, Heinz Mandl, and Alexander Renkl. *Educational Psychology Review, 30,* 303–330 (p. 324).

3 Prinz, A., Zeeb, H., Flanigan, A., Renkl, A., & Kiewra, K. A. (2020). Conversations with five highly successful female educational psychologists: Patricia Alexander, Carol Dweck, Jacquelynne Eccles, Mareike Kunter, and Tamara van Gog. *Educational Psychology Review, 33,* 763–795 (p. 777).

Tell Students Not to Forget Their Advisor

1 Fong, C. J., Flanigan, A. E., Hogan, E., et al. (2022). Individual and institutional productivity in educational psychology journals from 2015 to 2021. *Educational Psychology Review, 34,* 2379–2403.

2 Flanigan, A., Kiewra, K. A., & Luo, L. (2018). Conversations with four highly productive German educational psychologists: Frank Fischer, Hans Gruber, Heinz Mandl, and Alexander Renkl. *Educational Psychology Review, 30,* 303–330.

3 Kiewra, K. A., Luo, L., & Flanigan, A. (2021). Educational psychology early career award winners: How did they do it? *Educational Psychology Review, 33,* 1981–2018 (p. 1989).

Teach Students the Hidden Curriculum

1 Kiewra, K. A., Luo, L., & Flanigan, A. (2021). Educational psychology early career award winners: How did they do it? *Educational Psychology Review, 33,* 1981–2018 (p. 1998).

2 Kiewra, K. A., Hasnin, S., Soundy, J., Premkumar, P. K., & Labenz, C. (2023). Graduate student award winners in educational psychology: What made them successful? *Educational Psychology Review, 35,* Article 90.

3 Ibid.

Teach Students to Self-Regulate

1 Patterson-Hazley, M., & Kiewra, K. A. (2013). Conversations with four highly productive educational psychologists: Patricia Alexander, Richard Mayer, Dale Schunk, and Barry Zimmerman. *Educational Psychology Review, 25,* 19–45 (p. 35).

2 Ibid.

Tell Students to Pay It Forward

1 Bembenutty, H. (2022). *Contemporary pioneers in teaching and learning*, Vol. 2. Charlotte, NC: Information Age Publishing, Inc. (p. 100).
2 Ibid., p. 251.

7 | *Write Like a Star*

There is nothing to writing. Ernest Hemingway said: "All you do is sit down at the typewriter and bleed."[1] Dr. Suess said: "Every word is a struggle and every sentence is like the pangs of birth."[2] And Nathaniel Hawthorne said: "Easy reading is hard writing."[3]

Make Writing a Habit

Robert Puller wrote: "Good habits, once established, are just as hard to break as are bad habits."[1]

Academics might be good thinkers, even creative, but none of that matters if they don't put their ideas in writing and eventually get them published. Writer Sylvia Plath said: "Nothing stinks like a pile of unpublished writing."[2]

Productive scholars make writing a habit. Logan Fiorella said: "It is really important to establish a writing habit, doing it at the same time and place day after day, where it's just what you do, and it feels like no big deal."[3] Ming-Te Wang said much the same: "I force myself to write every day even if it's just an hour or two or a single paragraph. Psychologically, I know I'm making progress. Moreover, when I put something aside for a few days, it is really difficult for me to find the thread and pick back up."[4] John Glover had a writing routine and he exhorted students to follow his lead. Former colleague Bob Brown said: "It was John's routine to arrive early to the office each day and immediately begin writing, before his coat stopped swinging on the hook."[5] Former Glover student Alice Corkill said that John's mantra was to: "Write every day! He told students to get in the habit of writing every day – five pages a day."[6] Somehow, someway, carve time out of your day to write every day. Keep the writing train moving.

Even when regular writing is a habit, some scholars find it difficult to dive into a new writing project. Karen Harris said that her husband jokes that "the house is never cleaner than when I need to start the first draft of a manuscript."[7] I recommend that you set a launch date for beginning that new writing project and stick to it. Author Wolfgang von Goethe said: "Whatever you think you can do or believe you can do, begin it. Action has magic, grace and power in it."[8] The philosopher Hillel simply said: "If not you, who? If not now, when?"[9] Quoting Paulo Coelho: "One day or day one? You decide."[10]

Organize Your Writing Plan

Most of the information I present in this book came from seven published research articles concerning twenty-seven productive scholars. Let me describe my four-step method for organizing this information in preparation for writing.

1. I created a document I called "Productive Scholar Notes." This was about seventy-five pages of single-spaced notes chronicling the content in each of the seven articles. For each article, I noted sequentially all important information, representative quotations, and page numbers where that information appeared in the article. I used organizational headings to classify the notes. Here is an example:

Healthy work–life balance, female scholar article, pp. 17–18.

Van Gog takes lunch walk. Spends one day a week free from work. Kunter takes lunch break away from office. Keeps weekends free, not even checking emails. Kunter said: "I need clear breaks. If I'm always involved in work, that isn't good for my well-being. When I work, I work hard and fully concentrated, but I try to keep parts of my life free from work." Dweck said:

"For some people, working all the time becomes unproductive. Maybe you feel good if you are putting in the hours and maybe you feel guilty if you are not putting in the hours – but are all those hours efficient? And might they be more efficient if you took a little time for something else? So just working, day after day, without a break, is probably not the most efficient way. And, you may not be as likely to bring new perspectives and ideas to what you are doing."

Scholars mentioned leisure activities. Dweck, Kunter, and van Gog mentioned sports like running and yoga, cultural activities, and spending time with families and friends. Alexander and Eccles said it is difficult to detangle from work.

2. I created a second document I called "Potential Topics and Advice." I created this by finding unique or reoccurring topics of importance throughout the notes I had created. There were about a hundred potential topics, such as: Healthy Work-Life Balance, Administrative Role Need Not Deter Productivity, Seek Out a Strong Advisor, Get Plenty of Sleep, Don't Worry about Sleep, Work Long Hours, Work Normal Hours ... For each potential topic, I scanned my "Productive Scholar Notes" and listed scholars who had something to contribute or say about this topic along with the page number in "Productive Scholar Notes" where that information could be found. Here is an example:

Collaborate

Pressley, 3; Mayer, Zimmerman, Schunk, and Alexander, 14; female scholars, 24; Eccles the collaborator, 25; Eccles, Anderson, Fischer, 29; Collie, 40; Lombardi, 43, 44; early scholars, 48–49.

3. I created "Potential Sections" by grouping "Potential Topics and Advice" into about twenty sections, each with a superordinate heading, such as Research Productivity Methods, Writing Methods, Time Management, Mentorship, Collaboration, and Advising. Here is a sample section for Lifestyle:

Lifestyle

- Create stability. 4
- Live on the edge. Pressley, Alexander, Gruber, 4; Wang, 35; Lombardi, 43
- Play the hand you're dealt, or don't. Alexander's illness, 11
- Make sacrifices, pack with the devil. Pressley, Alexander, 11; female scholars, 27; Patall, 46
- Work–life balance. Anderson and others, 4; Zimmerman, 11; female scholars, 29; Wang, 35
- Lead healthy lifestyle. Exercise and running, 4; Zimmerman, 11; Schunk, 12; Mayer, 12; Dweck, 27; van Gog, 27; Fiorella, 32; Wang, 35; Collie, 41; Lombardi, 42–43
- Build in breaks. Schunk, 12; van Gog, Kunter, Dweck, 27
- Put family first. Don't let work consume you. Mayer, 11, 12
- Difficulty disengaging from work. Alexander, Eccles, 27; Lombardi, 43; Patall, 45

- Women have more difficult lifestyle than men. Female scholars, 30

4. I used the "Productive Scholar Notes" and the "Potential Topics and Advice" documents to write much of the book. When I wrote a section on Work–Life Balance, for example, the "Potential Topics and Advice" document told me exactly where I could find relevant information and quotations in the "Productive Scholar Notes" document. From those notes, I wrote that section, which in some cases was later renamed.

Now imagine had I not used this organizational process to make sense of the seven articles. How would I proceed? Perhaps I would review one of the articles and see that mentorship is an important topic. I would collect that information and then search the other six articles for mentorship information before writing that section. Not too bad one time, but I would need to repeat this check-every-article approach for each of the approximately one hundred topics included in the book. Rather than proceed through each article one time, finding and collecting information, I might need to proceed through each article a hundred times, perhaps seven hundred searches in all. This is inefficient as it adds perhaps a hundred times the work.

I have used much the same process for writing literature reviews. Here was the process I used for writing the literature review on lecture note taking for my dissertation:

1. I read through a small sample of note-taking articles to determine the key variables in note-taking studies. I found that there were note-taking variables such as whether students recorded notes or only listened to the lecture or were provided notes; lecture variables such as topic, length, and rate; review variables such as review placement and length; test variables such as type and placement; and note-taking indices such as idea units and words noted.

2. I created a "Note-Taking Framework" based on these variables. As shown in Table 7.1, the framework has headings such as Lecture, subheadings such as Topic, and space to record relevant information.

3. As I reviewed dozens of note-taking articles, I used the Note-Taking Framework to record notes for each article, as shown in

Table 7.1 *Note-taking framework*

Note-Taking Manipulation:
Lecture:
      Topic:
      Length:
      Rate:
Review:
      Placement:
      Length:
Test:
      Type:
      Placement:

Note-Taking Indices:
      Ideas:
      Words:

Table 7.2, leaving me with a comparable set of notes for each article reviewed.

4. I next created a "Master Matrix," shown in Table 7.3, for comparing information across articles. The matrix listed each article along the top row and each note-taking variable down the left side. In the matrix cells, I recorded what was done or found in each article for each variable. For example, in the "Article A by Lecture Rate" cell was information showing that lecture rate was 120 words per minute. In the "Article B by Note-taking Ideas" cell was information showing that note takers recorded 25 percent of lecture ideas.

5. Because a good review is more than a laundry list of study-by-study descriptions and findings, I next analyzed the Master Matrix horizontally across rows looking for patterns. Doing this across a single row, I might see that lecture length varied from eight to fifty minutes. Good to know that this variable can vary widely. Looking across multiple rows, I might notice that notes were more complete and more wordy when lecture rates were slower versus faster. Really good to know.

6. This analysis and the observed patterns were the basis for writing an integrative review, with headings like How Lecture Rate Affects Note Taking, rather than producing a laundry list

Table 7.2 *Completed note-taking framework for sample article*

Note-Taking Manipulation: Take notes versus listen only
Lecture:
        Topic: Educational measurement
        Length: 35 min
        Rate: 120 wpm
Review:
        Placement: Immediately following lecture
        Length: 15 min
Test:
        Type: Recall and recognition
        Placement: Immediate (after review) and delayed (2 days later)
Note-Taking Indices:
        Ideas: 35% of lecture ideas recorded
        Words: 10 words/idea unit

---

of study-by-study findings. Integrative writing might sound like this:

> A review of note-taking studies suggests there is a pattern between lecture rate and note taking. In general, when lecture rates were rapid (150 wpm or greater), lecture note taking was restricted with students recording about 25 percent of lecture ideas. When lecture rates were slower (e.g., 100–125 wpm), however, lecture note taking was more complete, with students recording between 35 percent and 45 percent of lecture ideas.

You must organize information, whether that's findings from a literature review or group means from an experiment, to see patterns, the big picture, the forest through the trees.

Frame Your Writing

Productive scholars use frameworks to organize their writing. Rebecca Collie frames a manuscript's discussion section by addressing these four questions:[1]

1. What was found?
2. Why is it important?
3. How does it contribute to theory and practice?
4. Why might the finding have occurred?

Table 7.3 *Master matrix for comparing articles*

		Article A	Article B	Article C	Article D	Article E
Note-Taking Manipulation		Take v. Listen	Take v. Listen	Take only	Take v. Listen	Take v. Provided
Lecture						
	Topic	Educ. Meas.	Operant Learning	Wildcats	Trees	Geometry
	Length	35 min	50 min	10 min	8 min	50 min
	Rate	120 wpm	150 wpm	100 wpm	100 wpm	175 wpm
Review						
	Placement	Following lecture	None	Following lecture	Before test	Following lecture and before test
	Length	15 min		5 min	5 min	20 min
Test						
	Type	Fact recall & recognition	Fact and concept	Free recall	Fact recognition	Problem-solving
	Placement	Immediate & delayed	Immediate	Immediate	2-day delay	1-week delay
Note-Taking Indices						
	Ideas	35%	25%	40%	45%	25%
	Words	10/idea unit	6/idea unit	14/idea unit	12/idea unit	6/idea unit

153

Table 7.4 *Zimmerman's planning framework*

	Question 1	Question 2	Question 3
Psychological Dimensions			
Self-Regulation Attributes			
Self-Regulation Dimensions			

Table 7.5 *Matrix framework to guide writing*

	Method 1	Method 2	Method 3
Selection			
Organization			
Integration			

Dale Schunk begins with an outline that contains some level of detail about what each section of a manuscript will contain. Schunk said: "The outline will probably change once I start writing but that's okay because I just want to get something down that will serve as a framework."[2]

Before self-regulation researcher Barry Zimmerman writes, he lays out his writing ideas in a matrix framework containing (a) research questions, (b) psychological dimensions underlying those questions, (c) self-regulation attributes associated with each dimension, and (d) self-regulation dimensions designed to influence each attribute, as shown in Table 7.4.[3]

When writing a review article or the literature review of a research report, Richard Mayer often frames ideas in a clear and simple parallel structure. For example, if writing about instructional methods, he might create and complete the matrix framework in Table 7.5 that guides him in addressing how each method influences the selection, organization, and integration processes of learning.[4]

Don't Start at the Beginning

In *The Sound of Music*, actress Julie Andrews, playing the role of a nanny teaching children how to go about their chores, sang Rogers and Hammerstein's famous line: "Let's start at the very beginning, a very good place to start ..."[1] Good chore-completion advice perhaps, but not the advice scholars offer for composing a manuscript.

Tamara van Gog writes the theory and method sections first and actually writes them before she conducts the study.[2] Doing so helps her to detect potential theory or method issues that might make her rethink her study's design and methods before the study is run. All too often, researchers lament their research plan during the poststudy writing phase when they realize that their study would have been stronger had they done this or that. Scholars should do their best to close the barn door before mistakes run loose. Prewriting the methods and theory sections, as van Gog advises, is one way to offset potential poststudy problems.

When writing a research report, Rich Mayer does not start at the beginning either. He follows this plan: First, he creates the data tables and graphics that contain the main ideas he wants to convey. Mayer's own multimedia principle of text design supports the use of graphics as humans learn best from words and images rather than words alone. Next, he writes the methods section because "that is the easiest part; it's morale boosting."[3] Mayer then writes the results, introduction, and discussion sections in that order.

When writing the introduction, Mayer sometimes begins that in a nonconventional way, by dropping an anchor. Mayer leads with a concrete example reflective of the study's purpose, such as Mayer's example below foreshadowing his study to remedy difficulties students have remembering and applying scientific explanations. Starting with concrete examples gains readers' attention and provides an anchor for better understanding the study's purpose.

Consider the following scenario. A student who is inexperienced in meteorology reads a textbook lesson explaining the cause-and-effect chain of events involved in how lightning storms develop. The explanation is clearly contained within the 600 words and five illustrations of the lesson. A few minutes later, we ask the student to write down the explanation (as a retention test) and to solve some problems that require using the explanation from the lesson (as a transfer test) ... Despite exerting considerable effort, the student performs poorly on both the retention and transfer tasks, indicating a lack of understanding of the process of lightning. Unfortunately, this is not a made-up example, but rather a pattern of results obtained frequently in our research laboratory at Santa Barbara ...[4]

Like Mayer, Patricia Alexander often begins her writing with a metaphor or analogical reference that gains reader interest, activates appropriate schema, and serves as a connective thread throughout the manuscript. Here's one example taken from an Alexander commentary about writing, titled "Why I Think You Can Write":

I think it's fascinating to learn that fleas can be trained. Picture the little critters in a jar with a lid on it. At first, the fleas will jump up and down, bopping their heads on the lid. Ouch! Eventually, an interesting thing happens: They figure out they can avoid the pain if they just shorten their jump ... Sometimes humans are just like those fleas. Many people think they can't write because of some comment that made them feel criticized ... That moment acts like that jar lid and causes pain. They decide they're not writers and never will be – and they'll never try again.[5]

Compose Rapidly without Judgment

According to the venerable Flower and Hayes writing model,[1] writing has three phases: planning, translating, and reviewing. The translating phase is where pen meets paper or fingers meet keyboard. This is the time to get one's ideas out and recorded for later review and revision. During the translation phase, writers should momentarily suspend judgment about the content and form of their writing and instead let their ideas flow. They should especially not get caught up in fixing grammatical mistakes that can wait until writing's reviewing phase. Ongoing editing can stifle creativity and prevent writers from discovering and generating new ideas while writing as their attention is diverted to writing form and mechanics.

Productive scholars tend to write the initial draft in this way, without concern for writing style or mechanics, knowing they will later revise their document to perfection. Dale Schunk advised scholars to "just get it written" without concern for writing quality.[2] John Glover did and advised the same. Former Glover student Alice Corkill said:

When John composed, he tried not to spend much time agonizing over the wording, tried not to spend much time editing. His writing strategy was to get his thoughts down on paper and then go back later and edit to perfection. I can hear John saying, "Don't worry about vocabulary, don't worry about wording. Instead, worry about making a logical and convincing case that the present study is necessary and important." It's always hard to start a writing task, but John would simply start by throwing a rambling-stream-of-consciousness-kind-of   -thing   onto   the   paper. He warned me more than once not to be a writer who sits and agonizes for hours over the first two sentences of an article they are trying to write. He said, "Well that's just ridiculous! Just start writing! Don't worry about the words, don't worry about the grammar, don't worry about trying to make it look nice, just get your ideas down on paper. Later, you can go back and figure out how to make it look like proper writing instead of a rambling stream of thoughts."[3]

Patricia Alexander is also a let-it-flow writer. Alexander sits down at the computer and composes rapidly, just as she would speak. She said: "It is a process. I let it flow, flow, flow as rapidly as it can flow. I call this throwing it up on the page." Naturally, Alexander spurns any editing when composing. She quipped: "People who try to edit sentence by sentence while they are building are constrained. It is almost like constipation, constraining oneself so tightly. You need to let the ideas out."[4]

Write with Style

Famous authors write with a distinct and recognizable style. Hemingway wrote with an efficient and economical style. His writings were straightforward and concise, free of flowery wordplay. Here's a sample from *The Sun Also Rises*:

In the morning I walked down the Boulevard to the rue Soufflot for coffee and brioche. It was a fine morning. The horse-chestnut trees in the Luxembourg gardens were in bloom. There was the pleasant early-morning feeling of a hot day. I read the papers with the coffee and then smoked a cigarette. The flower-women were coming up from the market and arranging their daily stock. Students went by going up to the law school, or down to the Sorbonne. The Boulevard was busy with trams and people going to work.[1]

Productive scholars also write with style. Patricia Alexander had a graduate school night job. She was a blues and jazz singer. No surprise, then, that her writing has a rhythm, a signature style. Alexander said: "The rhythm of a sentence matters to me. I used to think that my advisor, Ruth Garner, wrote using a jazz rhythm. Sentences were pretty truncated. There was not a lot of descriptive elaboration. There were not a lot of connections between sentences. It was brief and to the point, almost like jazz."[2] Alexander describes her own rhythm as more flowing, spiraling, elaborate, and dramatic.

Here are two brief passages. Can you tell which one Alexander wrote and which one Garner wrote?

Passage One

Half of the adults in our sample read the entire text with seductive details; half read it without. Recall of important information differed dramatically by condition. Whereas adults who read the text without seductive details recalled an average of 93% of the important generalizations about insect differences, adults who read the text with seductive details recalled an average of only 43%. In this latter group, readers recalled a combination of important and interesting information, and in no case did a reader recall all important generalizations, though this occurred frequently in the no-detail group.[3]

Passage Two

As we have suggested, engaging in this venture has been demanding and uncertain. For one thing, we are well aware of the limitations under which we operated. We recognize that ours is only one possible conceptualization of these knowledge terms. We realize that the evolution of knowledge about knowledge is continuous, as is the generation of labels needed to describe that evolution. Further, we understand that the framework we have devised has been significantly influenced by the literature we have examined and by our own research activities. However, we view this examination as a small, but critical, step in a developmental process.[4]

The first passage was Garner's; the second passage was Alexander's.

John Glover had an attention-getting style that included flowerful language and clever titles. Former Glover colleague Barbara Plake commented on Glover's word choice:

John liked to use flowerful words. He had a great vocabulary, and he used words that would not typically be used in scientific reporting. I remember one time he was writing about something having many varieties and referred to it as a kaleidoscope. You usually don't run into kaleidoscope in technical writing. One time he used the word calliope, which means beautifully voiced. John just loved words, especially multiple-syllabic words, and used words in a colorful attention-capturing way.[5]

Regarding his clever titles, former Glover student Alice Corkill said: "John liked to joke around with titles. He wanted to have interesting titles for his articles. He told students that the title was what was going to catch readers' attention and invite them to browse the article."[6] Here are a couple humorous and attention-capturing Glover titles: "Nobody Knows How to Remember That Prose" and "First Letter Mnemonics: DAM (Don't Aide Memory)."

To create your own defining writing style, try doing what novices have done for centuries in fields like music and writing. Study the masters and emulate their styles. Take what you like, a bit here and a bit there, from the experts until you hone and distinguish your personal style. When I pen a research article, I like to begin with a concrete example the way Mayer does. Here are the opening lines from a talent study I coauthored on Olympic speedskaters:[7] "Speed skaters are fascinating to watch, with their fluid movements, bent-forward posture to minimize draft, and breakneck speed. They are considered the fastest humans on Earth who use neither gravity nor a mechanical device to aid their speed." I also follow Mayer's lead in referring readers to the exact table or figure section I want them to see, for example, "as shown in the middle-row of Table 4." When I title an article, I sometimes try to emulate Joel Levin, the king of clever titles. He was responsible for this pun-riddled title for a work we coauthored combining our research interests on mnemonics and matrices: "Fishing for Text Facilitators: The Lure of the Mnematrix."[8]

Signal the Reader

My college educational psychology professor was a cue-dispensing savant. If a point was important, he'd alert students by saying: "This is ab-sol-ute-ly crit-ic-al," with each syllable delivered in staccato fashion. Another way he signaled importance was with this cue medley: Foot perched on desk, elbow to knee, chin resting in hand, jaw jutted, eyebrows raised, and then, and only then, several rapid and vehement head nods. When this cue assortment was delivered, students knew to record notes feverishly ... once it was established that the professor was not having a seizure.

Effective writers deliver cues too. They take readers by the hand, leading them clearly and unmistakably through their ideas and arguments. Signals help accomplish this. Richard Mayer's writings are filled with clarifying signals such as questions, headings, and specific directives. In an article on multimedia learning, Mayer organizes and signals his thoughts using questions such as:[1]

- What is the multimedia effect?
- What is the spatial contiguity effect?
- What is the temporal contiguity effect?

Many research reports contain a results section where findings are reported en masse without headings or with only general topical headings, like Recall Findings and Recognition Findings, that divulge little about what's to come. Now, consider the specificity and clarity of some of Mayer's headings:[2]

- *Labeled illustrations improved recall of explanative but not other information.*
- *Explanative illustrations improved transfer but not verbatim recognition.*

Similarly, writers often refer readers to tables and figures in this general way: "See Table 1" or "As shown in Figure 2." Now see how Mayer directs readers to a specific location and describes what they will see:[3]

- The left panel of Figure 3 shows the proportion of explanative and nonexplanative idea units recalled by the illustrations and no-illustrations groups.
- The right panels of Figure 3 show the proportion of creative answers on the transfer posttest for each group.
- To build a useful mental model of the system, a reader must attend to the relevant information as indicated by the italicized text in Table 1, build internal connections as indicated by in the middle

portion of Table 1, and build external connections as indicated in the lower portion of Table 1.

Patricia Alexander relies on text signals to organize and bridge ideas. Words like: first, next, stages, types, similar, although, moreover, furthermore, and whereas help convey a text's organization and transitions. Following is a paragraph written by Alexander and colleagues. I have highlighted the authors' hand-holding signals:[4]

Further, Bandura described human functioning as the interaction between person, behavior, and environment. **Specifically,** self-regulation emphasizes the reciprocal determinism of the environment on the person, mediated through behavior. **Person variables include** the distinct self-processes that interact with the environment through one's actions. **For example,** Bandura's self-reinforcement processes in Social Learning Theory (SLT) are predominately motivational. **These motivational dimensions include** evaluative dimensions of performance, personal standards, valuations of activities, and attributions. **However,** the act of self-regulation does not occur without the interaction of the person with the environment. **Although these contextual factors may play a smaller role than the person processes,** these interactions are critical to the self-regulation process. **This theoretical focus** appears different than with metacognition, involving a type of exogenous constructivism. **Specifically,** in SLT, the emphasis is placed on the derivation of knowledge from the environment. **Moreover, while Flavell and metacognition researchers** appear to have been more **influenced by** the cognitive orientation of his predecessors, **Bandura and other self-regulation researchers** appear to have been more **influenced by** neobehaviorism, which takes its cues from more empiricist frameworks.

Tell a Story

John Glover told a good story. Former Glover colleague Barbara Plake commented:

John was a superb writer able to communicate ideas in compelling and interesting ways. He told a story. There was foreshadowing at the beginning, good connections throughout, and clear focus on the question he was answering. John put all the pieces of the puzzle together for the reader, so that when they finished reading, it all came together. It was a skill that I admired and tried to duplicate in my writing.[1]

John Hattie also strives to make his scientific writing tell a clear, coherent, and memorable story that ties the parts together. He makes sure his students do the same. In every session with students, they hear the same question: "What's the story today?" indicating that Hattie wants them to get beyond their data by interpreting it and making meaning. Hattie said: "The work is not about the data but about my interpretation of these data and trying to develop and weave a compelling story." He wants students to adopt and live the motto: "So what's the story today?"[2]

Research findings are often poorly told. My hunch is that many journal readers skip the Results section and go right to the Discussion. Why? Because most Results sections are a blur of statistical jargon devoid of meaning. Here is an example:

For the learning concept Spurious Correlation, we found a significant omnibus effect of the experimental condition on the nonisomorphic conceptual understanding posttest, X^2 (3) = 11.37, p=.008.

Clear as mud, right? This is what Mayer said about presenting results in story fashion:

I try to have each section of the Results section focus on one of the research questions and predictions ... I begin by stating what the prediction or question was and try to describe the results in words, and then also refer the reader to a [certain spot in] a figure or table to document that. I think it's important to say in words what the results were before presenting statistics.[3]

Here, Mayer pulls out all his signaling and storytelling tricks to lead readers comfortably and coherently through results before providing the confirming statistics:[4]

Prediction 2: Explanative illustrations improve creative problem solving but not verbatim retention. The top-right portion of Figure 5 shows the proportion correct response for low prior-knowledge students in each treatment group on problem solving and verbatim retention. As can be seen, the parts-and-steps group outperformed the control group on problem solving (47% versus 28%) but not on verbatim retention (66% versus 68%). Consistent with prediction 2, separate t-tests conducted on these data revealed that the groups differed in problem solving performance, $t(28) = 3.51$, $p < .01$, but not on verbatim retention, $t(28) < 1$.

Now, that's a clear story.

Avoid Acronyms

And now the news:

In college sports, USC battles BYU on ABC with the winner holding the inside track to the CFP. FYI, CNN reported that a TWA flight out of JFK encountered a UFO. The AFA and FBI are investigating. The KGB denied involvement. There was an accident on the LIE. It was reported by NPR that a driver with ADD was checking his PDA and consuming a BLT when he crashed his BMW SUV into a farm animal that wandered onto the roadway. An ENT on the scene administered CPR following AMA guidelines and HIV precautions. The driver could not be revived and arrived DOA at the hospital. Services are TBA; May he RIP. CSI, ADA, FFA, and AAA officials are investigating.

OMG!

I find it especially frustrating when writers invent and use needless and confusing acronyms. Here's a fictitious but representative example for a study examining computer versus longhand note taking, with or without review, when lecture rates are either fast or slow. Here are the eight groups identified in the method section and their given acronyms:

1. Computer note taking, review, slow rate: CNT/R/SR
2. Computer note taking, no review, slow rate: CNT/NR/SR
3. Computer note taking, review, fast rate: CNT/R/FR
4. Computer note taking, no review, fast rate: CNT/NR/FR
5. Longhand note taking, review, slow rate: LNT/R/SR
6. Longhand note taking, no review, slow rate: LNT/NR/SR
7. Longhand note taking, review, fast rate: LNT/R/FR
8. Longhand note taking, no review, fast rate: LNT/NR/FR

Now imagine if these meaningless acronyms appear without reference thereafter in the results and discussion sections:

- The CNT/R/FR and LNT/R/FR groups achieved more than the LNT/NR/FR and CNT/NR/SR groups but not the CNT/R/SR group.
- Researchers should exercise caution in interpreting findings involving the CNT/NR/FR group because . . .

Say what? Avoid uncommon, self-created, and confusing acronyms. WIO . . . that means: Write It Out!

Be Simple and Concise

Author David Holbrook pointedly wrote: "Remember that brevity is the soul of wit. In each section, paragraph, and sentence of your paper, shun excessive length as diligently as you would avoid paying extra interest expenses on your credit card. Say exactly what you need to say, no more, and then stop. Like this."[1]

Richard Mayer said: "I try to be as concise and focused as possible. Having a lot of extraneous material is what confuses people. If there is a lot of detail that must be reported, I try to add it as a footnote or appendix to keep the text body as clear, concise, and flowing as possible."[2]

Below are examples of long-winded, word-salad writing submitted by graduate students **that I revised**, hopefully making the writing simpler and more concise, and ultimately more clear. See what you think.

- Then the teacher would give the students a blank version of the organizer after the text reading, which the students were to use what they had learned to make the organizer complete. **After students read the text, the teacher had them complete a blank organizer.**

- The concept mapping tool used was a computer-based program which was utilized for the purpose of content concept review. **The computer-based concept-mapping tool assessed students' concept knowledge.**

- The study examined the effects of instruction of graphic organizers on students' application of those visual aids in a text and on their attitudes towards reading. **This study examined how graphic organizer instruction impacts students' graphic organizer use and attitudes.**

- The focus of this study was to answer the following research question: Do explicit instruction and graphic organizers lead to increased learning of social studies content compared with a typical practice baseline phase? **The research question was: Does graphic organizer instruction produce increased social studies learning?**

One editing technique I used here to make students' writing more concise and powerful was eliminating unnecessary prepositional phrases, such as "for the purpose" or "to answer." Final Prepositional Phrase Score: Students, 16 – Kiewra, 0. Among my tongue-in-cheek writing tips is this one: Eliminate unnecessary phrases *of* preposition. Change: "Performance *on* the test *of* recall showed that girls *in* high school scored higher than boys *in* high school," to "High school girls recalled more than boys." 4–0. Change: "Efforts *to* reform education *in* public schools *in* inner cities is *of* growing public interest," to "Inner-city public-school education reform interest is growing." 4–0.

I'm stopping.

Write with Clarity

Author David Holbrook also wrote:

Speak clearly. Don't write in a style that sounds like mumbling. Don't let your thoughts come tumbling out in the order in which they occur to you. Rather, impose order on them. Shape your paper into a coherent structure and do everything possible to reveal that structure to your reader using an introductory preview, clear headings and subheadings, and a transparent concluding summary.[1]

Productive scholar Richard Anderson spent two years writing a manuscript trying to achieve clarity. Anderson said:

I work very hard on my writing, and I'd like to think of myself as a good professional writer. I work at the clarity of making the arguments stand out, but when I find that it isn't standing out clearly, that may mean the thinking behind it is murky. I like writing that has some interest but first it must be clear before it is appealing and interesting. I think many writers and much of the writing in our field is poor because too much is taken for granted. The elements and arguments are left out and the slogans of the day that seem to be laden with meaning are empty of meaning. If you cannot say it without using special slogans, you must ask yourself, is there really any meaning there?[2]

As a journal editor, editorial board member, and ad hoc reviewer, I have seen more than my share of mumbling, unclear arguments, confusing jargon, and murky writing. Writing so weak that it precluded publication. Here are a few obscure and poorly structured mumblings from submitted manuscripts that escaped comprehension and publication. This is not the clear and coherent writing Holbrook or Anderson envisioned.

- Importantly, note taking can support self-regulated studying of previously taught material through self-reflection on whether the material from the lectures was understood and from including reviewing notes in study plans as a goal-setting behavior.
- Seek clarification from relevant teaching and learning leads on the expectation for equivalence and inform students as to whether they should expect an equivalent experience from lecture capture.

- Furthermore, long-term programs, in prioritizing future success over immediate rewards, are more likely to be equipped to appropriately anticipate, discount, and manage performance-level fluctuations over one's athletic development emerging from various mental and physical impediments.
- For professional programs to force social support as a contributor to professional accomplishment is an ethically problematic issue, and will likely detract from the growth of an organic, contingent support structure.
- The model regards the process as a transformation of latent abilities into specific skills relevant to a given activity, of which intrapersonal factors work alongside the environment to catalyze or impede the transformation.

Say What?

Productive scholars understand that disseminating their scholarly ideas depends on perfecting the written word. No easy task, because, as Rebecca Collie said, writing is a "tremendously complex process."[3] To be successful, Logan Fiorella said that he must be a "stickler for writing" and work hard to "tell a coherent and flowing story" that is "clear and concise."[4] Heinz Mandl stressed writing quality. His former student and productive scholar Frank Fischer said: "What I learned from Heinz and pass along to my students is the importance of writing quality. It is important to write in understandable ways so the text can be understood as easily as possible by others. Heinz would ask us, 'Are you more concerned with sounding intelligent or being understood by your audience?'"[5] Richard Mayer told a humorous story about the importance (and dangers) of clarity. Early on in graduate school, Mayer submitted some written work to his advisor, Jim Greeno, who responded: "I don't understand what you are saying." Mayer revised the work making sure he wrote it clearly and resubmitted it to Greeno who responded: "Now that it is written clearly, I don't think you have a very good idea." Mayer said: "I didn't understand when I was a student how important writing is. I thought you just do good research and that was it. But you actually have to explain it to other people."[6]

Write for Your Friends

I once asked *Journal of Educational Psychology* editor Joel Levin how he knows when he has a manuscript worth publishing. He said that in addition to the manuscript making an important contribution and meeting technical necessities, it must pass the Friend Test. He would sometimes give the manuscript to an educated friend (or reviewer) unfamiliar with the topic area, and the friend must find the paper understandable, interesting, and memorable days later for Levin to consider publishing it. Good idea because much of what's published in scientific journals is jargon-laden, incomprehensible, and no fun to read. It's as though it was written for about a dozen like-minded people and the writer's mother. Moms read everything their kids write. But I doubt even she enjoyed it.

Writer David Holbrook also advises scholars to make their writing interesting and understandable:

Do not hesitate to make your paper interesting. Avoid use of the dull, lifeless, empty-sounding style that some writers affect when they want to sound scientific or scholarly. Try to use active verbs, colorful language, and vivid imagery. Remove passive verbs from your prose as carefully as you would remove bits of broken eggshell from an omelet that you plan to eat or pieces of slivered glass from an ice-cream cone that you intend to lick. Up to the limits imposed by science and scholarship, try to make your writing come alive. Try to make it dance and sing. In short, strive for a more poetic and less prosaic voice.[1]

Patricia Alexander writes for a common audience. She wants people outside her domain to understand her writing, not just her academic peers. To aid reader understanding and interest, Alexander often begins her writing with a metaphor or analogical reference that gains reader interest, activates appropriate schema, and serves as a connective thread throughout the manuscript. In one article where Alexander and colleagues addressed the imprecision and confusion surrounding three seemingly interchangeable psychological terms, the authors begin the article using a linking metaphor by describing a 1922 work touting that language be used with great care and precision. Alexander and colleagues reference this older work to make their related point that educational literature today lacks linguistic clarity and specificity. The authors return to this 1922 work later in their article to bring their argument full circle.[2]

Karen Harris writes for three audiences. She said:

When I write now, there are various readers very alive in my mind. One of these readers is quite new to the topic, and therefore I must be clear yet concise. Another reader lives in my mind as that person who is quite likely to misinterpret what I say or twist what I mean. A third reader is one who is predisposed to dislike what I do and is quite critical about it. As I write, read what I have written, and revise, each of these readers in my mind takes turns, and I see the text as best I can through their eyes.[3,4]

Back Off a Bit but Don't Let Your Writing Get Cold

If you were tiling your bathroom floor or painting the living room, it makes little sense to stretch those jobs out longer than need be. Letting them sit uncompleted for a time breaks momentum, delays completion, and just plain looks bad. The same is generally true for writing. Once started, it's generally best to stick with it by writing some most every day until completion.

That said, productive scholars do occasionally pause from writing in order to gain perspective and see their writing with fresh eyes. Sabina Neugebauer said: "Sometimes I intentionally back away from my written work for two or three days or even a week to avoid paralysis and to improve the work's arguments or conceptualization."[1] Karen Harris said: "It is important to step away from your work, take breaks, and see it fresh."[2] Rebecca Collie also occasionally seeks distance from her writing. Collie steps away from the manuscript for a week or so in order to return to it with fresh eyes, which allows her to identify any remaining sore spots and make additional edits. Collie actually budgets the stepping away time into her writing timeline. She clarified that it is good to step away while polishing, but not good to step away and interrupt momentum when creating the initial draft.[3]

When Collie does step away, she makes sure that she parks her writing on a hill, a hidden-curriculum writing strategy she learned from her graduate school advisor. For example, knowing that it can be difficult to restart a task on Monday morning, Collie tries to complete difficult tasks on Thursday or Friday and save Monday morning for less cognitively taxing work. She also creates outlines or rough drafts before finishing for the day so she can return to writing more readily the next workday.[4]

Doug Lombardi also advocates writing pauses. He advised scholars to: "Write early, then think about it. Let it incubate, percolate, and then come back to it."[5]

Ming-Te Wang, like Collie, emphasizes the importance of writing momentum and seeing the initial draft through to completion before stepping away. Wang cautions: "When I put [an uncompleted project] aside for a few days, it's really difficult for me to find the thread and pick back up."[6]

Don't let your writing sit too long and get cold.

Don't Stop until You're Finished

Another way to approach writing is to set writing goals for the day and not stop until you're finished. It is rumored that writer Victor Hugo would give his clothing to a valet before sitting down to write. Hugo told the valet not to return his clothes until the completed text was placed outside his door. This might be a writing-completion strategy best enacted when writing from home rather than the office.

Erika Patall feels guilty when she does not reach her daily writing goal. Patall said: "It's a little bit crazy, but I cannot just stop halfway through a task because I'll feel guilty about stopping or I won't be able to sleep if I didn't get to a logical stopping point. I feel bad if I don't get things done."[1]

Learn as You Write

When you read, you think you understand; when you write, you know if you understand.

Writing involves more than producing a product, it is also a process for learning. Karen Harris said:

Much of writing is about learning. I love that part. I love searching, collecting, and reading articles, chapters, reports, and so on. Our jobs are so busy that sometimes it is hard to get the time to read, think, and learn unless you are getting ready to write ... As I search, read, and plan recursively, I often go off on tangents. I find related work that's of great interest but not necessary right now. I file it and make notes to myself of where it can be useful. I have always found these tangents useful over time.[1]

Embrace Feedback

In the cartoon strip *Zits*, teenage son Jeremy asks his mother what she thinks of his written work. She returns his paper heavily stained in red ink and says: "I made a few edits." Jeremy's response: "When I said I was open to feedback, I meant compliments."[1]

Don't we all. As a rule, we tend to shun critical feedback. It bruises our ego and commands that more work be done. Educational researcher James Popham neatly summed up the importance of feedback and offered this sage advice to fellow scholars:

Find a colleague who will provide candid reactions to your work; then venerate that individual ... It will someday be demonstrated unequivocally by social anthropologists that when it comes to criticizing a coworker's efforts, most colleagues are wimps. Faced with such widespread wimpiness, it is inordinately difficult to find a colleague whom you can trust to tell you when your shabby efforts are, in truth, shabby. Yet, because most of us – beginners as well as veterans – become professionally enamored with our creations, it is uncommonly helpful to have someone who is honest enough to tell you that your most recent "breakthrough" manuscript should be sent to the paper shredder. If you find someone whose spine is not supple, a person who's occasionally willing to spend time honestly critiquing your work – revere that individual.[2]

When a colleague tells you "your work is great" and nothing more, that is no help at all. Scholars need critics, not cheerleaders. Like Popham suggests, find colleagues willing to spend time scrutinizing your work and giving you honest and detailed feedback. Anything short of that will not help you prepare a better manuscript and grow as a scholar. If colleagues won't lay it on the line and say it like it is, perhaps check with your mother.

Scholars I interviewed recognize the value of critical feedback and seek it out. Ming-Te Wang said: "Receiving feedback is sometimes painful, but you just need to get over it because no one is a perfect writer and feedback is what makes you better."[3] Sabina Neugebauer too depends on the critical feedback she receives from her writing group colleagues, recognizing that their criticism "fortifies you for submitting your work to journals and for addressing the difficult comments you get during the review process."[4] Seasoned scholar Michael Pressley said much the same about feedback received following manuscript submission: "I always spend time with the reviews and try to figure out what they are telling me. Every one of those points is always telling me something, and we try to react to that and respond to it."[5]

Revise, Revise, Revise

Writer Robert Graves said: "There is no such thing as good writing, only good rewriting."[1] Writer Stephen King offered much the same message: "To write is human, to edit is divine."[2]

Productive scholars got the message. They edit and edit their manuscripts to perfection, until they sparkle. Michael Pressley comments on revision:

I never sit down and write [a manuscript] until I know a lot of what I want to put down . . . At one point, I kept track and I was doing like 40 revisions after the first draft. Now I would say there's always two or three monstrous revisions and then tons of tons of fine tuning . . . You don't let it get out of your presence until the fine tuning.[3]

Most productive scholars suspend judgment as they compose, necessitating the need for serious editing later. As mentioned earlier, Patricia Alexander likes to let her initial draft writing "flow, flow, flow as rapidly as I can let it flow."[4] When composing a manuscript on his computer, Dale Schunk also tries to get his ideas down on paper, "just get it written,"[5] without concern for revision. After composing the manuscript, he goes old school on it. He prints it and makes revisions by hand before making changes on the computer. He repeats this revision process three or more times until the document is in top shape.

Speaking of old school, John Glover literally performed cut-and-paste editing before it was a word-processing thing. Former Glover student Alice Corkill said: "When revising his work before computers were readily available, John would cut bits and pieces from the manuscript he was writing and tape them together in new ways trying to find the best fit for his writing segments."[6]

Hans Gruber noted that he learned the importance of manuscript revision while working in Heinz Mandl's group. Gruber said that Mandl was known for going through papers ten or fifteen times and always looking for inconsistencies and weak points.[7] Group member Frank Fischer agreed, noting that Mandl would sometimes review up to a dozen versions of Fischer's manuscripts before agreeing to submit them for publication. Now, Fischer uses a similar process with his graduate students. Fischer said: "I'm trying to guide my students toward effective writing. They compose a draft and I give them feedback. We have up to fifteen feedback rounds before we submit our papers."[8]

Rebecca Collie said: "People tend to assume that writers get it right the first time, but that is not the case. It's just editing, editing, and editing."[9] This perspective helps Collie to view multiple rounds of editing as a necessary practice. She said: "Knowing that every writer needs editing is important, because I don't view myself as a failure for needing to edit many, many times."[10] Collie is certainly in good company. Even Rich Mayer, who has published more than six hundred works, struggles with the revision process. Mayer said, after writing the initial manuscript draft: "I revise and go through multiple, multiple drafts. That's the painful part of writing."[11]

A Few Words about Length: Not Too Long, Not Too Short

How's this for a title: "A Note on Sadomasochism in the Review Process: I Hate When That Happens."[1] In that article, Morris Holbrook penned a satirical look at the incompetency and unsympathetic criticisms that consume the review process. Holbrook also tried to help by offering suggestions for authors and reviewers. Here are a couple of his writing suggestions pertaining to manuscript length.

1. "Adjust the overall length of your paper to the magnitude of its contribution. Do not attempt to inflate a routine replication of some small study into a 50-page magnum opus in which you dutifully repeat all previous researchers' citations of every extant reference that bears even tangentially on the topic at issue."[2]
2. "Don't carve your work too thin and thereby sell yourself short. Specifically, don't go for 'twofers' by chopping one cohesive study into several pieces that you then attempt to publish separately in hopes of extending the length of your vita."[3]

Be like Goldilocks and find comfort in Mama Bear's just right.

A Few More Writing Tips

Here is a bit of tongue-in-cheek writing advice I've culled along the way:

- *Paper*: Unless you are referring to something written in high school, try "manuscript," "article," "thesis," "report," or "dissertation."
- *Contractions*: Don't use contractions in formal writing unless writing about the birth process.
- *Double negatives*: Do not use no double negatives. They are a no-no.

- *Verbs has to agree with their subjects*: So don't tell me that data *is* never flawed. "Data" is plural.
- *Do not verb nouns*: I strategized and dialogued about this writing pitfall.
- Never *utilize* a long word when a *diminutive* word will do. Use "use."
- *Future tense*: Use sparingly. Do not write: "This article will explore three main points." The article is here and now. Write: "This article explores three main points."
- *Citations*: Kiewra (2024) says to begin paragraphs and sentences with ideas, not with citations.
- *Quotations*: Use quotations only when the author's exact words are needed. "Use your own words," Kiewra advises. In qualitative research, do report rich quotations. Let the interviewees speak.
- *Commas*: Use commas to separate three items such as Anderson, Alexander, and Fiorella. Do not use them unnecessarily, and inappropriately.
- *I think*: I am sure that you do, but I believe you mean "I believe."
- *I feel*: Again, I believe you mean "I believe." Most readers, I am sorry to say, are not concerned with your sense of touch or physical well-being.
- *Very*: A very vague and unnecessary adjective. Drop it entirely or replace it with a descriptive adjective if one is needed. I heard a newscaster report that an event was "very unprecedented." Mark Twain offered this damn good advice: "Substitute 'damn' every time you're inclined to write 'very'; The editor will delete it and the writing will be as it should be."[1]
- Avoid the phrase "*highly* significant." Differences are significant or they are not. Think "pregnant."
- *Can, may, might*: Not exactly interchangeable. Can means capable, may means allowed, and might means possible.
- *Center around*: A physical impossibility. The correct phrase is "center on."
- *While and since*: Use only in relation to time; otherwise use "although" or "whereas" for "while," and use "because" for "since," so says the American Psychological Association.[2]
- *Proofread* carefully to see if you any words out.

Do your best to follow these damn helpful writing tips.

Join a Writing Group

Consider joining a writing group, especially while in graduate school or early in your scholarly career. Ming-Te Wang credits his writing group while a Harvard University graduate student for making him a good professional writer today. Wang's writing group met regularly, reviewed one another's written products, and provided critical feedback that led to revisions and subsequent rounds of critiques and revisions.[1]

Sabina Neugebauer also credited her Harvard University graduate student writing group for shaping her writing knowledge and skills. Now well into her career, Neugebauer is still a dedicated member in two female writing groups. These groups guide her research and writing and provide an avenue for supporting female scholars in the academy. Neugebauer said: "I have always had a writing group, [and being part of these groups] plays an enormous role in my professional development and productivity." One group is comprised of qualitative researchers who share a commitment to social justice research in education, engage Neugebauer's experimental work, and make her "explain ideas that could otherwise be taken for granted by someone using similar experimental methods." The other group contains mostly pre-tenure scholars, where Neugebauer can discuss "cutting-edge methods" that new faculty members bring with them fresh from their graduate training.[2]

Each of Neugebauer's groups meets once a month. Members are required to submit their writing beforehand for review. Feedback is given to members about a week before meetings, giving members time to "absorb the feedback and think of any questions to ask the reviewers." Feedback focuses on all aspects of the manuscript – argumentation, design, and analysis are all fair game. At the meeting, about thirty minutes are devoted to discussing each member's writing, with five minutes set aside for a personal check-in on one's academic successes or struggles. Neugebauer described her experiences with writing groups as "transformative – an incredible process that fortifies you for submitting your work to journals and for addressing the difficult comments you get during the review process. It helps you build the tough skin needed in the academy."[3]

Here are a few general reasons why writing groups are beneficial:[4]

1. Motivation: Preparing for meetings motivates you to write and meet writing goals.

2. Inspiration: Reading the work of others inspires you to write more.
3. Constructive criticism: Feedback from others shapes and improves your writing.
4. Support and encouragement: Others take an interest in your writing and encourage you to write more.
5. Networking: You connect with others who can guide you and help open opportunity doors.
6. Critiquing others. You have the opportunity to critique others, an important mentoring and professional reviewer skill.

References

Write Like a Star

1 Hemingway, E. *BrainyQuote*. www.brainyquote.com/quotes/ernest_hemingway_384744.
2 Oh! The places you'll go! If only you try! (August 27, 2015). *The Picture Book Professor*. www.picturebookprofessor.com/the-picture-book-professor/oh-the-places-youll-go/.
3 Hawthorne, N. *BrainyQuote*. www.brainyquote.com/quotes/nathaniel_hawthorne_108636.

Make Writing a Habit

1 Puller, R. *r/quotes*. www.reddit.com/r/quotes/comments/e705k/good_habits_once_established_are_just_as_hard_to/.
2 Plath, S. *creativeshadows*. https://creative-shadows.com/2012/08/11/nothing-stinks-like-a-pile-of-unpublished-writing-sylvia-plath/.
3 Kiewra, K. A., Luo, L., & Flanigan, A. (2021). Educational psychology early career award winners: How did they do it? *Educational Psychology Review*, *33*, 1981–2018 (p. 2013).
4 Ibid., p. 1992.
5 Kiewra, K. A., & Kauffman, D. (2023). John Glover: A long overdue account of his productive scholarship methods. *Educational Psychology Review*, *35*, Article 56.
6 Ibid.
7 Bembenutty, H. (2022). *Contemporary pioneers in teaching and learning*, Vol. 2. Charlotte, NC: Information Age Publishing, Inc. (p. 139).
8 Von Goethe, W. *Goodreads*. www.goodreads.com/quotes/991527-whatever-you-think-you-can-do-or-believe-you-can.
9 Hillel. *Goodreads*. www.goodreads.com/quotes/983886-if-not-you-then-who-if-not-now-when.
10 Coelho, P. (March 19, 2009). *Anne LaFollette*. www.annelafolletteart.com/blog/2019/03/19/one-day-day-one-you-decide.

Frame Your Writing

1 Kiewra, K. A., Luo, L., & Flanigan, A. (2021). Educational psychology early career award winners: How did they do it? *Educational Psychology Review, 33,* 1981–2018.
2 Patterson-Hazley, M., & Kiewra, K. A. (2013). Conversations with four highly productive educational psychologists: Patricia Alexander, Richard Mayer, Dale Schunk, and Barry Zimmerman. *Educational Psychology Review, 25,* 19–45 (p. 32).
3 Ibid.
4 Patterson-Hazley, M., & Kiewra, K. A. (2013). Conversations with four highly productive educational psychologists: Patricia Alexander, Richard Mayer, Dale Schunk, and Barry Zimmerman. *Educational Psychology Review, 25,* 19–45.

Don't Start at the Beginning

1 Do-re-mi. *Songfacts.* www.songfacts.com/lyrics/julie-andrews/do-re-mi.
2 Prinz, A., Zeeb, H., Flanigan, A., Renkl, A., & Kiewra, K. A. (2020). Conversations with five highly successful female educational psychologists: Patricia Alexander, Carol Dweck, Jacquelynne Eccles, Mareike Kunter, and Tamara van Gog. *Educational Psychology Review, 33,* 763–795.
3 Patterson-Hazley, M., & Kiewra, K. A. (2013). Conversations with four highly productive educational psychologists: Patricia Alexander, Richard Mayer, Dale Schunk, and Barry Zimmerman. *Educational Psychology Review, 25,* 19–45 (p. 33).
4 Mayer, R. E., Bove, W., Bryman, A., Mars, R., & Tapangco, L. (1996). When less is more: Meaningful learning from visual and verbal summaries of science textbook lessons. *Journal of Educational Psychology, 88,* 64–73 (p. 64).
5 Alexander, P. (April 7, 2021). Why I think you can write. *The Paso Robles Press.* https://pasoroblespress.com/commentary/why-i-think-you-can-write/.

Compose Rapidly without Judgment

1 Flower, L., & Hayes, J. R. (1981). A cognitive process theory of writing. *College Composition and Communication, 32,* 365–387.
2 Patterson-Hazley, M., & Kiewra, K. A. (2013). Conversations with four highly productive educational psychologists: Patricia Alexander, Richard Mayer, Dale Schunk, and Barry Zimmerman. *Educational Psychology Review, 25,* 19–45 (p. 32).

3 Kiewra, K. A., & Kauffman, D. (2023). John Glover: A long overdue account of his productive scholarship methods. *Educational Psychology Review, 35*, Article 56.

4 Patterson-Hazley, M., & Kiewra, K. A. (2013). Conversations with four highly productive educational psychologists: Patricia Alexander, Richard Mayer, Dale Schunk, and Barry Zimmerman. *Educational Psychology Review, 25*, 19–45 (p. 33).

Write with Style

1 Hemingway, E. *Goodreads*. www.goodreads.com/quotes/854999-in-the-morning-i-walked-down-the-boulevard-to-the.

2 Patterson-Hazley, M., & Kiewra, K. A. (2013). Conversations with four highly productive educational psychologists: Patricia Alexander, Richard Mayer, Dale Schunk, and Barry Zimmerman. *Educational Psychology Review, 25*, 19–45 (p. 33).

3 Garner, R. (1993). "Seductive details" and adults' learning from text. In S. R. Yussen & M. C. Smith (eds.), *Reading across the life span: Recent research in psychology* (pp. 215–222). New York: Springer.

4 Alexander, P. A., Schallert, D. L., & Hare, V. C. (1991). Coming to terms: How researchers in learning and literacy talk about knowledge. *Review of Educational Research, 61*, 315–343.

5 Kiewra, K. A., & Kauffman, D. (2023). John Glover: A long overdue account of his productive scholarship methods. *Educational Psychology Review, 35*, Article 56.

6 Ibid.

7 Ott Schacht, C. L., & Kiewra, K. A. (2018). The fastest humans on Earth: Environmental surroundings and family influences that spark talent development in Olympic speedskaters. *Roeper Review, 40*, 21–35.

8 Kiewra, K. A., Kim, S., Meyers, T., Levin, J. R., Renandya, W. A., & Hwang, Y. (1994). *Fishing for text facilitators: The lure of the mnematrix*. New Orleans, LA: American Educational Research Association.

Signal the Reader

1 Mayer, R. E. (2002). Multimedia learning. *Psychology of Learning and Motivation, 41*, 85–139.

2 Mayer, R. E. (1989). Systematic thinking fostered by illustrations in scientific text. *Journal of Educational Psychology, 81*, 240–246.

3 Ibid.

4 Dinsmore, D. L., Loughlin, S. M., & Alexander, P. (2008). Focusing the conceptual lens on metacognition, self-regulation, and self-regulated learning. *Educational Psychology Review, 20,* 391–409 (p. 393).

Tell a Story

1 Kiewra, K. A., & Kauffman, D. (2023). John Glover: A long overdue account of his productive scholarship methods. *Educational Psychology Review, 35,* Article 56.
2 Bembenutty, H. (2022). *Contemporary pioneers in teaching and learning,* Vol. 2. Charlotte, NC: Information Age Publishing, Inc. (pp. 161, 164, 178).
3 Kiewra, K. A., & Creswell, J. W. (2000). Conversations with three highly productive educational psychologists: Richard Anderson, Richard Mayer, and Michael Pressley. *Educational Psychology Review, 12,* 135–161 (p. 145).
4 Mayer, R. E., & Gallini, J. (1990). When is an illustration worth ten thousand words? *Journal of Educational Psychology, 82,* 715–727 (p. 722).

Be Simple and Concise

1 Holbrook, M. B. (1986). A note on sadomasochism in the review process: I hate when that happens. *Journal of Marketing, 50,* 104–108 (p. 106).
2 Patterson-Hazley, M., & Kiewra, K. A. (2013). Conversations with four highly productive educational psychologists: Patricia Alexander, Richard Mayer, Dale Schunk, and Barry Zimmerman. *Educational Psychology Review, 25,* 19–45 (p. 32).

Write with Clarity

1 Holbrook, M. B. (1986). A note on sadomasochism in the review process: I hate when that happens. *Journal of Marketing, 50,* 104–108 (p. 107).
2 Kiewra, K. A., & Creswell, J. W. (2000). Conversations with three highly productive educational psychologists: Richard Anderson, Richard Mayer, and Michael Pressley. *Educational Psychology Review, 12,* 135–161 (pp. 151–152).
3 Kiewra, K. A., Luo, L., & Flanigan, A. (2021). Educational psychology early career award winners: How did they do it? *Educational Psychology Review, 33,* 1981–2018 (p. 2001).
4 Ibid., p. 2013.
5 Flanigan, A., Kiewra, K. A., & Luo, L. (2018). Conversations with four highly productive German educational psychologists: Frank Fischer, Hans

Gruber, Heinz Mandl, and Alexander Renkl. *Educational Psychology Review*, 30, 303–330 (p. 317).
6 Patterson-Hazley, M., & Kiewra, K. A. (2013). Conversations with four highly productive educational psychologists: Patricia Alexander, Richard Mayer, Dale Schunk, and Barry Zimmerman. *Educational Psychology Review*, 25, 19–45 (p. 32).

Write for Your Friends

1 Holbrook, M. B. (1986). A note on sadomasochism in the review process: I hate when that happens. *Journal of Marketing*, 50, 104–108 (p. 106).
2 Alexander, P. A., Schallert, D. L., & Hare, V. C. (1991). Coming to terms: How researchers in learning and literacy talk about knowledge. *Review of Educational Research*, 61, 315–343.
3 Bembenutty, H. (2022). *Contemporary pioneers in teaching and learning*, Vol. 2. Charlotte, NC: Information Age Publishing, Inc. (p. 140).
4 Patterson-Hazley, M., & Kiewra, K. A. (2013). Conversations with four highly productive educational psychologists: Patricia Alexander, Richard Mayer, Dale Schunk, and Barry Zimmerman. *Educational Psychology Review*, 25, 19–45 (p. 33).

Back Off a Bit but Don't Let Your Writing Get Cold

1 Kiewra, K. A., Luo, L., & Flanigan, A. (2021). Educational psychology early career award winners: How did they do it? *Educational Psychology Review*, 33, 1981–2018 (p. 1997).
2 Bembenutty, H. (2022). *Contemporary pioneers in teaching and learning*, Vol. 2. Charlotte, NC: Information Age Publishing, Inc. (p. 140).
3 Kiewra, K. A., Luo, L., & Flanigan, A. (2021). Educational psychology early career award winners: How did they do it? *Educational Psychology Review*, 33, 1981–2018.
4 Ibid.
5 Ibid., p. 2004.
6 Ibid., p. 2014.

Don't Stop until You're Finished

1 Kiewra, K. A., Luo, L., & Flanigan, A. (2021). Educational psychology early career award winners: How did they do it? *Educational Psychology Review*, 33, 1981–2018 (p. 2006).

Learn as You Write

1 Bembenutty, H. (2022). *Contemporary pioneers in teaching and learning*, Vol. 2. Charlotte, NC: Information Age Publishing, Inc. (p. 139).

Embrace Feedback

1 Scott, J., & Borgman, J. (March 7, 2022). *Zits*. King Features Syndicate.
2 Popham, W. J. (1991). Research news and comment: A slice of advice. *Educational Researcher, 20*, 18.
3 Kiewra, K. A., Luo, L., & Flanigan, A. (2021). Educational psychology early career award winners: How did they do it? *Educational Psychology Review, 33*, 1981–2018 (p. 2013).
4 Ibid.
5 Kiewra, K. A., & Creswell, J. W. (2000). Conversations with three highly productive educational psychologists: Richard Anderson, Richard Mayer, and Michael Pressley. *Educational Psychology Review, 12*, 135–161 (p. 152).

Revise, Revise, Revise

1 Graves, R. *Goodreads.* www.goodreads.com/quotes/9084374-there-is-no-such-thing-as-good-writing-only-good.
2 King, S. *Goodreads.* www.goodreads.com/quotes/299449-to-write-is-human-to-edit-is-divine.
3 Kiewra, K. A., & Creswell, J. W. (2000). Conversations with three highly productive educational psychologists: Richard Anderson, Richard Mayer, and Michael Pressley. *Educational Psychology Review, 12*, 135–161 (p. 152).
4 Patterson-Hazley, M., & Kiewra, K. A. (2013). Conversations with four highly productive educational psychologists: Patricia Alexander, Richard Mayer, Dale Schunk, and Barry Zimmerman. *Educational Psychology Review, 25*, 19–45 (p. 33).
5 Ibid., p. 32.
6 Kiewra, K. A., & Kauffman, D. (2023). John Glover: A long overdue account of his productive scholarship methods. *Educational Psychology Review, 35*, Article 56.
7 Flanigan, A., Kiewra, K. A., & Luo, L. (2018). Conversations with four highly productive German educational psychologists: Frank Fischer, Hans Gruber, Heinz Mandl, and Alexander Renkl. *Educational Psychology Review, 30*, 303–330.

8 Ibid., p. 321.
9 Kiewra, K. A., Luo, L., & Flanigan, A. (2021). Educational psychology early career award winners: How did they do it? *Educational Psychology Review*, *33*, 1981–2018 (p. 2013).
10 Ibid., p. 2014.
11 Patterson-Hazley, M., & Kiewra, K. A. (2013). Conversations with four highly productive educational psychologists: Patricia Alexander, Richard Mayer, Dale Schunk, and Barry Zimmerman. *Educational Psychology Review*, *25*, 19–45 (p. 33).

A Few Words about Length: Not Too Long, Not Too Short

1 Holbrook, M. B. (1986). A note on sadomasochism in the review process: I hate when that happens. *Journal of Marketing*, *50*, 104–108.
2 Ibid., p. 106.
3 Ibid., p. 107.

A Few More Writing Tips

1 Lee, K. K. (November 30, 2012). Mark Twain on writing: "Kill your adjectives." *Forbes*. www.forbes.com/sites/katelee/2012/11/30/mark-twain-on-writing-kill-your-adjectives/?sh=6ea8d2df40e8.
2 APA Fact of the Week: While and Since. Complete Dissertation. www.statisticssolutions.com/apa-fact-of-the-week-while-and-since/.

Join a Writing Group

1 Kiewra, K. A., Luo, L., & Flanigan, A. (2021). Educational psychology early career award winners: How did they do it? *Educational Psychology Review*, *33*, 1981–2018.
2 Ibid., p. 1996.
3 Ibid., pp. 1996–1997.
4 Stein, C. (June 2, 2022). 10 reasons to join a writing group. *thinkwritten*. https://thinkwritten.com/10-resons-why-you-should-join-a-local-writing-group/.

8 | *Handle the Review Process*

Become a motivator of writing, not the butcher of it; similarly, become an editor, not the copy editor.

A. K. Kuykendall[1]

I have submitted scores of manuscripts, served on nearly a dozen editorial boards, and did a five-year stint as editor-in-chief, so I know a thing or two because I've seen a thing or two when it comes to the review process. In this section, you'll see that the review process is flawed (like you don't know that already) and how to handle submissions that were rejected or given a second chance.

Understand That the Review Process Is Flawed

Although I've seen the review process work flawlessly on the backs of industrious, insightful, and helpful reviewers and editors, a lot of what I've witnessed is not pretty. From my perch as writer, reviewer, and editor, I have witnessed many reviewers who set out to show how smart they are, picking at a manuscript until it bleeds. And their smart ideas are often off track, things best left for a different study. In Morris Holbrook's classic article about the sadomasochism of the review process, he jokes (sort of) about authors receiving "12 pages of technically incompetent and hopelessly unsympathetic criticisms from three mutually inconsistent reviews."[1] Holbrook offers this advice to reviewers: "The human tendency toward criticizing others dwells so strongly in our constitutions that we find it much easier to recognize flaws than to discover virtues. Allow yourself the pleasure of saying something nice or paying a compliment once in a while."[2]

But, the real problem, I believe, lies with editors who sometimes behave like managers instead of scholars. They seem reluctant to get involved in the review process. Oftentimes, editors respond like this to authors: "I did an independent review of your manuscript and am in

182

agreement with the reviewers ..." Really? If you did an independent review, how can you agree with erroneous statements reviewers made due to careless reading? How can you agree with irrelevant or incomprehensible ideas? How can you agree with reviewers who disagree? I do not mean to dump on all editors, but the field could certainly use more editors like former *Journal of Educational Psychology* editor Joel Levin who closely read a manuscript, who did not patently agree with reviewers and let reviewers and authors know that, and who took a more developmental approach, trying to improve and polish work that had potential rather than outright dismissing it.

Here are a couple of my personal review process war stories.

I submitted a manuscript to a top-tier journal and it was rejected, which is a clear signal to move on to a second-tier journal. On this rare occasion, however, I pushed on instead of moved on. Here's why. Reading the reviewers' comments, none of them seemed fatal and all of them seemed like simple matters to address. I wrote a polite letter to the editor expressing that view, describing how I might handle each comment, and asking if I might submit a revision ... silence. I waited a month and wrote again ... silence. Another month ... silence. No one appreciates being ignored, and I'm not a quitter. I contacted the journal's publisher and chronicled the decision–request–silence events. Within hours, the editor wrote to me and apologized, saying: "I had never had such a request and did not know how to handle it." "Maybe by communicating," I thought. I was given an opportunity to revise, and my revised manuscript was accepted for publication.

My colleagues and I submitted a manuscript to a top-tier journal. It took eight months to get a revise and resubmit decision letter and reviews. Part of the delay might have occurred because there were, unexplainably, five reviewers, each offering about 10–20 comments. We revised and resubmitted within a month's time and included a response letter addressing each of the reviewers' points. Another seven months passed before we again received a revise and resubmit decision letter and five reviews. Only this time, most reviewers said that so much time had passed since they first read the manuscript and there were so many changes that they read the revised manuscript as if it was a new submission. That led to a whole new list of criticisms to address similar in size to the first. Again, we revised and resubmitted within a month and waited another six months for a decision, which again was revise and resubmit, with more *Catch-22* new criticisms to address.

The main fault here is with the editor for allowing so much time to run off the publishing clock with each submission, for including five reviewers when two or three would do (too many cooks in the kitchen), and for not being more involved. The editor should do more than collect reviews and pass them onto authors. The editor, in this case, could have been more punctual, warned reviewers to judge a resubmission based on its handling of previous comments, and made second or third revision judgments without reviewer input.

If Your Manuscript Is Rejected

First, join the club. The rejection rate for top-tier journals is about 90 percent, so don't get discouraged. As was reported back in the Frame Failure section in Chapter 5, even Rich Mayer, the most productive educational psychologist on the planet, has work rejected. Mayer said: "I've probably had more papers rejected from the *Journal of Educational Psychology* than anyone in the history of that journal ... In this field, you have to learn how to take criticism and rejection because we're pretty critical of each other and reviewers can sometimes be brutal."[1] Recall too that Ming-Te Wang offered this rejection-handling advice: "All academics must get used to rejection, and young scholars must realize that rejection is something all scholars must live with and learn from no matter how senior. Receiving feedback is sometimes painful, but you just need to get over it." He jokingly added that young scholars would better understand that no scholars are immune from rejection "if we all published a CV of rejections."[2]

Second, consider submitting your work to another journal. Ming-Te Wang said: "You can always find a home for a paper in a second-tier journal."[3] Before submitting your manuscript a second or third time, it's vital that you pay attention to the reviewers' comments from previous submissions. Those serve as blueprints for strengthening your work and upping publication possibilities. Heed those suggestions. There's another reason you should not submit the same manuscript to a second journal unchanged: It might well land in the same reviewer's hands. Editors are fairly astute at inviting qualified reviewers, and there are likely a small set of qualified reviewers to evaluate your submission. That might explain why I once received a manuscript that seemed eerily familiar. I checked my "Reviews" file and sure enough, there was the same manuscript, word for word. The sobering first line to my new review was this: "I have reviewed this manuscript before for another journal. None of my previously recommended changes were made. Therefore, my review letter is also unchanged as is my recommendation to reject publication."

Third, perhaps cut your losses. Rich Mayer said: "Although rejection hurts, I try not to take it personally. Reviewers have valid comments that can help, so I try to apply their input and move on, because the important thing is continuing to pursue my research questions and to disseminate the findings. I continue to believe in my acquired abilities and tell myself to keep trying."[4]

If Your Manuscript Passes Muster

It's unlikely that you'll ever have a manuscript "accepted with no revisions" or even a "revise and resubmit with minor revisions" decision. When you ask three or more reviewers to review a manuscript, you can expect an arms race of criticisms and recommendations, which means your most realistic hope is for a "major revisions, revise, and resubmit" decision. But that's actually fantastic news.

Most first-time manuscript submitters don't realize this, as was the case for former *Educational Psychology Review* editor-in-chief Dan Robinson, who said this about his first journal submission experience:

The initial decision letter was "major revisions, revise, and resubmit." As a young author, when I first read these words, it was very discouraging, devastating, deflating, and so forth. But I eventually realized that the editor had, in fact, allowed me to slip my foot in the door. I had been given a roadmap showing me how to get closer to an acceptance. The editor was essentially saying, if you do a good job revising the paper according to the reviewer concerns, I will consider this further. So, I tackled the revisions diligently, paying close attention to the reviewers' suggestions and making sure that I did not simply dismiss or pay lip service to the concerns. By doing so, my paper was strengthened and eventually accepted.[1]

Rebecca Collie first learned about the revise and resubmit decision from her graduate school advisor, who said:

Once you have submitted the manuscript, you have only done about 50% of the work. When you get it back, you have to do the other half. If you get a revise and resubmit, that's the editor saying they are willing to pursue this with you. So don't give up. Don't get disheartened by the massive number of comments. Just work through them one by one. Eventually, you'll realize you have handled them all.[2]

It goes beyond obvious to say that you must revise your foot-in-the-door manuscript in line with reviewers' feedback. This is the only pathway to publication. This might mean bolstering your literature review, framing your theoretical argument, more fully expounding methods, reanalyzing data, linking findings to theory and practice, and adding limitations and future research directions. Heck, nominate Reviewer A for a reviewing award, if that's what it takes. Less obvious perhaps is the importance of the "response to reviewers" letter that accompanies your revision. This might actually determine your publication chances as much as or more than the revised manuscript. Let's see what this letter should contain.

1. **Provide an overview.** After acknowledging the editor and reviewers for their insightful and helpful guidance, provide a summary of changes with emphases on major criticisms, such as: weak theoretical foundation, low scoring reliability, and inappropriate analyses and their handling.
2. **Be polite and respectful.** You might find the reviewers' comments off target and off-putting, and you might be right. So what? The fate of your manuscript rests in the reviewers' hands. No sense biting the hand that publishes you. Be polite, respectful, and appreciative of their insightful and helpful suggestions whether you're submitting Revision 1 or 5. Certainly, don't let your frustrations with the review process boil over into a scathing response letter opening like this one humorously penned by scholar Gene Glass:

   Dear Sir, Madame, or Other:
   Enclosed is our latest version of Ms. #1996-02-22-RRRRR, that is the re-re-re-revised revision of our paper. Choke on it. We have again rewritten the entire manuscript from start to finish. We even changed the g-d-running head! Hopefully, we have suffered enough now to satisfy even you and the bloodthirsty reviewers.[3]

   In a more serious tone, Morris Holbrook offers this advice:

   Accept the reviewers' criticisms gracefully and behave as if every word of their comments offered a pearl of wisdom ... Cultivate a posture of humility.[4]

3. **Respond to all points raised.** Scholar Michael Pressley recognizes the value of reviewer feedback. Pressley said: "I always spend time with the reviews and try to figure out what they are telling me. Every one of those points is always telling me something, and we try to react to that and respond to it."[5]

Follow Pressley's lead even if you disagree with or find reviewers' points difficult to handle. Respond to each one. Also, be sure to unpack all the reviewers' points, which could be bunched together in a lengthy paragraph. Give each point a number and name (such as, Reviewer 1, Comment 2: Missing Explicit Hypotheses) and respond to it. But, not like Gene Glass does here:

> One perplexing problem was dealing with suggestions 13–28 by Reviewer B. As you may recall (that is, if you even bother reading the reviews before sending your decision letter), that reviewer listed 16 works that he/she felt we should cite in this paper. These were on a variety of different topics, none of which had any relevance to our work that we could see. The only common thread was that all 16 were by the same author, presumably someone whom Reviewer B greatly admires and feels should be more widely cited. To handle this, we have modified the Introduction and added, after the Review of Relevant Literature, a sub-section entitled "Review of Irrelevant Literature" that discusses these articles.[6]

In a more serious tone, Morris Holbrook offers this advice:

> Act in good faith by trying to fix all aspects of the paper with which [reviewers] have found fault. If they disagree with each other, seek a resolution of this conflict. Forget your righteous indignation over what seems like the incompetence, insensitivity, and mutual inconsistency of the reviewers' comments ... Refuse to make suggested changes only if they are, literally, either impossible or destructive to the paper's contribution.[7]

4. **Accept the blame.** Even when a reviewer can't or does not read, missing something as obvious as the nose on their unobservant face, accept the blame. Recently a reviewer commented: "It still remains the case that explicit hypotheses were not put forward." My response: "Although explicit hypotheses appeared in the Present Study section on pp. 7–8, I see that they are easily overlooked among the many ideas in this section. The revised

manuscript now divides the Present Study section into three subsec-
tions, each with a descriptive heading. Hypotheses now appear
under the p. 8 subheading 'Hypotheses.'"

5. **Make each response complete and self-contained.** Strive to pen
responses that address a reviewer's comments right then and there
rather than send the reviewer back to the manuscript. This is
absolutely critical. Reviewers are primarily looking to see if you
followed their previous suggestions. If they can get this information
from the response letter alone, it reduces their reading of the revised
manuscript. The less they read your revised manuscript, the less
likely they are to harp on previous issues or uncover new things to
complain about. So, do something like this.

Reviewer 3, Comment 7: Provide a fuller description of the lecture
characteristics such as lecture length and rate.

Response: Additional information about lecture characteristics: length,
rate, and idea units appears on p. 9, line 17 in the Materials subsection of
the revised manuscript as follows: "The lecture contained 121 idea units,
lasted 45 minutes, and was presented at an average rate of 150
words per minute."

If the change is too long to quote in the response letter, be sure to
describe the change fully and lead reviewers to the exact pages and
spots where it can be found. Don't leave them to wander about the
manuscript. For example:

Response: As per Reviewer 2's suggestion, separate ANOVAs assessing
note-taking outcomes were replaced by a MANOVA. Findings stemming
from this new analysis appear throughout the Note-Taking Findings
section on pp. 15–16 in the revised manuscript. Although minor changes
occurred with regard to significance values, all comparisons again
reached statistical significance using MANOVA, as was true when
ANOVAs were used originally.

6. **Be thankful and positive.** Thank the editor and reviewers for their
insightful and helpful comments that have resulted in a much
improved manuscript hopefully worthy of publication. Also let
them know that you're willing to make further modifications to
strengthen the manuscript if need be. Certainly don't end your
response letter this Gene Glass way:

Assuming you accept this paper, we would also like to add a footnote acknowledging your help with this manuscript and to point out that we liked the paper much better the way we originally submitted it, but you held the editorial shotgun to our heads and forced us to chop, reshuffle, hedge, expand, shorten, and in general convert a meaty paper into stir-fried vegetables. We could not – or would not – have done it without your input.[8]

References

Handle the Review Process

1 Kuykendall, A. K. *Goodreads*. www.goodreads.com/quotes/tag/editor.

Understand That the Review Process Is Flawed

1 Holbrook, M. B. (1986). A note on sadomasochism in the review process: I hate when that happens. *Journal of Marketing*, *50*, 104–108 (p. 105).
2 Ibid, p. 107.

If Your Manuscript Is Rejected

1 Kiewra, K. A., Walsh, J., & Labenz, C. (2023). Moving beyond fulfill-ment: Wisdom years stories of passion, perseverance, and productivity. *Educational Psychology Review*, *35*, Article 20, p. 20.
2 Kiewra, K. A., Luo, L., & Flanigan, A. (2021). Educational psychology early career award winners: How did they do it? *Educational Psychology Review*, *33*, 1981–2018 (p. 1993).
3 Ibid.
4 Kiewra, K. A., Walsh, J., & Labenz, C. (2023). Moving beyond fulfill-ment: Wisdom years stories of passion, perseverance, and productivity. *Educational Psychology Review*, *35*, Article 20, p. 20.

If Your Manuscript Passes Muster

1 Robinson, D. H. (2022). *Bloody Mary for the AERA attendee's soul*. Charlotte, NC: Information Age Publishing (p. 66).
2 Kiewra, K. A., Luo, L., & Flanigan, A. (2021). Educational psychology early career award winners: How did they do it? *Educational Psychology Review*, *33*, 1981–2018 (p. 1998).
3 Glass, R. L. (2000). A letter from the frustrated author of a journal paper. *The Journal of Systems and Software*, *54*, 1.

4 Holbrook, M. B. (1986). A note on sadomasochism in the review process: I hate when that happens. *Journal of Marketing*, 50, 104–108 (p. 107).

5 Kiewra, K. A., & Creswell, J. W. (2000). Conversations with three highly productive educational psychologists: Richard Anderson, Richard Mayer, and Michael Pressley. *Educational Psychology Review*, 12, 135–161 (p. 152).

6 Glass, R. L. (2000). A letter from the frustrated author of a journal paper. *The Journal of Systems and Software*, 54, 1.

7 Holbrook, M. B. (1986). A note on sadomasochism in the review process: I hate when that happens. *Journal of Marketing*, 50, 104–108 (p. 107).

8 Glass, R. L. (2000). A letter from the frustrated author of a journal paper. *The Journal of Systems and Software*, 54, 1.

9 | *Manage Time and Life*

Time is really the only capital that any human has, and the only thing he cannot afford to lose.

Thomas Edison[1]

The bad news is time flies. The good news is you're the pilot.

Michael Altshuler[2]

Preserve Morning Hours for Scholarly Activities

When's the best time of day for you to handle creative tasks like designing a study or writing a manuscript? Is it predawn when song-birds sound their alarm, a bit later after the morning's first caffeine burst tingles your synapses, perhaps midday following lunch and a nap, in the evening after the day's dust settles, or later still when the night owl calls?

A few scientists have raised this question. In one study,[1] researchers analyzed the test scores from half a million college exams administered at either 9:00 a.m., 1:30 p.m., or 4:30 p.m. over a five-year period in the United Kingdom. Scores were highest in the 1:30 p.m. period. Does this mean that a human's creative sweet spot is in the early afternoon, post-lunch? Isn't this when many people around the world drop what they are doing, drop into bed, and go full-on siesta?

By now, you probably recognize the study's flaws. First, participants were college students who never heard the axioms "early to bed and early to rise" or "the early bird gets the worm." They were likely shedding their PJs just an hour or two before those 1:30 p.m. exams. Second, is test taking in any way akin to a scholar's creative endeavors? Hardly.

Productive scholars establish a routine, a rhythm, that boosts prod-uctivity. For most, their creative peak is morning. They preserve morning hours to tackle their most intellectually demanding tasks and push more routine tasks like meetings and teaching (sorry students) to the afternoon.

The way that Barry Zimmerman, Dale Schunk, Richard Mayer,[2] and Carol Dweck[3] structure time is eerily similar. All work about fifty hours per week with about half that time focused on research activities. All preserve and protect the morning hours for writing because all contend that they are fresher in the morning and writing is their most important activity, deserving of their best effort. All contend that ideas and words flow more easily. Setting aside daily time for writing pays big dividends over the long haul. Mayer, for example, is happy to produce just three or four written pages a day. All put off other more rudimentary tasks like teaching, meetings, correspondence, and administrative duties until the afternoon whenever possible. They sometimes bring their work home and spend a portion of some evenings and weekends reading professional literature or reviewing manuscripts or student work. Mayer said:

I have a segmented day and week that works for me. I have breakfast with my wife in the morning. From 8:30 until noon, I'm in my office on campus writing. I have lunch with my colleagues or with a research group each day. Then in the afternoon, from 12:30 until 5:00 or so, I teach, conduct office hours, meet with students, do service work, and try to get a little more writing done if I can. After work, I have dinner with my wife, walk the dog or something, and later use part of the evening reading or reviewing student work.[4]

Mayer's former student Logan Fiorella adopted Mayer's front-loaded workday approach. Fiorella said: "I try to work on the most important task, such as writing a manuscript or a grant proposal, for the first two or three hours. If I do that, it's already a productive day … A couple of hours a day for a month really add up." He added: "It's really important to establish a writing habit, doing it at the same time and place day after day, where it's just what you do, and it feels like no big deal."[5]

German scholars Heinz Mandl, Alexander Renkl, Frank Fischer,[6] and Mareike Kunter[7] also pack scholarly tasks into morning hours while at their mental peaks. Afternoons are for less demanding and less important tasks. Renkl writes in the morning from home. He also uses down moments throughout the day to write and revise. Fischer is department chair. He has his assistant hold calls while he works on scholarly tasks most mornings. Fischer also works on scholarship in his home office in the evening. Kunter creates to-do lists to guide her morning writing tasks and documents time spent writing, words written, and if goals were met. Kunter said: "You must ruthlessly defend your writing time."[8]

Ming-Te Wang has also developed a morning writing habit. Wang said: "I force myself to write every day even if it's just an hour or two or a single paragraph. Psychologically, I know I'm making progress. Moreover, when I put something aside for a few days, it is really difficult for me to find the thread and pick it back up." Wang pushes classes and meetings to the afternoon and calls meetings "time killers."[9]

Erika Patall[10] takes a slightly different approach, preferring to clear the deck of mundane tasks before shifting to more intellectual tasks. At the start of each day, which can begin as early as 4:30 a.m., Patall focuses on easier tasks that can be completed quickly, such as cleaning out her email inbox and addressing small administrative tasks. Then, attention is turned toward research and writing as she spends most of the day completing tasks on her scholarly to-do list. Evenings are spent with her husband and two young children. Once the family is asleep, though, Patall often returns to her work until between 10:00 p.m. and midnight before going to bed.

Michael Pressley[11] was not much of a sleeper either, sleeping just five hours most nights. Pressley found time pockets in the mornings and evenings to do his scholarly work. Pressley woke up early each morning to write. By mid-morning, he was in schools doing research observations. Late mornings found him at the university attending to his journal editor responsibilities. Afternoon hours were reserved for handling his department chair duties. Evenings were spent with family. Pressley settled in for a brief nap when his family went to bed. Upon awakening, he wrote for a couple more hours before going to bed. Rinse and repeat.

As a graduate student at Harvard University, Carly Robinson rose with the birds and got down to work. Robinson said: "I was most efficient in the morning. I felt fresh and could tackle things efficiently and productively early in the day. An early start also allowed me to have evenings free for my social life, like seeing friends and working out."[12]

Unlike the other scholars, Patricia Alexander's productivity does not hinge on the morning hours. Alexander said: "I know that some people say they write better in the morning. I do not. I can write anywhere, anytime. I can write on the fly. I write whenever I have time to write. That works just fine for me."[13] Alexander rises each day around 6:00 a.m. and is rarely in bed before 1:00 a.m. She spends three to four hours writing every day but, unlike the others, is not tied to the morning hours for this. In fact, when she was completing her master's degree, she also performed as a blues/jazz singer. Throughout an evening, she performed several forty-minute sets on stage interspersed by twenty-minute breaks. Alexander would write during those short breaks.

In the end, it might not matter so much when work is completed or if one's work schedule is strict or fluid. Whether the work drum sounds in the morning, evening, or night, scholars must march to their own beat and become masters of their time.

Work Normal or Long Hours

Some scholars log normal workdays and weeks. John Glover logged normal workday hours and then spent evenings with family. Former Glover student Alice Corkill said: "John was a nine-to-five kind of guy. He'd come to the office every day, Monday through Friday, and stay all day. He didn't sacrifice time with his family. He had his work schedule and his home schedule, and he didn't take a lot of work home. When he went home, he spent time with his family."[1]

Rich Mayer works a normal eight-hour day and usually takes evenings and weekends off to spend time with family and relax. Mayer does occasionally steal a bit of off-time to review manuscripts for several journals, admitting that doing so is "kind of fun and doesn't feel like work."[2] Apparently, the apple does not fall far from the tree. Logan Fiorella,[3] Mayer's former advisee, holds the same nine to five work schedule as Mayer, leaving evenings and weekends free as well. Rebecca Collie[4] also works a normal eight-hour day. Work hours decreased for Sabina Neugebauer and Ming-Te Wang post-tenure. Neugebauer[5] worked ten-hour days pre-tenure but has worked seven-hour days post-tenure, while also working sparingly on weekends. Ming-Te Wang admits that he "worked like a dog for the first seven years of his career,"[6] from 7:00 a.m. to 4:00 p.m. and then again from 9:00 p.m. until midnight. Those twelve-hour days were reduced to six-hour days post-tenure.

Some scholars exceed a forty-hour work week. As a graduate student at Harvard University, Carly Robinson often logged sixty-hour weeks.[7] Erika Patall said she is consumed by her work and routinely works ten to twelve hours each weekday plus another four to eight hours on weekends. Patall sometimes starts her work at 4:00 a.m. She admits that her work commitment "is a little bit crazy."[8] Doug Lombardi admits that he "works all the time because I love what I do. I think about this stuff all the time."[9] Patricia Alexander is much the same way. She said: "I'm a workaholic. I really do not do leisure." Alexander works a nine to five schedule and then works at home in the evening until midnight or later. Her time management motto is "work fast, work a lot."[10] Jacquelynne Eccles[11] also works at the office from nine to five plus evenings and weekends. Tamara van Gog[12] works in the office from 7:30 a.m. till 3:30 p.m., goes for a run, and does more work each evening. She also preserves one weekend day for writing. German scholars Hans Gruber, Alexander Renkl, and Frank Fischer[13] all work long hours. Fischer works from 8:00 a.m. to 8:00 p.m. each weekday in his university office. Renkl works eight to ten hours a day. Gruber logs seventy-hour work weeks. The three of them learned their work habits from their advisor, Heinz Mandl, who worked fifty-plus hours a week. Gruber said: "Heinz would arrive at the office sometime between 5:00 and 7:00 a.m. ... Heinz was certainly a workaholic. He never asked us to be similar, but we certainly learned that from him."[14]

Be a Planner But Don't Overdo It

If you aim for nothing, you'll hit it every time.

Unknown

A goal without a plan is just a wish.

Antoine de Saint Exupery[1]

Productive scholars set goals and orchestrate plans for reaching them. Self-regulation researcher Dale Schunk[2] naturally relies on goal setting and planning. Schunk sets five- or six-yearly project goals each August along with plans and timelines for completing them. Monthly, Schunk monitors his progress toward those goals and modifies his goals, plans, and timelines accordingly. Schunk sets weekly goals each Sunday and writes detailed plans for completing them. Every night he lists daily goals for things he wants to accomplish the next day.

Mareike Kunter[3] is also a goal setter and planner. Kunter creates long-term goals and detailed to-do lists with time allocations for completion. She keeps track of her weekly and daily progress and enjoys crossing completed tasks from her to-do list.

Rebecca Collie[4] has a to-do list application that helps her organize and prioritize her multiple research projects, due dates, and reminders. Collie reviews the app each morning and decides how to best allocate time. Doug Lombardi[5] uses several ongoing to-do lists to help him stay on top of the various tasks he juggles. Lombardi creates separate to-do lists for research, grants, editorial work, and service duties. He examines all the lists each morning, prioritizes tasks, and sets daily goals and time allocations.

When she was a graduate student, Carly Robinson used a to-do list to plan and took advantage of small time pockets. Robinson said: "I am a planner. I always plan and decide what I need to prioritize and work on next. This helped me be a productive graduate student. Even if I only had 15 minutes of free time, I could always pull from my to-do list and make progress on small tasks in an efficient and effective manner."[6]

Scholars should consider a note of caution in their planning: Don't overplan. This cautionary note comes to you from computer scientists who try to figure out how to get computers to make the best decisions and to complete work most efficiently. In 1997, the National Aeronautics and Space Administration (NASA) landed the rocket *Pathfinder* on the moon where it was to carry out a number of scientific tasks. Unfortunately, *Pathfinder* came down with a bug in its scheduler, which determines what tasks to work on and when to switch tasks. The bug caused *Pathfinder* to procrastinate, to behave busily but avoid its most important work.[7] Humans, of course, do this often as we surf the Internet, grab a snack, and even fold laundry to avoid the work we should prioritize. Sometimes our failure to prioritize is more subtle but equally harmful. Suppose you vow to get to work after handling some email. In handling email, you decide that you can't respond right now but you'll rank the emails in importance and vow to first handle the most important ones later. If you do this, you are making two procrastination errors. One, you are dealing with email instead of your work. Two, taking the time to prioritize emails is a waste of time. You're better off simply handling them chronologically or even randomly than taking time to prioritize them. What does all this have to do with scholarly planning? Be careful that you are not robotically spending too much time formulating plans and allocating time versus getting down to work.

Get Down to It

When I was in college, I had a hallmate nicknamed Winkle because he slept about as much as Rip Van Winkle. Every evening after dinner, Winkle would return to the residence hall and promptly tell us how much work he intended to do that night ... "Two hours of Chem, another hour of English Lit, and then cram till morning for tomorrow's Econ exam." It never happened. Before getting down to work, Winkle had to shower, make a few calls to buddies back home, and grill up a couple cheese dogs in his electric cooker. Eventually, he kicked back on his bed, cracked open a book, and soon drifted off to sleep. Winkle was a procrastinator.

Productive scholars don't procrastinate, they get down to it. According to former student Alice Corkill, John Glover was an efficient worker: "John was efficient. He didn't waste time in the office. He didn't spend a lot of time going around and chatting with people. When he was at the office he worked, and when he was at home he was at home."[1]

Reporting on her work efficiency, Mareike Kunter said: "I'm self-disciplined. I can concentrate well and I can focus well."[2] Her self-discipline is reflected in the strategies she uses for managing her time and research. For example, she follows short- and long-term plans and keeps careful records of her writing progress.

Tamara van Gog is also a go-getter. She said: "I'm quite good at getting things done, not hesitating too long but just doing it."[3] Van Gog explained that her straightforward approach to accomplishing things originated during her childhood while living in a working-class surrounding. Even as a child, her stepfather told her: "If you want to get ahead in life, you have to get a move on."[4]

Rebecca Collie does not let grass grow under her feet either. Collie has two children and limited time to get things done. She said: "When

I'm at work, I have to work, and I just get on with it. There can be no procrastination, no wasted time, because as soon as my children get home from school or daycare, I need to be a mom."[5]

As a graduate student, Hyewon Lee carved out large chunks of time to accomplish important things and gave short shrift to less important things. Lee said: "For cognitively demanding work, I fiercely preserved chunks of uninterrupted time, usually four hours. One to two hours was not enough for me to get into deep concentration." When it came to lower-priority work, Lee told herself, "I'll get this work done within one hour, and I will not spend any more time on it than that." Another Lee time-saver was working from home. Lee said: "I rarely traveled to campus. I didn't want to waste my time traveling."[6]

One way Ming-Te Wang and other scholars remain efficiently productive is by avoiding meetings or limiting meeting durations. Wang calls meetings "time killers."[7] University faculty are notorious for scheduling meetings to dispense information that could be dispensed electronically and for handling matters best handled by an individual or small group. I recall a nightmarish meeting where twenty-five faculty members wordsmithed a document. Such inefficiency explains why so many faculty I observe are handling other business on their laptops during meetings.

Say No

When it comes to saving money, experts tell you to pay yourself first. Be sure the first bite out of that monthly paycheck goes toward your priorities before paying the electric company. Since time is money, you should also prioritize spending sufficient time pursuing your goals, not someone else's. Here is how a creative individual responded to an invitation to participate in a study on creativity:

I hope you will not think me presumptuous or rude if I say that one of the secrets of productivity is to have a VERY BIG waste paper basket to take care of ALL invitations such as yours. Productivity in my experience consists of NOT doing anything that helps the work of other people but to spend one's time on the work the good Lord has fitted one to do, and to do it well.[1]

Sometimes productive scholars say "no" in order to spend their time on the work the good Lord has fitted them to do.

Tamara van Gog's work choices are guided by this question: "What do I have to get involved in, what do I want to get involved in, and what do I not want to get involved in?"[2] For instance, van Gog chooses to spend time securing grants and conducting grant-funded research over time spent teaching. She also chooses to keep at least one weekday plus weekends free for writing. To do so, she says "no" to other opportunities or invitations that could interfere.

Other scholars also mentioned the need to say "no" to competing tasks that can pull them off track. You read earlier how John Glover avoided university committees and service obligations, preferring to spend his energy on research. Logan Fiorella finds that making too many commitments, even small ones, distracts him, as do unfinished things that linger.[3] Ming-Te Wang said: "I needed to learn to say 'no' to people and stay true to the goals I wanted to accomplish." Wang turned down research collaboration opportunities and associate editorship invitations early in his career. Wang said: "Early on, I focused on my own work rather than getting lost exploring different collaborations with different people. I was highly cautious about what collaborations I accepted or pursued, only choosing those I found promising and doable. In general, I chose to avoid multiple collaborations during my pre-tenure years to raise productivity." As for editorial positions, Wang remarked: "Those positions are difficult and time consuming. I didn't want to become an editor until I was a full professor."[4]

Still think you can't say "no"? Try these replies:

- I'm honored you asked me, but I don't have the time to commit to that now.
- Thanks for the invitation, but this is not something that is a strength for me. You'd be better off inviting someone else.
- I wish I could, but I have other commitments I must fulfill.

If those don't work, and you want to discourage future invitations, you might try these replies:

- My spirit animal advises I don't do this.
- Perhaps I could after my skin lesions heal.
- Would it be okay if my probation officer joins us?

Use Time Pockets

While the scholars generally carve large blocks of time, especially in the morning, to work on their scholarly tasks, they also take advantage of smaller time pockets throughout the day to get things done. As mentioned earlier, Patricia Alexander boasts: "I can write anywhere, anytime. I can write on the fly. I write whenever I have time to write. That works just fine for me."[1]

Dale Schunk spent more than half his career as an administrator but still published over a hundred works during that administrative span. He did so by finding time pockets for scholarly work. Schunk said: "My free time to work on research and writing was very limited, so I planned time carefully and used breaks in my schedule for scholarship. For example, I took copies of manuscripts with me to my administrative work and worked on them during small breaks."[2] When possible, Schunk also preserved time outside of work hours for writing manuscripts, reading journals and books, attending conferences, and staying connected with colleagues and graduate students.

Alexander Renkl[3] works exclusively on writing at his home each morning. Afternoons are spent on teaching and administrative tasks at the university. Whenever Renkl has a few down moments throughout the afternoon, he returns to his scholarly work to write or revise.

With the explosion of laptops, tablets, smartphones, and cloud computing, the down moments Renkl references can be filled quickly with work-related uploads and downloads. Time spent in a doctor's waiting room, on hold with a voiceless business, or during a four-minute sports TV time out can be spent taking care of business.

Of course, one can also go old school during down moments and work off-line. That's what Carly Robinson did on her train commutes from Providence, RI to Harvard University while in graduate school. Robinson said: "The internet service on the train was not great, so I did not get distracted by responding to emails or opening up different browsers. That was good focus time for me to read, work on course assignments, or dive into my research data."[4]

Doug Lombardi even finds time pockets while grooming or walking. No kidding. You'll recall that Lombardi said: "A lot of my writing is done when I'm taking a shower, washing my hair, or brushing my teeth. A lot of writing is done on my walks with (wife) Janelle, because I think about this stuff all the time."[5]

Deter Distractions

Creativity scholar Mihaly Csikszentmihalyi, who interviewed dozens of creative people, offered this advice: "Erect barriers against distractions, dig channels so that energy can flow more freely, find ways to escape outside temptations and interruptions."[1] And to think he wrote this before smartphones and other digital devices.

Computers, smartphones, and other digital devices certainly help us do our work. I remember a time long ago when my dissertation was prepared by a professional typist. Edits were made using correction tape, Wite-Out, or retyping entire sections. There was no digital record of the defense product, so I made umpteen copies and preserved them in my apartment (in the refrigerator in case of fire), university office, car, and bank safe-deposit box. Three close friends were also given maps to these locations. As an assistant professor, I wrote manuscripts by hand and snail mailed them to collaborators around the country, who would mark them with their highlighters and pens, and ship them back for further revision.

Although our computers and digital devices now offer on-the-go, all-the-time access to our work, they are also life's major distraction. If you're a student or instructor, here are some sobering in and out of class data:[2]

1. Students engage in off-task computer activities nearly two-thirds of class time.
2. Seventy to ninety percent of students text during class.
3. In-class texting decreases note taking by up to 40 percent and achievement by 50 percent.
4. More than 60 percent of students become distracted by digital devices when they study.
5. Students studying during a three-hour time block were distracted by digital devices thirty-five times on average.
6. Digital distractions while studying decrease student study time, schoolwork completion, assignment quality, course grades, and cumulative grade-point average. It also makes students more stressed while studying.

Things are no better in the workplace. Rosen and Samuel write: "Digital overload may be the defining problem of today's workplace. All day and night, on desktops, laptops, tablets, and smartphones, we're bombarded with so many messages and alerts that even when we want to focus, it's nearly impossible. And when we're tempted to procrastinate, diversions are only a click away."[3] Here are some sobering workplace distraction data:

- People juggling several streams of content do not pay attention or manage tasks as well as those who focus on one thing at a time. Multitasking is a myth.[4] Our brains can focus on just one task at a time.
- When workers switch to an electronic task unrelated to their work, it takes about twenty minutes to return to the work-related task.
- Workers waste more than two hours a day using their phones.
- Most of that wasted time is spent checking personal email and surfing the Internet, particularly sites for entertainment, games, and shopping.

It is difficult for most people to escape from the temptations of mobile devices because their overuse reflects obsession or compulsion. What draws us to our digital devices? Perhaps one or more of these anxieties:

- FOMO: Fear of missing out
- FOBO: Fear of being offline
- Nomophobia: Fear of being out of mobile phone contact.

Such anxieties are likely the root for many people checking their smartphones every fifteen minutes or less and feeling anxious if they don't.

Computer scientists believe that computers experience the same problems as humans as they handle distractions. Each time a computer switches from one task to another, it must bookmark existing work, move existing data out of memory, and move new data in. Doing so allows the computer to be quickly responsive to new tasks but at the cost of productivity. This is akin to humans pausing their work to read and respond to incoming texts or emails. Computer scientists have learned that the best solution is for computers to do what's termed interruption coalescing.[5] This happens when the computer pools interruptions, ignores them for a time, and then switches to handle the accumulated interruptions all at once before switching back to the primary work task. Humans should do the same: Work without interruption while incoming messages silently and blindly pool behind the scenes and then handle the accrued interruptions at one time, perhaps once per hour.

So beware of the distractions wrought by technology, and don't be a cyber-slacker. Here are some simple-to-dispense, but perhaps hard-to-enact, tips for reducing digital distractions:

- Wean yourself from digital devices when working by initially shutting down unnecessary devices for thirty minutes by setting an alarm. When it rings, allow yourself a couple minutes for a tech check-in. Gradually extend the off-grid time to an hour or more.
- Take a recharging break from work every ninety minutes (in line with our natural rest–activity cycle) and take a ten-minute break to listen to music, exercise, or meditate. Try to do these or other calming activities outside in nature if possible.
- Turn off phone notifications and place phones out of sight and out of reach. Even having phones in-pocket or nearby is a temptation that makes people less productive.
- Use one computer screen instead of two. More screen real estate invites more windows and programs and potential distractions.

To deter distractions also consider where your work is done. Scholars Alexander Renkl,[6] Carol Dweck,[7] and Logan Fiorella[8] are among the productive scholars who work from home most mornings. Working at home, they say, is less distracting than working at the office. Rich Mayer[9] works at the office throughout the day but closes his door in the morning to block distractions when engaged in research and writing activities. Frank Fischer[10] is department chair but still preserves office time for scholarly work. During those work periods, he has his assistant hold all calls and not allow visitors. Fischer also works on writing manuscripts in the evenings and on weekends in a small, private room on the top floor of his house that is free from family distractions. Perhaps a bit of white noise technology is helpful. Although David Berliner has a penchant for being able to "turn things off when I write," he said, "I put on classical music (no voices – too distracting) and just do it."[11] Similarly, Karen Harris[12] prefers writing with low-volumed music or with the television playing in the background rather than with complete silence.

Finally, recognize that mundane routines like showering, dressing, and driving can distract us from our work. Consider this: For every 5 minutes you drive one-way to work, you spend 5 (minutes) × 46 (work weeks) × 5 (weekdays) × 2 (trips per day) totaling 38.3 hours of yearly commuting time. That's an entire work week. If you live 25 minutes from work, you spend nearly 200 hours commuting a year. That's five 40-hour weeks tossed to the curb. Give consideration to how you might preserve time. Can you work from home more often? Can you arrange to drive to and from work when traffic is light instead of heavy? Can you arrange to exercise first thing in the morning so that just one shower (after exercising) is needed instead of one before work and another after exercising later in the day? And can you understand why Albert Einstein wore the same old sweater and baggy trousers each day? Mihaly Csikszentmihalyi writes:

Einstein wasn't trying to upset anybody. He was just cutting down on the daily effort involved in deciding what clothes to wear, so that his mind could focus on matters that to him were more important ... Suppose it takes only two minutes each day to decide how to dress. That adds up to 730 minutes, or 12 hours a year. Now think about all the repetitive things we have to do throughout the day – comb hair, drive cars, eat, and so on. And then think not only of the time it takes to do each of these things but of the interruption in the train of thought they cause, both before and after. Having to choose a tie could derail a whole hour's worth of reflection! No wonder Einstein preferred to play it safe and wear the same old clothes.[13]

Maintain a Work–Life Balance

As the saying goes, "all work and no play makes Jack a dull boy." It also makes him less effective, less healthy, and less happy. People who work the brain also need to work the body. Chess players, who spin their gray matter for hours at a time when playing tournament chess, know this.[1] Legend has it that the 1984 World Chess Championship was called off after five months and forty-eight games because defending champion Anatoly Karpov had lost twenty-two pounds and "looked like death," according to grandmaster and commentator Maurice Ashley. In 2004, winner Rustam Kasimdzhanov lost seventeen pounds during the six-game championship. The realization that intensive mental work creates physical problems has sent many a chess player to the gym, pool, or running trails seeking better health and a sharper mind.[2]

I can relate. I've been an endurance and nature disciple since I laced up my first running shoes in 1978. Since then, I've logged more than 100,000 miles running, hiking, and walking, mostly on nature's trails. This routine has kept me healthy and happy and has provided opportunity to reflect and think. Some of my best ideas have evolved on the trails.

Productive scholars I interviewed also recognize that all work and no play is not the best course for maintaining productivity or a happy life.

Instead, most seek a work–life balance that includes time for family, mental rejuvenation, and physical activity.

Earlier you read about John Glover's commitment to research. Former Glover colleague Barbara Plake said: "John had a non-stop commitment to scholarship . . . He would come early and stay late; we were in research production around the clock." But then Plake added: "Now, I have to say that this sounds like a driven person that has no life outside of academia, but John was one of the most devoted family people that I knew, so he managed to focus his energies on his family but still keep his passion for research."[3] Glover colleague Bob Brown added: "John was completely devoted to his home life and two young daughters."[4]

Rich Mayer might be the world's most productive educational psychologist, but he is certainly not all work and no play. Mayer said: "I put my family first and my job second."[5] Mayer usually works a full day but spends evenings and weekends focused on family. When his children were younger, he drove them to school and was involved in their school and community activities. Now that they are grown, there are daily phone calls and trips from California to Michigan to visit children and grandchildren.[6] For leisure, Mayer enjoys walking his dogs and mountain biking in picturesque Santa Barbara, California. He goes to the movies with his wife and tries to figure out his latest technology gadgets. Mayer joked: "I like learning to use my computer, I-Pad, and Smart Phone. Those give me plenty of hours of wasted time."[7]

Similarly, Logan Fiorella, who is married and has a young daughter, said that he puts family first. Fiorella works a conventional nine to five schedule and rarely works evenings or weekends. To balance his academic work, Fiorella exercises regularly after lunch in his home gym and enjoys playing golf.[8]

Ming-Te Wang is finding more time for leisure post-tenure. Wang said: "For the first seven years of my career, I worked like a dog." He worked from 7:00 a.m. until 4:00 p.m., again from 9:00 p.m. until midnight, plus more time on weekends, logging about sixty work hours per week. Since then, he realized: "I cannot do this for the rest of my life," and he sought a "better work-life balance."[9] Now Wang works about six hours a day Monday through Friday and rarely on weekends. For exercise and renewal, Wang runs thirty to forty minutes a day.

Hans Gruber is also a dedicated runner who often breaks up his twelve-hour workdays with a midday run. Gruber said: "My colleagues often say, 'It's so early in the afternoon, you can't leave already.' But, they leave at six in the evening and I sometimes continue on until one in the morning."[10]

Richard Anderson enjoys life outside academia. He enjoys "efficiently putting on a nice meal with every course done nicely and without having to drop everything for a day and dirty every pot and pan to get it done."[11] He and his wife share an interest in photography. Anderson especially enjoys aquatic sports and bringing his pioneering research spirit to the outdoors. Anderson said:

I went to Northern Wisconsin where we have a cottage and I spent two days sailing all by myself. I spent three days and two nights on a personal camping trip in a wilderness area where I carried my canoe and all my gear from lake to lake up in the Sylvania wilderness area in the upper peninsula of Michigan. And then I read an old book on canoeing about how the explorers got upstream in their canoes using a pole. So, I decided I'd like to try that so I went to a local pole vault manufacturer and got a 14-foot fiberglass pole and made a special mount on each end with a two-inch stainless steel pin in it, and I poled up a river one day. It was more exhausting than I thought it would be and I didn't get as far as I wanted to and then I poled back down the river. So, it's a nice way that a lone individual can do a canoe trip.[12]

Self-regulation scholars Barry Zimmerman and Dale Schunk also seek work–life balance. Zimmerman exercises for one to two hours most afternoons and enjoys leisure activities such as tennis, snow skiing, New York City music performances, and traveling abroad. Schunk commented that he builds break time into his days. He said: "I have to have breaks. I can't work all the time. I schedule the breaks just like I schedule the work. If I don't schedule breaks, the work will fill up that time."[13] Schunk likes to work around the yard and spends three to five hours doing that most weeks. He jogs a few miles every morning and enjoys reading novels, going to shows and movies, visiting friends, and traveling.

Productive female scholars depend on taking daily and weekly breaks to maintain a healthy work–life balance and sustained vigor when they do work.[14] Tamara van Gog takes a daily walk during her lunch break and spends one day a week free from work. Mareike Kunter takes lunch breaks away from the office and keeps weekends free, not even checking emails. Kunter said: "I need clear breaks. If I'm always involved in work, that isn't good for my well-being. When

I work, I work hard and fully concentrated, but I try to keep parts of my life free from work."[15] Carol Dweck said:

For some people, working all the time becomes unproductive. Maybe you feel good if you are putting in the hours and maybe you feel guilty if you are not putting in the hours – but are all those hours efficient? And might they be more efficient if you took a little time for something else? So just working, day after day, without a break, is probably not the most efficient way. And, you may not be as likely to bring new perspectives and ideas to what you are doing.[16]

Dweck, Kunter, and van Gog also mentioned that outside of work they enjoy sports like running and yoga, cultural activities, and spending time with families and friends.

Maintaining a work–life balance might be more difficult for women than men given their unbalanced contributions in the home. A gender gap report revealed that women spend two to ten times more time providing unpaid care work than men.[17] Closer to academia, some of the productive male scholars I interviewed reported that their wives accomplished up to 95 percent of family and household chores.[18]

Among the female scholars,[19] several seemed to bear the brunt of homeland responsibilities. Patricia Alexander was a single parent. Jacquelynne Eccles raised two children on her own. Mareike Kunter took a year off after having twins and then chose to work reduced hours after that. Kunter said:

It wasn't much of a problem to take a year off and to now work reduced hours because I'm not in this phase in which I have to qualify or fight for a position. I've done this before . . . But witnessing other female colleagues who have children, I think family responsibilities take time away from them that male colleagues can spend on their career.[20]

Patricia Alexander said:

There is a choice to be made between devoting time to building a family and building a career. Many women understand the need to give up on certain things in order to raise a family. Women are nurturers and that takes energy away. If you look at the men on the list [of top educational psychologists], in most cases, they've all been married and have wives who understand and support their careers.[21]

Rebecca Collie feels pressure to be productive during her 8:30–5:00 workday – taking only one twenty-minute break for lunch – because of her impending childcare obligations.

As mentioned earlier, Collie said: "When I'm at work, I have to work, and I just get on with it. There can be no procrastination, no wasted time, because as soon as my children get home from school or daycare, I need to be a mom."[22]

Sirui Wan[23] emphasized that it is also vital for graduate students to look after their personal health and emotional well-being. Wan noted that as a graduate student he spent time outdoors and participated in a rowing club as a way of staying healthy and refreshed. Wan emphasized that graduate students should take one full day off per week, where they do no research or classwork or work-related activities, to support their personal health and emotional well-being.

On the work–life balance flip side, some scholars find it difficult to disengage from work. Doug Lombardi said: "I really like what I do. I really enjoy it. I don't take a lot of time disengaging from what I do. I have to schedule my off time. If I want to disengage, I schedule that."[24] For example, he and his wife schedule a "date day" once every week in the summer and once every month during the semester to disengage from work. Patricia Alexander said: "I sometimes joke that I've got a socially acceptable addiction: I just love to work. There's always some burning issue that I've got to deal with."[25] Alexander admitted that a work–life balance is not her preference or style. She said: "I really do not do leisure. Even if I am watching TV, I am watching TV and writing or grading papers. I cannot not work. I am a workaholic. That is not a good thing, but it is who I am." Alexander has tried to build leisure activities into her life. Once she took up crocheting because people said it would relax her. She ended up crocheting two Afghans in a week. Another time she tried painting and painted fifty portraits in about a month. "Whatever I do," she lamented, "gets out of hand."[26]

With a hard-driving work ethic comes sacrifice. German scholar Hans Mandl said that he sacrificed having a social life in favor of his work.[27] His protégé, Frank Fischer, said: "What I sacrifice are the evening hours, the evening hours that many people spend with their families or friends … When my children were younger, all of them were asleep when I came home. I thought of that as a sacrifice always."[28] Regarding sacrifice, Alexander said that she has lived most of her life as a single woman but is content. Her family, including her parents, son, daughter-in-law, and beloved grandchildren are important parts of her life. Always the academic, Alexander added: "I am devoted to my students and my work. They are my family too. The rewards have been plenty."[29]

Create Stability or Live on the Edge

Most of the productive scholars have stable lives marked by routine. On the stability side, Richard Anderson[1] wakes up every morning at 5:25 to exercise. He alternates his exercise routine between weight lifting, which he has done for the past ten years, and running, which he has done for more than the past twenty years. He arrives at the university every day at 8:30 and begins work. Richard Mayer reported in 2000 that he drives his daughter to school each morning and plans his workday as he drives to the university. He too arrives and begins work at 8:30. Hmmm, 8:30? Mayer works on scholarly tasks every morning, with the door closed and technology silenced. Most days he eats lunch with his colleagues or research group. He spends afternoons fulfilling teaching, advising, and service duties. His nightly 6:00 family dinner anchors his day. After dinner he spends time with family relaxing or exercising. Later in the evening, he might spend time reviewing manuscripts or student work. Mayer touts the importance of stability: "There's been a lot of stability in my life. I had a stable family as a kid and I have a very supportive wife and family as an adult that I get a lot of satisfaction from. I put my family first and my job second."[2]

On the live-on-the-edge side are Michael Pressley and Patricia Alexander. Unlike other scholars who have typically held just one or two academic positions, Pressley moved about holding posts at Michigan State University, University of Albany, Western Ontario University, University of Maryland, and Notre Dame University. Pressley's daily life was no less varied and harried. As reported earlier, Pressley[3] slept just five hours nightly. He'd wake up early each morning and work on writing articles and books for a few hours before fulfilling other professorial duties at schools or at the university. Evenings were spent with family. When the family went to bed, Pressley would nap for a bit and then rise to write for a couple hours before going to bed. Pressley's on-the-edge lifestyle was perhaps linked to his illness and a desire to produce while he could. At the time, Pressley had twice battled cancer and lost about six months to treatment. Pressley eventually overcame a third cancer battle before succumbing to the disease in 2006 at the age of fifty-five.

Patricia Alexander and Michael Pressley were colleagues for a time at the University of Maryland. Not sure what they served in the dining hall there, but the two of them shared on-the-edge similarities. Alexander too slept just four or five hours a night and quipped: "That is kind of the Michael Pressley model. Michael and I used to match each other on that."[4] Alexander rises each day around 6:00 a.m. and rarely retires to bed before 1:00 a.m. Her workdays hold minimum structure. Unlike other scholars who routinely write in the mornings, Alexander reported that she writes anytime the mood strikes or when a few minutes are at hand. As mentioned, Alexander does not have a leisure routine either. It is difficult for her to relax and disengage from work. She said: "I cannot 'not work.' I am a workaholic. That is not a good thing, but it is who I am."[5] Alexander, like Pressley, was also diagnosed with a terminal disease, which prompted her to race through graduate school. For Alexander, the race never ended. She said: "I lived every day as if I were dying, and I still do. I never take any day for granted. And to this day, I never lost that 'live like you are dying' mentality."[6]

Guilt Can Motivate

There are two kinds of guilt: The kind that drowns you until you're useless, and the kind that fires your soul to purpose.

Sabaa Tahir[1]

Guilt can be a motivator.

Erika Patall's feelings of guilt move her to task completion. Patall said:

If you were to ask my family what encapsulates a large portion of my personality, they would say that I work really, really hard and really long on anything that seems important to me. My husband, who I've known since fourth grade, says that I work harder than anyone he's ever known. It's a little bit crazy, but I cannot just stop halfway through a task because I'll feel guilty about stopping or I won't be able to sleep if I didn't get to a logical stopping point. I feel bad if I don't get things done.[2]

When asked what motivates him to be productive, scholar David Berliner said: "I like working with others – the guilt associated with not letting down your friends is enormous. Writing with a colleague is my best motivation – I am social and don't want to disappoint my colleague, so I try to meet the deadlines we jointly set. Guilt is my foremost motivator."[3] In a similar guilt-induced vein, Michael Mayrath[4] recommends creating social deadlines for your collaborative projects so that others also hold you accountable for getting things done. Karen Harris concurs, saying: "Deadlines are both my worst enemies and best friends. Writing with or for others helps create those deadlines."[5]

I too was motivated by guilt as I raced through graduate school – from B.A. to Ph.D. in three years. After graduating college, at my parents' expense, I became a third-grade teacher. My parents and I saw this position as a crowning achievement and as my ticket to financial independence. So, when I quit teaching after just two years to attend graduate school, partly funded by my parents, I felt guilt. Guilt that I was delaying my full entrance into adulthood. Guilt that I was shirking my self-sufficiency obligation. And guilt that I was once again sponging off my hardworking parents. All that guilt spurred me to get in and get out of graduate school as quickly as possible.

References

Manage Time and Life

1 Edison, T. *Vantage Circle*. https://blog.vantagecircle.com/time-management-quotes/
2 Altshuler, M. *Vantage Circle*. https://blog.vantagecircle.com/time-management-quotes/

Preserve Morning Hours for Scholarly Activities

1 Mitra, M. (September 18, 2020). Scientists have pinpointed the most productive time of the day, and it's not the crack of dawn. *Money*. https://money.com/most-productive-time-of-day/.
2 Patterson-Hazley, M., & Kiewra, K. A. (2013). Conversations with four highly productive educational psychologists: Patricia Alexander, Richard Mayer, Dale Schunk, and Barry Zimmerman. *Educational Psychology Review, 25,* 19–45.
3 Prinz, A., Zeeb, H., Flanigan, A., Renkl, A., & Kiewra, K. A. (2020). Conversations with five highly successful female educational psychologists: Patricia Alexander, Carol Dweck, Jacquelynne Eccles, Mareike

Kunter, and Tamara van Gog. *Educational Psychology Review*, 33, 763–795.

4 Patterson-Hazley, M., & Kiewra, K. A. (2013). Conversations with four highly productive educational psychologists: Patricia Alexander, Richard Mayer, Dale Schunk, and Barry Zimmerman. *Educational Psychology Review*, 25, 19–45 (p. 30).

5 Kiewra, K. A., Luo, L., & Flanigan, A. (2021). Educational psychology early career award winners: How did they do it? *Educational Psychology Review*, 33, 1981–2018 (p. 1989).

6 Flanigan, A., Kiewra, K. A., & Luo, L. (2018). Conversations with four highly productive German educational psychologists: Frank Fischer, Hans Gruber, Heinz Mandl, and Alexander Renkl. *Educational Psychology Review*, 30, 303–330.

7 Prinz, A., Zeeb, H., Flanigan, A., Renkl, A., & Kiewra, K. A. (2020). Conversations with five highly successful female educational psychologists: Patricia Alexander, Carol Dweck, Jacquelynne Eccles, Mareike Kunter, and Tamara van Gog. *Educational Psychology Review*, 33, 763–795.

8 Ibid., p. 780.

9 Kiewra, K. A., Luo, L., & Flanigan, A. (2021). Educational psychology early career award winners: How did they do it? *Educational Psychology Review*, 33, 1981–2018 (p. 1992).

10 Kiewra, K. A., Luo, L., & Flanigan, A. (2021). Educational psychology early career award winners: How did they do it? *Educational Psychology Review*, 33, 1981–2018.

11 Kiewra, K. A., & Creswell, J. W. (2000). Conversations with three highly productive educational psychologists: Richard Anderson, Richard Mayer, and Michael Pressley. *Educational Psychology Review*, 12, 135–161.

12 Kiewra, K. A., Hasnin, S., Soundy, J., Premkumar, P. K., & Labenz, C. (2023). Graduate student award winners in educational psychology: What made them successful? *Educational Psychology Review*, 35, Article 90.

13 Patterson-Hazley, M., & Kiewra, K. A. (2013). Conversations with four highly productive educational psychologists: Patricia Alexander, Richard Mayer, Dale Schunk, and Barry Zimmerman. *Educational Psychology Review*, 25, 19–45 (p. 31).

Work Normal or Long Hours

1 Kiewra, K. A., & Kauffman, D. (2023). John Glover: A long overdue account of his productive scholarship methods. *Educational Psychology Review*, 35, Article 56.

2 Kiewra, K. A., Walsh, J., & Labenz, C. (2023). Moving beyond fulfill-ment: Wisdom years stories of passion, perseverance, and productivity. *Educational Psychology Review*, *35*, Article 20, p. 8.
3 Kiewra, K. A., Luo, L., & Flanigan, A. (2021). Educational psychology early career award winners: How did they do it? *Educational Psychology Review*, *33*, 1981–2018.
4 Ibid.
5 Ibid.
6 Ibid., p. 1992.
7 Kiewra, K. A., Hasnin, S., Soundy, J., Premkumar, P. K., & Labenz, C. (2023). Graduate student award winners in educational psychology: What made them successful? *Educational Psychology Review*, *35*, Article 90.
8 Kiewra, K. A., Luo, L., & Flanigan, A. (2021). Educational psychology early career award winners: How did they do it? *Educational Psychology Review*, *33*, 1981–2018 (p. 2006).
9 Ibid., p. 2012.
10 Patterson-Hazley, M., & Kiewra, K. A. (2013). Conversations with four highly productive educational psychologists: Patricia Alexander, Richard Mayer, Dale Schunk, and Barry Zimmerman. *Educational Psychology Review*, *25*, 19–45 (p. 31).
11 Prinz, A., Zeeb, H., Flanigan, A., Renkl, A., & Kiewra, K. A. (2020). Conversations with five highly successful female educational psycholo-gists: Patricia Alexander, Carol Dweck, Jacquelynne Eccles, Mareike Kunter, and Tamara van Gog. *Educational Psychology Review*, *33*, 763–795.
12 Ibid.
13 Flanigan, A., Kiewra, K. A., & Luo, L. (2018). Conversations with four highly productive German educational psychologists: Frank Fischer, Hans Gruber, Heinz Mandl, and Alexander Renkl. *Educational Psychology Review*, *30*, 303–330.
14 Ibid., p. 317.

Be a Planner but Don't Overdo It

1 De Saint-Exupery, A. *Goodreads*. www.goodreads.com/quotes/87476-a-goal-without-a-plan-is-just-a-wish.
2 Patterson-Hazley, M., & Kiewra, K. A. (2013). Conversations with four highly productive educational psychologists: Patricia Alexander, Richard Mayer, Dale Schunk, and Barry Zimmerman. *Educational Psychology Review*, *25*, 19–45.

3 Prinz, A., Zeeb, H., Flanigan, A., Renkl, A., & Kiewra, K. A. (2020). Conversations with five highly successful female educational psychologists: Patricia Alexander, Carol Dweck, Jacquelynne Eccles, Mareike Kunter, and Tamara van Gog. *Educational Psychology Review*, *33*, 763–795.

4 Kiewra, K. A., Luo, L., & Flanigan, A. (2021). Educational psychology early career award winners: How did they do it? *Educational Psychology Review*, *33*, 1981–2018.

5 Ibid.

6 Kiewra, K. A., & Kauffman, D. (2023). John Glover: A long overdue account of his productive scholarship methods. *Educational Psychology Review*, *35*, Article 56.

7 Singh, P. (August 26, 2020). How to manage your time more effectively (according to machines). *Prakhar Singh*. https://prakharr.medium.com/how-to-manage-your-time-more-effectively-according-to-machines-18a94aca6b5a.

Get Down to It

1 Kiewra, K. A., & Kauffman, D. (2023). John Glover: A long overdue account of his productive scholarship methods. *Educational Psychology Review*, *35*, Article 56.

2 Prinz, A., Zeeb, H., Flanigan, A., Renkl, A., & Kiewra, K. A. (2020). Conversations with five highly successful female educational psychologists: Patricia Alexander, Carol Dweck, Jacquelynne Eccles, Mareike Kunter, and Tamara van Gog. *Educational Psychology Review*, *33*, 763–795 (p. 774).

3 Ibid.

4 Ibid.

5 Kiewra, K. A., Luo, L., & Flanigan, A. (2021). Educational psychology early career award winners: How did they do it? *Educational Psychology Review*, *33*, 1981–2018 (p. 2000).

6 Kiewra, K. A., Hasnin, S., Soundy, J., Premkumar, P. K., & Labenz, C. (2023). Graduate student award winners in educational psychology: What made them successful? *Educational Psychology Review*, *35*, Article 90.

7 Kiewra, K. A., Luo, L., & Flanigan, A. (2021). Educational psychology early career award winners: How did they do it? *Educational Psychology Review*, *33*, 1981–2018 (p. 1992).

Say No

1 Csikszentmihalyi, M. (1996). *Creativity: Flow and the psychology of discovery and intention*. New York: HarperCollins (p. 14).

2 Prinz, A., Zeeb, H., Flanigan, A., Renkl, A., & Kiewra, K. A. (2020). Conversations with five highly successful female educational psychologists: Patricia Alexander, Carol Dweck, Jacquelynne Eccles, Mareike Kunter, and Tamara van Gog. *Educational Psychology Review*, *33*, 763–795 (p. 778).
3 Kiewra, K. A., Luo, L., & Flanigan, A. (2021). Educational psychology early career award winners: How did they do it? *Educational Psychology Review*, *33*, 1981–2018.
4 Ibid., p. 1993.

Use Time Pockets

1 Patterson-Hazley, M., & Kiewra, K. A. (2013). Conversations with four highly productive educational psychologists: Patricia Alexander, Richard Mayer, Dale Schunk, and Barry Zimmerman. *Educational Psychology Review*, *25*, 19–45 (p. 31).
2 Ibid., p. 37.
3 Flanigan, A., Kiewra, K. A., & Luo, L. (2018). Conversations with four highly productive German educational psychologists: Frank Fischer, Hans Gruber, Heinz Mandl, and Alexander Renkl. *Educational Psychology Review*, *30*, 303–330.
4 Kiewra, K. A., Hasnin, S., Soundy, J., Premkumar, P. K., & Labenz, C. (2023). Graduate student award winners in educational psychology: What made them successful? *Educational Psychology Review*, *35*, Article 90.
5 Kiewra, K. A., Luo, L., & Flanigan, A. (2021). Educational psychology early career award winners: How did they do it? *Educational Psychology Review*, *33*, 1981–2018 (p. 2004).

Deter Distractions

1 Csikszentmihalyi, M. (1996). *Creativity: Flow and the psychology of discovery and intention*. New York: HarperCollins (p. 351).
2 Luo, L. & Kiewra, K. A. (2022). Applying SOAR strategies to curb digital distractions while note taking and studying. In A. Flanigan and J. Kim (eds.), *Digital distractions in the college classroom* (pp. 161–188). Hershey, PA: IGI Global.
3 Rosen, L., & Samuel, A. (2015). Conquering digital distractions: Two experts on managing the overload. *Harvard Business School Press*, *93*, 110.
4 Napier, N. K. (May 12, 2014). The myth of multitasking. *Psychology Today*. www.psychologytoday.com/us/blog/creativity-without-borders/201405/the-myth-of-multitasking.

5 Singh, P. (August 26, 2020). How to manage your time more effectively (according to machines). *Prakhar Singh*. https://prakharr.medium.com/how-to-manage-your-time-more-effectively-according-to-machines-18a94aca6b5a.

6 Flanigan, A., Kiewra, K. A., & Luo, L. (2018). Conversations with four highly productive German educational psychologists: Frank Fischer, Hans Gruber, Heinz Mandl, and Alexander Renkl. *Educational Psychology Review, 30*, 303–330.

7 Prinz, A., Zeeb, H., Flanigan, A., Renkl, A., & Kiewra, K. A. (2020). Conversations with five highly successful female educational psychologists: Patricia Alexander, Carol Dweck, Jacquelynne Eccles, Mareike Kunter, and Tamara van Gog. *Educational Psychology Review, 33*, 763–795.

8 Kiewra, K. A., Luo, L., & Flanigan, A. (2021). Educational psychology early career award winners: How did they do it? *Educational Psychology Review, 33*, 1981–2018.

9 Kiewra, K. A., & Creswell, J. W. (2000). Conversations with three highly productive educational psychologists: Richard Anderson, Richard Mayer, and Michael Pressley. *Educational Psychology Review, 12*, 135–161.

10 Flanigan, A., Kiewra, K. A., & Luo, L. (2018). Conversations with four highly productive German educational psychologists: Frank Fischer, Hans Gruber, Heinz Mandl, and Alexander Renkl. *Educational Psychology Review, 30*, 303–330.

11 Bembenutty, H. (2022). *Contemporary pioneers in teaching and learning*, Vol. 2. Charlotte, NC: Information Age Publishing, Inc. (p. 23).

12 Ibid. (no page numbers designated).

13 Csikszentmihalyi, M. (1996). *Creativity: Flow and the psychology of discovery and intention*. New York: HarperCollins (p. 351).

Maintain a Work–Life Balance

1 Kumar, A. (November 25, 2022). The secret these chess champions use to win isn't skill – it's physical workouts. *Reader's Digest*. www.rd.com/article/train-like-a-master/.

2 How physical activity can help you play better chess? *WooChess*. https://woochess.com/en/lesson/how-physical-activity-can-help-you-play-chess-better.

3 Kiewra, K. A., & Kauffman, D. (2023). John Glover: A long overdue account of his productive scholarship methods. *Educational Psychology Review, 35*, Article 56.

4 Ibid.

5 Kiewra, K. A., & Creswell, J. W. (2000). Conversations with three highly productive educational psychologists: Richard Anderson, Richard Mayer, and Michael Pressley. *Educational Psychology Review*, *12*, 135–161 (p. 149).

6 Kiewra, K. A., Walsh, J., & Labenz, C. (2023). Moving beyond fulfillment: Wisdom years stories of passion, perseverance, and productivity. *Educational Psychology Review*, *35*, Article 20.

7 Patterson-Hazley, M., & Kiewra, K. A. (2013). Conversations with four highly productive educational psychologists: Patricia Alexander, Richard Mayer, Dale Schunk, and Barry Zimmerman. *Educational Psychology Review*, *25*, 19–45 (p. 31).

8 Kiewra, K. A., Luo, L., & Flanigan, A. (2021). Educational psychology early career award winners: How did they do it? *Educational Psychology Review*, *33*, 1981–2018.

9 Ibid., p. 1992.

10 Flanigan, A., Kiewra, K. A., & Luo, L. (2018). Conversations with four highly productive German educational psychologists: Frank Fischer, Hans Gruber, Heinz Mandl, and Alexander Renkl. *Educational Psychology Review*, *30*, 303–330 (p. 318).

11 Kiewra, K. A., & Creswell, J. W. (2000). Conversations with three highly productive educational psychologists: Richard Anderson, Richard Mayer, and Michael Pressley. *Educational Psychology Review*, *12*, 135–161 (p. 150).

12 Ibid.

13 Patterson-Hazley, M., & Kiewra, K. A. (2013). Conversations with four highly productive educational psychologists: Patricia Alexander, Richard Mayer, Dale Schunk, and Barry Zimmerman. *Educational Psychology Review*, *25*, 19–45 (p. 30).

14 Prinz, A., Zeeb, H., Flanigan, A., Renkl, A., & Kiewra, K. A. (2020). Conversations with five highly successful female educational psychologists: Patricia Alexander, Carol Dweck, Jacquelynne Eccles, Mareike Kunter, and Tamara van Gog. *Educational Psychology Review*, *33*, 763–795.

15 Ibid., p. 778.

16 Ibid.

17 Ferrant, G., Pesando, L. M., & Nowacka, K. (December 2014). Unpaid care work: The missing link in the analysis of gender gaps in labour outcomes. *OECD Development Centre*. www.oecd.org/dev/develop ment-gender/Unpaid_care_work.pdf.

18 Flanigan, A., Kiewra, K. A., & Luo, L. (2018). Conversations with four highly productive German educational psychologists: Frank Fischer, Hans Gruber, Heinz Mandl, and Alexander Renkl. *Educational Psychology Review*, *30*, 303–330.

19 Prinz, A., Zeeb, H., Flanigan, A., Renkl, A., & Kiewra, K. A. (2020). Conversations with five highly successful female educational psychologists: Patricia Alexander, Carol Dweck, Jacquelynne Eccles, Mareike Kunter, and Tamara van Gog. *Educational Psychology Review*, 33, 763–795.

20 Ibid., p. 781.

21 Patterson-Hazley, M., & Kiewra, K. A. (2013). Conversations with four highly productive educational psychologists: Patricia Alexander, Richard Mayer, Dale Schunk, and Barry Zimmerman. *Educational Psychology Review*, 25, 19–45 (p. 37).

22 Kiewra, K. A., Luo, L., & Flanigan, A. (2021). Educational psychology early career award winners: How did they do it? *Educational Psychology Review*, 33, 1981–2018 (p. 2000).

23 Kiewra, K. A., Hasnin, S., Soundy, J., Premkumar, P. K., & Labenz, C. (2023). Graduate student award winners in educational psychology: What made them successful? *Educational Psychology Review*, 35, Article 90.

24 Kiewra, K. A., Luo, L., & Flanigan, A. (2021). Educational psychology early career award winners: How did they do it? *Educational Psychology Review*, 33, 1981–2018 (p. 2002).

25 Prinz, A., Zeeb, H., Flanigan, A., Renkl, A., & Kiewra, K. A. (2020). Conversations with five highly successful female educational psychologists: Patricia Alexander, Carol Dweck, Jacquelynne Eccles, Mareike Kunter, and Tamara van Gog. *Educational Psychology Review*, 33, 763–795 (p. 778).

26 Patterson-Hazley, M., & Kiewra, K. A. (2013). Conversations with four highly productive educational psychologists: Patricia Alexander, Richard Mayer, Dale Schunk, and Barry Zimmerman. *Educational Psychology Review*, 25, 19–45 (p. 31).

27 Flanigan, A., Kiewra, K. A., & Luo, L. (2018). Conversations with four highly productive German educational psychologists: Frank Fischer, Hans Gruber, Heinz Mandl, and Alexander Renkl. *Educational Psychology Review*, 30, 303–330.

28 Ibid., p. 318.

29 Patterson-Hazley, M., & Kiewra, K. A. (2013). Conversations with four highly productive educational psychologists: Patricia Alexander, Richard Mayer, Dale Schunk, and Barry Zimmerman. *Educational Psychology Review*, 25, 19–45 (p. 31).

Create Stability or Live on the Edge

1 Kiewra, K. A., & Creswell, J. W. (2000). Conversations with three highly productive educational psychologists: Richard Anderson, Richard Mayer, and Michael Pressley. *Educational Psychology Review*, 12, 135–161.

2 Ibid., p. 149.
3 Ibid. (no page numbers designated).
4 Patterson-Hazley, M., & Kiewra, K. A. (2013). Conversations with four highly productive educational psychologists: Patricia Alexander, Richard Mayer, Dale Schunk, and Barry Zimmerman. *Educational Psychology Review, 25,* 19–45 (p. 31).
5 Ibid.
6 Ibid., p. 30.

Guilt Can Motivate

1 Tahir, S. *Goodreads.* www.goodreads.com/quotes/6644111-there-are-two-kinds-of-guilt-the-kind-that-drowns.
2 Kiewra, K. A., Luo, L., & Flanigan, A. (2021). Educational psychology early career award winners: How did they do it? *Educational Psychology Review, 33,* 1981–2018 (p. 2006).
3 Bembenutty, H. (2022). *Contemporary pioneers in teaching and learning,* Vol. 2. Charlotte, NC: Information Age Publishing, Inc. (p. 23).
4 Mayrath, M. (2008). Attributions of productive authors in educational psychology journals. *Educational Psychology Review, 20,* 41–56.
5 Bembenutty, H. (2022). *Contemporary pioneers in teaching and learning,* Vol. 2. Charlotte, NC: Information Age Publishing, Inc. (p. 140).

10 | *Seek and Lend Support*

Help others achieve their dreams and you will achieve yours.

Les Brown[1]

Seek Institutional Support

If you're a scholar, where you work matters. The greater the resources and support, the greater the likelihood you'll be productive and successful.

The University of Georgia is highly supportive of Logan Fiorella's research, providing him with a manageable course load, reducing service obligations, and nominating him for awards.[1] Fiorella's advisor, Rich Mayer, credited his university for his own success: "I had good luck landing at University of California, Santa Barbara. It's been a great environment and has certainly had an incredibly positive influence on my life."[2] At the University of Pittsburg, Ming-Te Wang's dean established a motivation center and appointed Wang director. That center positions Wang to seek grants, partner with schools, and fund staff and student positions. It also provides Wang with a lab manager to handle administrative tasks.[3] Sabina Neugebauer commented that resource-rich institutions set one up for success. They provide a brand name that attracts prominent scholars and talented students with whom to collaborate. They also provide the infrastructure and financial resources to get things done.[4]

The best time to get support is when offered a job. That's when you hold the cards. The institution has already spent considerable time and resources securing a position, assembling a search committee, combing through applications and reference letters, conducting remote and campus interviews, and determining a winner ... you! They want you. They don't want to backtrack through the hiring process or, heaven forbid, begin anew. So, once the offer is in hand, lay your cards on the table. Tell them politely all the things you'd like in order to be content and successful, things like a higher annual salary, a summer stipend prior to your fall appointment, moving expenses, yearly travel money, start-up money for your lab, lab space and equipment, research assistants, course reductions, four calling birds, and three French hens. They'll tell you that some things, mostly monetary things, either cannot be negotiated or would put you in an awkward position relative to your new colleagues who don't have these perks. Don't buy it. Everyone negotiates and lands the best deal they can. All they can say is no to some requests; they can't withdraw the offer.

Be careful, though, not to tip your hand or play your cards too early. It's okay to casually ask about resources when interviewed, but that is not the time to press or negotiate. Wait until the offer is in hand before playing your cards.

Arrange Personal Support

Graduate students and productive scholars rely on the support of family or others to free up time to work. Graduate student scholar Carly Robinson leaned on her family for child-rearing support. Robinson said: "My family came and cared for the baby and were very happy to help."[1] Robinson also enlisted the part-time help of a nanny. Graduate student scholar Hyewon Lee eliminated some personal responsibilities by leaning on her church. Lee said: "I got a lot of support from my church." They helped her with childcare, cooking, and household chores. Lee also used food catering services to "save my time as much as I could."[2]

German scholars Frank Fischer and Alexander Renkl have spouses who handle the bulk of family chores. Fischer's spouse handles about 95 percent of the childcare and household chores, and Renkl's spouse handles about 90 percent.[3] Ming-Te Wang's spouse quit her position as a nurse to be a full-time care provider for their children, which allows Wang more time to focus on his work.[4]

As mentioned previously, women in academia have traditionally and unfairly taken on the bulk of homeland chores. Some of the productive female scholars I studied found ways to enlist support and turn that tide. Erika Patall credits her husband, a museum director in Los Angeles where the family resides, for supporting her heavy work schedule. She said: "He lets me work. He does more of the regular daily tasks such as getting breakfast going in the morning, getting the kids ready for school, and handling the children's drop-offs while I'll try to prepare for my day."[5] Patall's mother, who lives across the country, also helps the family with household responsibilities from time to time. Patall said: "She'll come to town and help with the kids if I need help or if I need to travel."[6]

Female scholars Rebecca Collie and Sabina Neugebauer[7] along with Carol Dweck, Mareike Kunter, and Tamara van Gog[8] all share household duties fairly equally with their spouses. Collie said: "I couldn't do what I do without his support. I couldn't be as productive. I just couldn't. He does half the drop-offs for the kids and cooks half the meals."[9] Neugebauer credits her husband with being a supportive partner and father and the household chef. Some of the female scholars also reported that they and their partners rely on support from outside the family, such as the support provided by childcare centers, caregivers, cleaning services, and food preparation services.

Both Logan Fiorella and Doug Lombardi[10] are married to spouses also in the academy. Fiorella and his spouse both work full time and share life chores like cleaning and childcare equally, allowing each other the time to be productive. Lombardi's spouse, Janelle Bailey, is also a professor in science education and offers support as a collaborator and emotional confidant. The couple takes a three-mile walk every morning and often discuss research. Moreover, their home office desks are in the same room and adjacent, allowing Lombardi to easily discuss ideas with Bailey throughout the day. Lombardi said: "I talk to her about research questions and bat ideas around with her when we do our morning walks around the neighborhood. At home, I just lean over and ask her a question, and we'll go off [talking about our ideas]." As a confidant, Lombardi said: "Janelle often pulls me back from the edge of the abyss .... Every kind of weird thing that I wanted to do or bridge that I wanted to burn, she said, 'Don't do it! Don't do that! Just keep going, keep plugging away.'"[11]

Speaking of emotional support, Wang was part of two groups that lent emotional support. One was a person-of-color group and the other a Christian Fellowship group. The person-of-color group was composed of five men representing diverse backgrounds such as African American, Asian, and Latinx. They met weekly for lunch to discuss their work and how they could support one another socially and professionally. Similarly, the Christian Fellowship group allowed Wang to share strengths and concerns with others and helped him cope with stress and anxiety.[12]

Lend Support: Pay It Forward

You have probably heard the fable about the ant and the dove. It goes something like this. An ant falls into a brook and is drowning. A dove sees this and drops a leaf near to the ant. The ant climbs aboard and floats to safety. Soon after, a hunter is about to shoot the dove. The ant sees this and stings the hunter, causing him to miss, and the dove flies to safety. The moral? One good turn deserves another.

There have been and will be times in your career when you need a leaf. Should a leaf fall, embrace it, and ride it to the shore. Once upon the shore look for opportunities to return the favor or to pay it forward to someone else in need.

As mentioned earlier, Ivar Braten observed a doctoral student who had just defended her dissertation warmly thanking her advisor Claire Weinstein for all her academic and personal support. Weinstein replied: "You remember this when you become a professor."

Michael Pressley believed in paying it forward. Pressley said: "You want to orient yourself to the students and to the people younger than you are because that really is your future … What you're really supposed to be doing at the university is nurturing talent."[1,2]

One way that John Glover lent support was by promoting and crediting his collaborators. Former Glover collaborator Barbara Plake said: "It was always a rich research environment where John made his colleagues feel like they were smart, did good work, and were valued. Afterward John promoted the people he worked with and shared the credit, always saying 'this was the team's work' never 'my work.' I felt honored that he wanted to work with me."[3]

There are many ways – big and small – to lend support. Here are just a few:

- Invite junior colleagues and students to join your research project.
- Volunteer to review a colleague's manuscript before submission.
- Write unsolicited notes of praise about someone to their supervisor.
- Go out of your way to talk to graduate students and junior faculty at a conference.
- Volunteer to help a graduate student prepare for a job interview.
- Reveal aspects of the hidden curriculum to junior faculty and students.

I recall two support-lending incidents that perhaps altered careers. One occurred when I was on my department's graduate committee. We were asked to rubber stamp a doctoral student dismissal. Her supervisory committee believed she was not making satisfactory progress toward completion. Our vote was 4–1 in favor of dismissal. I cast the dissenting vote. Prior to our meeting, I had closely reviewed the student's partially completed dissertation and found it more than satisfactory. Despite our committee's confirming vote for dismissal, I wrote an unsolicited letter to the university graduate committee voicing my dissent and asking them to reconsider the dismissal. They did. And more. The graduate school dean asked if I would advise the student. I agreed, though I had never met the student, and her work was well outside my area. I worked with the student and her reconstituted committee, and six months later she successfully defended her dissertation.

Another support-lending incident occurred in much the same way. I was a member of my college's promotion and tenure committee. A faculty member I did not know was voted down for promotion and tenure 6–1, with my vote being the dissenting vote. I believed that the faculty member's file had been mishandled and misconstrued at both the department and college level and that the candidate had met all standards. Again, I wrote an unsolicited letter of support to the college dean and to administrators who would review the file up the line. That faculty member was tenured and promoted.

Anyone can make a difference if they try.

References

Seek and Lend Support

1 Brown, L. *35 Helping Others Quotes on Success*. www .awakenthegreatnesswithin.com/35-helping-others-quotes-on-success-2/.

Seek Institutional Support

1 Kiewra, K. A., Luo, L., & Flanigan, A. (2021). Educational psychology early career award winners: How did they do it? *Educational Psychology Review*, *33*, 1981–2018.

2 Patterson-Hazley, M., & Kiewra, K. A. (2013). Conversations with four highly productive educational psychologists: Patricia Alexander, Richard Mayer, Dale Schunk, and Barry Zimmerman. *Educational Psychology Review*, *25*, 19–45 (p. 29).

3 Kiewra, K. A., Luo, L., & Flanigan, A. (2021). Educational psychology early career award winners: How did they do it? *Educational Psychology Review*, *33*, 1981–2018.

4 Ibid.

Arrange Personal Support

1 Kiewra, K. A., Hasnin, S., Soundy, J., Premkumar, P. K., & Labenz, C. (2023). Graduate student award winners in educational psychology: What made them successful? *Educational Psychology Review, 35*, Article 90.

2 Ibid.

3 Flanigan, A., Kiewra, K. A., & Luo, L. (2018). Conversations with four highly productive German educational psychologists: Frank Fischer, Hans Gruber, Heinz Mandl, and Alexander Renkl. *Educational Psychology Review, 30*, 303–330.

4 Kiewra, K. A., Luo, L., & Flanigan, A. (2021). Educational psychology early career award winners: How did they do it? *Educational Psychology Review, 33*, 1981–2018.

5 Ibid., p. 2007.

6 Ibid.

7 Ibid.

8 Prinz, A., Zeeb, H., Flanigan, A., Renkl, A., & Kiewra, K. A. (2020). Conversations with five highly successful female educational psychologists: Patricia Alexander, Carol Dweck, Jacquelynne Eccles, Mareike Kunter, and Tamara van Gog. *Educational Psychology Review, 33*, 763–795.

9 Kiewra, K. A., Luo, L., & Flanigan, A. (2021). Educational psychology early career award winners: How did they do it? *Educational Psychology Review, 33*, 1981–2018 (p. 2007).

10 Ibid. (no page numbers designated).

11 Ibid., p. 2002.

12 Ibid. (no page numbers designated).

Lend Support: Pay It Forward

1 Bembenutty, H. (2022). *Contemporary pioneers in teaching and learning*, Vol. 2. Charlotte, NC: Information Age Publishing, Inc. (p. 251).

2 Kiewra, K. A., & Creswell, J. W. (2000). Conversations with three highly productive educational psychologists: Richard Anderson, Richard Mayer, and Michael Pressley. *Educational Psychology Review, 12*, 135–161 (p. 153).

3 Kiewra, K. A., & Kauffman, D. (2023). John Glover: A long overdue account of his productive scholarship methods. *Educational Psychology Review, 35*, Article 56.

11 | *Climb Down from the Tower*

academia: (n.) terminal condition in which the head gradually swells while the heart slowly atrophies.

Sol Luckman[1]

Intellect is a savage thing, not some cozy, peaceful pet to be shut away in institutions for the mild-mannered.

Mike Hockney[2]

Serve the Field

The academics I studied are more than productive scholars, they are multiskilled and multicommitted to serving their communities, universities, and professions. Rich Mayer is a prime example: An editor for two journals, editorial board member for eleven others, and holding an office in twenty-nine professional organizations and twenty-two campus organizations. Mayer has also served his local school board for four decades. Off the record, I can affirm that he completes manuscript reviews for journals in a matter of days, not weeks or months as some do, and he responds to emails the same day they are received. Ask him for a letter of support and it's delivered the next day. As the famous saying goes: "If you want something done, ask Rich Mayer to do it."

Michael Pressley was more than a productive scholar. He was also committed to teaching and educational service. But, for Pressley, these were not three targets, but one. Pressley called himself an "interpenetrater." His research activities penetrated his teaching and service activities. Pressley said: "I doubt there has been in the last ten years a single graduate course that I taught where there hasn't been some important written product that I did or a student did with me . . . There's been some important piece of writing or some important piece of research in every course."[1] For instance, when Pressley taught a course on motivation for the first time, he used that instructional opportunity to scour the motivation literature, publish a literature review on motivation to help inform and direct the field, publish a motivation chapter to serve practitioners, and gave talks on motivation to serve the educational community. For Pressley, teaching, research, and service moved in one direction. There were no wasted steps.

Doug Lombardi also maximizes his contributions by efficiently integrating research, teaching, and service activities. For example, he said: "As a result of my research on information weaponization, I developed a freshman seminar course on that topic. As I'm doing research on information weaponization, I'm teaching about it."[2] And, because Lombardi's research depends largely on teacher involvement, he served on the boards of the Pennsylvania State Science Teachers Association and the National Earth Science Teachers Association, which allowed him to network with and involve teachers in his work.

Rebecca Collie does much the same by conducting research-oriented service. Collie spends 10–15 hours a week on service that complements her research, such as serving as an associate editor and on several editorial boards. Collie also serves students and educators with her invited talks in schools and applied articles for a general readership. For example, Collie creates 800-word summaries of her journal articles and publishes them in a free online magazine for practitioners.[3]

Like Collie, Karen Harris makes it a priority to make her research findings accessible to practitioners. Roughly seventy of her publications are written for teachers. Harris also provides free workshops and instructional materials to schools.[4]

For me, my goal has always been to both advance new knowledge through my scholarship and to disseminate that knowledge to the practitioners who can use it – take educational psychology to the people. I have done this in a number of ways, such as: directing my university's Academic Success Center; developing a university-wide study skills class; making more than five hundred invited presentations to students, educators, scholars, and parents; writing a weekly newspaper column; and teaching chess in schools and in the community, including a club for children with autism and their parents.

Be an Editor, Certainly a Reviewer

Although I was critical of the manuscript review process earlier in the section "Understand That the Review Process Is Flawed" in Chapter 8, one of the best ways to serve your field is by being a journal reviewer or perhaps even an editor. Thoughtful and helpful scholars are needed to carry out these vital professional roles.

Patricia Alexander has served as an editor for one journal or another the past twenty-seven years. Here is her perspective:

[There is a] great deal of labor involved in editing a journal, but it is a role I honestly enjoy and take very, very seriously. An editor is a gatekeeper of sorts for the field. You labor to ensure that the best work, the best ideas find their way into print; that researchers' dedication translates into better educational and psychological outcomes for society. However, an editor must be a nurturer, encouraging the thinking and writing of newer community members; providing a platform for creative or innovative ideas that might not otherwise find their way into the community psyche; and offering opportunities to voices or views that might go unnoticed.[1]

Karen Harris served as editor for *Journal of Educational Psychology*. As editor, she saw her role as being "more than a vote counter but rather decision maker." She warns that being an editor is time-consuming, "much more work than you initially expect," and requires "giving up aspects of your own work."[2] For Harris, this meant taking secondary positions in research collaborations, less grant writing, and saying no to invitations and requests more often.

I served as editor of *Educational Psychology Review* for five years. I agree with Harris that being an editor is time-consuming and hard work. It was especially difficult during my tenure because the submission and review process had not yet gone electronic. This meant that manuscripts took the slow boat from author to editor to reviewers to editor to author. This meant that I painstakingly edited and marked manuscripts by hand. Still, it was a once-in-a-lifetime opportunity and one of the best professional opportunities in my career.

As for reviewing, here are Alexander's thoughts:

Every submitter deserves the most thoughtful, instructive feedback I can offer – whether I find the piece worthy of publication or not. When I sign on as an editorial board member, I do so with the promise that my reviews will offer the best of my thinking and provide the researcher with whatever guidance I can provide – and I promise to be timely.[3]

Teaching and learning scholar Brian Coppola offers a similar developmental approach to reviewing. He said:

I see editorial work divided between two goals. The first goal is to identify and develop manuscripts of promise and significant contribution, which can serve as exemplars of excellent work. The second goal is to provide as much educative guidance to manuscripts that have future potential. Triaging work that is either unacceptable or inappropriate to the venue is also part of the job, but less intellectually engaging.[4]

Taking on editorial positions not only serves the field, doing so helps you grow as a scholar. Rebecca Collie, who serves as an associate editor, said: "It's truly a privilege to be an associate editor and to serve on several editorial boards. I learn a lot. It helps introduce me to new theories, findings, and statistical approaches. Examples of outstanding writing also improve my writing."[5]

Ivar Braten, who has served as a reviewer for more than forty international peer-reviewed journals and presently sits on the review board for eight major journals, agrees that reviewing, although time-consuming, prompts learning. He said:

Quite a few weekends are spent reading and evaluating other people's work. Mostly, but not always, I read studies that interest me and from which I can learn something, so this also helps me keep abreast of what's happening in my field. Moreover, I learn from reading other reviewers' evaluation of a manuscript, and not least from how authors handle revision. Sometimes I also learn what not to do, both as an author and as a reviewer.[6]

As a reviewer, I have reviewed about ten to twenty-five manuscripts a year throughout my career, with each requiring about half a day to read and record notes and then write the review letter, which is ordinarily two to four pages. I always try to remain positive but also try to offer detailed feedback that can help authors improve their research and writing now and with future submissions.

It's Okay to Administrate

Surprisingly, about a quarter of the productive scholars I investigated also served administrative roles at some point during their careers.

Why is this? Perhaps this is the Peter Principle at work, wherein people are promoted up the academic ladder until they finally reach a level for which they are incompetent. Let's be real. Most graduate training prepares scholars to conduct research, maybe teach a lick, but not administrate. Yet, a fair number of academics exchange their *APA Manual* for a cozy office and a summer stipend. Really, but why? Some might do it because it's simply their rotational turn to lead their department for a few years. This is sometimes the case in the German system. Some might be ready to leave the classroom and be free from academia's publish-or-perish demands. Some might seek career mobility. They have designs on becoming a dean, provost, or chancellor, power positions with attractive salaries and press box seating. And, some might do it to finally get back at colleagues who've made their academic lives miserable.

Some, of course, do it because they really want to make a difference. They want to make their departments or colleges a better and more productive place. They seek to build a strong faculty and better serve the educational community. Jacquelynne Eccles, who has published nearly four hundred books, journal articles, and book chapters, is presently associate dean at California, Irvine, because she wanted to "facilitate each of my colleagues' ability to do what they are best at and most interested in doing."[1] John Hattie, who published or presented more than 1,200 scientific papers, served as head of school or dean of research at four universities over twenty-five years because he wanted to make a difference. Hattie said: "You can make a difference by standing for quality research, quality resources and opportunities, opening up spaces for outstanding early-career academics, creating Ph.D. candidates as colleagues, not students, and bringing together colleagues who may not initially see connections."[2]

Whatever the transformative reason, the question raised here is: Can academics-turned-administrators remain productive like Eccles and Hattie and, if so, how?

Consider these fantastic numbers from Michael Pressley's annual evaluation one year: eighteen journal articles, three authored books, two edited books, two editorships, eleven editorial boards, and two major awards. Oh, did I mention he was also department chair? How did Pressley do it? A lot of hard work and not much sleep. As mentioned previously,[3] Pressley napped a bit when the family went to bed. He'd soon awaken and write for several hours before turning in. He'd rise early and write for a few more hours before returning to the schools. Not a healthy lifestyle but a productive one for Pressley during this administrative era. My former dean did much the same, rising at 4:30 each morning in order to write for a few hours before doing dean duties.

The German university system requires professors to cycle through administrative responsibilities, usually for two-year stints. Hans Gruber, Alexander Renkl, and Frank Fischer[4] all took their turns as department chairs and even college deans. The trio agreed that scholarly productivity naturally falls somewhat when administrative duties arise. Still, there are ways to keep the scholarship train chugging. Renkl said: "I think productivity will go down, but won't stop completely because of how much I collaborate with others. But, I won't be able to provide as much feedback and will need to be more cautious about beginning new collaborations."[5] Fischer said that he remains productive by assuming more of a director role with his research team. He meets regularly with the team, assigns tasks, reads their work, and provides several rounds of feedback until manuscripts are out the door. Being a collaborator and director can keep administrators productive.

Dale Schunk is a scholar turned long-time administrator. Schunk was department chair for eight years and college dean for another nine. Schunk spent more than half his time performing administrative duties but was still productive, publishing about a hundred works during this administrative span. As mentioned earlier, Schunk did so, in part, by practicing what his research program preached – effective goal setting and time management practices. Schunk said: "Being an administrator forced me to engage in goal setting and time management daily. My free time to work on research and writing was very limited so I planned time carefully and used breaks in my schedule for scholarship."[5] To maximize time, Schunk also shifted his empirical work from investigating K-12 students to investigating college students who were more accessible, and he emphasized conceptual writing over empirical work because the former is less time-consuming. Overall, Schunk viewed positively his dual role as administrator and scholar. He said that serving this dual role assured that he was putting his time to good use every day as he performed valuable public service and advanced new knowledge.

But, Prioritize Research

In baseball, major league scouts grade prospective players on their five tools: hitting, hitting for power, running, fielding, and throwing. The more tools the better. A five-tool player, a jack of all trades, is a rare and much sought-after commodity. While a five-tool player is desirous, a player with one outstanding tool, especially power hitting, is also valued. Nothing turns a game more quickly than a three-run blast.

What kind of academic player do you want to be? Perhaps one with multiple tools – research, teaching, and service – and even managerial skills for a new challenge or for when playing skills erode. Or perhaps one who swings for the fences, knocking out research article after article. It's no secret that universities value, reward, and taut their homerun-hitting scholars.

Which player are you? Your decision rests partly on your institution's expectations and partly on your values. Erika Patall's values prompt her to swing away. As reported earlier, Patall said: "You can't be a jack of all trades. To be a successful researcher, you must prioritize research over all else. You have to accept that you'll be less good at other things. I don't ever want to be bad at anything, especially teaching, but once I meet a threshold of good enough, I accept that."[1]

Whichever way you go, recall what Patricia Alexander said about research productivity:

Don't aim to be a prolific scholar; aim to be the best you can be. Trying to be prolific might be detrimental because it can lead you down a path of producing without meaning, where the numbers take precedence over the influence. Aspire to true scholarship whether that leads to 500 publications or 50 publications. Be sure that each publication represents your best thinking, is influential, and impacts others.[2]

References

Climb Down from the Tower

1 Luckman, S. *Goodreads*. www.goodreads.com/quotes/tag/ivory-tower.
2 Hockney, M. *Goodreads*. www.goodreads.com/quotes/tag/ivory-tower.

Serve the Field

1 Kiewra, K. A., & Creswell, J. W. (2000). Conversations with three highly productive educational psychologists: Richard Anderson, Richard Mayer,

and Michael Pressley. *Educational Psychology Review, 12,* 135–161 (p. 145).

2 Kiewra, K. A., Luo, L., & Flanigan, A. (2021). Educational psychology early career award winners: How did they do it? *Educational Psychology Review, 33,* 1981–2018 (p. 2004).

3 Ibid. (no page numbers designated).

4 Bembenutty, H. (2022). *Contemporary pioneers in teaching and learning,* Vol. 2. Charlotte, NC: Information Age Publishing, Inc.

Be an Editor, Certainly a Reviewer

1 Bembenutty, H. (2022). *Contemporary pioneers in teaching and learning,* Vol. 2. Charlotte, NC: Information Age Publishing, Inc. (p. 99).

2 Ibid., p. 137.

3 Ibid., p. 99.

4 Ibid., p. 224.

5 Kiewra, K. A., Luo, L., & Flanigan, A. (2021). Educational psychology early career award winners: How did they do it? *Educational Psychology Review, 33,* 1981–2018 (p. 1999).

6 Bembenutty, H. (2022). *Contemporary pioneers in teaching and learning,* Vol. 2. Charlotte, NC: Information Age Publishing, Inc. (p. 250).

It's Okay to Administrate

1 Bembenutty, H. (2022). *Contemporary pioneers in teaching and learning,* Vol. 2. Charlotte, NC: Information Age Publishing, Inc. (p. 72).

2 Ibid., p. 173.

3 Kiewra, K. A., & Creswell, J. W. (2000). Conversations with three highly productive educational psychologists: Richard Anderson, Richard Mayer, and Michael Pressley. *Educational Psychology Review, 12,* 135–161.

4 Flanigan, A., Kiewra, K. A., & Luo, L. (2018). Conversations with four highly productive German educational psychologists: Frank Fischer, Hans Gruber, Heinz Mandl, and Alexander Renkl. *Educational Psychology Review, 30,* 303–330 (p. 319).

5 Patterson-Hazley, M., & Kiewra, K. A. (2013). Conversations with four highly productive educational psychologists: Patricia Alexander, Richard Mayer, Dale Schunk, and Barry Zimmerman. *Educational Psychology Review, 25,* 19–45 (p. 37).

But, Prioritize Research

1 Kiewra, K. A., Luo, L., & Flanigan, A. (2021). Educational psychology early career award winners: How did they do it? *Educational Psychology Review, 33,* 1981–2018 (p. 2007).

2 Patterson-Hazley, M., & Kiewra, K. A. (2013). Conversations with four highly productive educational psychologists: Patricia Alexander, Richard Mayer, Dale Schunk, and Barry Zimmerman. *Educational Psychology Review, 25,* 19–45 (p. 39).

Conclusion

Let the views of others educate and inform you, but let your decisions be a product of your own conclusions.

Jim Rohn[1]

What conclusions have you drawn about being a more productive scholar?

Anyone Can Do This

Helen Keller said: "Believe. No pessimist ever discovered the secrets of the stars or sailed to an unchartered land or opened a new heaven to the human spirit."[1] Philosopher Ernest Holmes said: "Believe as though you are, and you will be."[2] An Arabic proverb advises: "Throw your heart out in front of you and run ahead and catch it."[3]

Speaking of running, recall that no one thought a runner would crack the four-minute barrier for the mile until Roger Bannister did it in 1954. After that, thirty-seven more runners beat the four-minute mark in the next year. Decades later, American miler Steve Scott broke the barrier 136 times. What might seem impossible usually is not.

Returning to productive scholars, what were the odds that children raised in poverty, in tenements or on cotton or poultry farms, by parents who were drug store clerks, cigar makers, or cobblers, and who faced racial segregation would have gone on to be highly productive scholars? But they did.[4]

What were the chances that Rebecca Collie,[5] who dropped out of college, or David Berliner,[6] who flunked out of college, would be among the most productive scholars of their generations? Slim at best, but they did. And what about Logan Fiorella[7] who was rejected for graduate school and who had a single job offer surface from about twenty applications. Now he is among his generation's most productive scholars.

235

You get the idea. There is really no barrier too high that you can't get over, around, or through. You can do what these productive scholars have done or whatever else it is you'd like to do. First, believe. Next, follow the advice found here or that from others who have succeeded. Then, make it happen.

You can do this but it takes sustained effort. Michael Pressley was famous for saying: "There are no quick fixes." Patricia Alexander also reminded us that good work requires hard effort over the long haul. Alexander said: "A burst of energy is not enough; it must be sustained."[8] Of course, it was my own advisor, Hal Fletcher, who routinely dispensed this sage parting advice: "Stay with it now!"

Take Heed of the Universe Conspiring

In the novel *The Alchemist* by Paulo Coelho, the protagonist Santiago is led to his treasure by a series of seemingly serendipitous events or signs because: "When you want something, all the universe conspires in helping you achieve it."[1] I have seen what might amount to universe conspiring impact others and me.

I interviewed the Wander Women, Kristy Burns and Annette Demel, for a project on how people remain productive in their wisdom years.[2] The Wander Women are famous for quitting their jobs, selling their homes, abandoning their possessions, and setting out to hike America. Among their travels are the Appalachian Trail (2,190 miles) stretching from Georgia to Maine, the Continental Divide Trail (3,028 miles) up and down America's central spine, and the Pacific Crest Trail (2,653 miles) linking Mexico and Canada along the Pacific Coast. The impetus for this transformation seemed universe conspiring. One afternoon, about eight years ago, the pair met with a financial advisor to plot their future. The advisor overwhelmed them with financial pie charts and employment timelines stretching into their seventies. They left the meeting wondering if the work-until-seventy path was right for them. That same afternoon, they met friends at a bookstore coffeeshop, where they stumbled upon a book called *Die Broke*[3] (Pollan & Levine, 1998), whose first line was: "Quit your job." They said:

We bought the book and read it that night. It talked about the value of time versus money. About the time you have left and how you want to spend it. About how you can compromise other parts of your life to have more time.

We thought, "That's what we're supposed to do, not work into our seventies. We should just sell everything we own and go adventuring." And from that point on, we never looked at the world the same. We saw our present lives as typical, predictable: Get educated, get a job, get a house, paint the porch, do the yardwork, buy stuff, and keep buying stuff. Suddenly, we didn't want our stuff and couldn't wait to get rid of it. Instead of stuff, we coveted rich experiences in nature. We made a five-year plan to sell all we owned, settle our debt, get a camper, and properly plan our lives. No pie charts, just trail maps.[4]

In the scholarly realm, Berkeley School of Education Professor Zeus Leonardo, who received the American Educational Research Association Scholars of Color Distinguished Career Contribution Award, might have never made it into a Ph.D. program if not for a universe-conspiring twist of fate. When he applied to graduate school, his intention was to earn a terminal master's degree. He, however, accidently checked the application box for the Ph.D. degree. Imagine his surprise when he learned that he was accepted into the doctoral program. Lombardo interpreted this as a stroke of fate and decided to pursue his Ph.D.

A similarly serendipitous event involving graduate school application happened to David Berliner. He applied to the doctoral program in experimental psychology at Stanford and was rejected. But someone at Stanford noted that Berliner had done some educational research and sent his application to the educational psychology program in the School of Education. The head of educational psychology reviewed it and knew one of the references. They were old friends. The two spoke on the phone, and Berliner was soon accepted into the Stanford educational psychology program without having applied.[5]

Scholar John Hattie was at least twice the product of fortuitous universe conspiracy. After Hattie's first year of college, while home for holidays, a letter came congratulating him on being awarded a new scholarship to attend university full time and to secure a full-time teaching position upon graduation. He called the school, confused, and told them he never applied for such a scholarship. But he had, when he thought he was signing the attendance roll in one of his classes. While employed as a teacher postgraduation, Hattie was walking to catch a weekend train when the head of education at the university drove by and offered him a ride. Their conversation led to the head of education inviting Hattie to come to his office on Monday where he offered Hattie a full-time job overseeing undergraduate seminars and earning a master's degree, which Hattie accepted.[6]

My University of Nebraska colleague, Dipti Dev, sought and followed a life-altering sign. She had just completed her doctoral degree at the University of Illinois and pondered two directions. One was a return to her native India to pursue a postdoc with her advisor, who was strongly pushing her in this direction. The second was to take an assistant professor position at the University of Nebraska–Lincoln where she had just interviewed. While walking across the Illinois campus, she hoped she would see a sign directing her. Suddenly, there was a bus stop sign reading: "From here to Lincoln." Though the sign was for Lincoln, Illinois, there was no mistaking its universe-conspiring message.

My own path to educational psychology professor had a serendipitous, universe-conspiring beginning. Following high school, I was interested in attending a private New York college but was rejected, leaving me with a short list of safety-net state colleges that I had never seen and had no interest in attending. My parents suggested that we take a weekend trip to visit Oneonta College in upstate New York, but I declined and they visited alone. They reported that the college was beautifully situated in rolling hills, had good food, and lighted tennis courts. "Okay, good enough," I groaned, "I'll go there." But it was there, and only there, that I could have discovered my educational psychology calling, thanks to Professor Nelson DuBois. The material he espoused was delicious, infectious, and he was the greatest instructor I had ever seen. I wanted to do what he was doing. No telling how my life might have turned had I not stumbled onto the Oneonta campus and into Professor DuBois' class.

Keep your radar tuned for universe-conspiring opportunities that arise. And, of course, make the best of them when they do arise. Here's hoping this book helps you find and benefit from untold opportunities for success and happiness.

References

Conclusion

1 Rohn, J. *AZ Quotes*. www.azquotes.com/quotes/topics/conclusion.html.

Anyone Can Do This

1 Keller, H. *Goodreads*. www.goodreads.com/quotes/1089482-believe-no-pessimist-ever-discovered-the-secrets-of-the-stars.
2 Holmes, E. *quotefancy*. https://quotefancy.com/quote/1241977/Ernest-Holmes-Believe-as-though-you-are-and-you-will-be.
3 Arab   proverb.   *egorunamok*.   https://egorunamok.tumblr.com/post/
    35911485044/throw-your-heart-out-in-front-of-you-and-run-ahead.
4 Bembenutty, H. (2022). *Contemporary pioneers in teaching and learning*,
    Vol. 2. Charlotte, NC: Information Age Publishing, Inc.
5 Kiewra, K. A., Luo, L., & Flanigan, A. (2021). Educational psychology
    early career award winners: How did they do it? *Educational Psychology
    Review, 33*, 1981–2018.
6 Bembenutty, H. (2022). *Contemporary pioneers in teaching and learning*,
    Vol. 2. Charlotte, NC: Information Age Publishing, Inc.
7 Kiewra, K. A., Luo, L., & Flanigan, A. (2021). Educational psychology
    early career award winners: How did they do it? *Educational Psychology
    Review, 33*, 1981–2018.
8 Patterson-Hazley, M., & Kiewra, K. A. (2013). Conversations with four
    highly productive educational psychologists: Patricia Alexander, Richard
    Mayer, Dale Schunk, and Barry Zimmerman. *Educational Psychology
    Review, 25*, 19–45 (p. 36).

Take Heed of the Universe Conspiring

1 Coelho, P. (1993). *The alchemist*. New York: HarperCollins (p. 40).
2 Kiewra, K. A., Walsh, J., & Labenz, C. (2023). Moving beyond fulfill-
    ment: Wisdom years stories of passion, perseverance, and productivity.
    Educational Psychology Review, 35, Article 20.
3 Levine, M., & Pollan, S. M. (1998). *Die broke: A radical four-part
    financial plan*. New York: HarperCollins.
4 Kiewra, K. A., Walsh, J., & Labenz, C. (2023). Moving beyond fulfill-
    ment: Wisdom years stories of passion, perseverance, and productivity.
    Educational Psychology Review, 35, Article 20, p. 27.
5 Bembenutty, H. (2022). *Contemporary pioneers in teaching and learning*,
    Vol. 2. Charlotte, NC: Information Age Publishing, Inc.
6 Ibid.

Appendix
Meet the Productive Scholars

Here is a thumbnail sketch of the referenced scholars' credentials.

- Patricia Alexander: Best known for the model of domain learning. Author of more than three hundred publications. Received the Thorndike Career Achievement Award in Educational Psychology (APA) and the Sylvia Scribner Career Award (AERA). Ranked second most productive educational psychologist.[1]
- Richard Anderson: A foremost scholar on reading. Published more than 250 articles and books. Received the Thorndike Career Achievement Award in Educational Psychology (APA).
- James Banks: Known as the Father of Multicultural Education. Banks has authored or edited more than twenty books, over sixty chapters, and about a hundred articles on multicultural education. He received AERA's inaugural Social Justice in Education Award.
- David Berliner: Best known for his work on educational policy, classroom teaching and learning, and coauthoring six editions of *Educational Psychology*.[2] Author of more than three hundred publications.
- Ivar Braten: Norwegian scholar. Best known for his work on epistemic cognition in multiple document literacy. Authored more than 160 articles and books.
- Rebecca Collie: Australian scholar. Best known for her work on motivation and well-being. She has about seventy publications since earning her doctoral degree in 2014. Early-career award-winning scholar. Ranked third among top-producing early-career scholars.[3]
- Brian Coppola: An organic chemist best known for his pioneering work on discipline-centered teaching and learning. He is the author of about a hundred articles and four books.
- Carol Dweck: Best known for her work on mindset and motivation. Author of nearly two hundred publications. Received the Thorndike Career Achievement Award in Educational Psychology (APA) and

APA's Distinguished Scientific Award for the Application of Psychology.

- Jacquelynne Eccles: Best known for her work on academic motivation. Author of more than three hundred publications. Received the Thorndike Career Achievement Award in Educational Psychology (APA) and APA's Distinguished Scientific Award for the Application of Psychology.
- Logan Fiorella. Best known for his work on generative learning strategies. Early-career award-winning scholar. Ranked third among most productive educational psychologists overall and first among early-career scholars.[4] Authored about fifty-five publications since earning his doctoral degree in 2015.
- Frank Fischer: German scholar. Best known for his work on collaborative learning. Authored more than 250 publications.
- John Glover: Published about a hundred articles and twenty-three books on topics pertaining to reading, memory, and creativity over a sixteen-year career shortened by his untimely death in 1989.
- Hans Gruber: German scholar. Best known for his work on expert performance, including workplace expertise. Authored more than 250 publications.
- Karen Harris: Pioneered the self-regulated strategy development model of writing instruction. She has authored fourteen books and more than two hundred journal articles and book chapters. Harris has received the AERA Sylvia Scribner Career Award.
- John Hattie: Australian scholar. Hattie is best known for his scholarly work on visible learning and its dissemination in thousands of schools. Hattie has authored thirty-eight books and has published or presented 1,200 research papers.
- Hyun Ji Lee: 2021 AERA Division C (Learning and Instruction) Graduate Research Excellence Award co-winner. Graduate of Korea University.
- Mareike Kunter: German scholar. Best known for her model of teacher competence. Authored more than 150 publications since earning her doctorate in 2004. Ranked sixth among most productive educational psychologists.[5]
- Carol D. Lee: Best known for her five decades of work helping students from minority backgrounds to excel. Lee received AERA's Distinguished Contributions to Research in Education Award.

She has published more than a hundred journal articles and books and has founded three African-centered schools.

- Hyewon Lee: 2021 AERA Division C (Learning and Instruction) Graduate Research Excellence Award co-winner. Graduate of Ohio State University.
- Zeus Leonardo: Best known for his work on race, class, and gender in education. He has authored ten books and about seventy articles and chapters. He received AERA's Scholars of Color Distinguished Career Contribution Award.
- Doug Lombardi: Best known for his work on epistemic cognition and science learning. He received early-career awards from AERA and APA. He earned his doctorate in 2012 and has authored about fifty publications.
- Heinz Mandl: German scholar. Best known for work in learning and cognition, including cooperative learning. He has authored more than 450 publications.
- Rich Mayer: Best known for his work on multimedia learning. Mayer is the author of more than six hundred publications, including forty books. He has been ranked the world's most productive educational psychologist over many years.[6] He has received numerous awards including the Thorndike Career Achievement Award in Educational Psychology (APA) and the James McKeen Cattell Award for a lifetime of outstanding contributions to applied psychological research.
- Sabina Neugebauer: Best known for her work on language and literacy development. She earned her doctorate in 2011 and has authored about thirty-five publications. She is an early-career award winner (AERA).
- Erika Patall: Best known for her work on motivation and choice. She earned early-career awards from AERA and APA. She earned her doctorate in 2009 and has authored about sixty publications.
- Michael Pressley: Best known for his research on memory development, strategy instruction, and reading comprehension. He received the Thorndike Career Achievement Award in Educational Psychology (APA). Pressley published over 350 articles and authored or edited thirty-three books over his thirty-year career. Pressley passed away in 2006 at the height of his career.

- Alexander Renkl: German scholar. Best known for his work on worked examples, instructional explanations, learning from multiple representations, and reflective writing. He has authored more than 350 publications.
- Carly Robinson: 2020 AERA Division C (Learning and Instruction) Graduate Research Excellence Award winner. Graduate of Harvard University.
- Dale Schunk: Best known for his work on social and instructional factors on learning, motivation, and self-regulation. He has authored about 125 publications, including sixteen books.
- Marilla Svinicki: Best known for her work in higher education and faculty development and for editing *McKeachie's Teaching Tips*. She has authored more than eighty works, including eleven authored or edited books.
- Tamara van Gog: German scholar. Best known for research on example-based learning and teacher assessment of student learning. She has authored about two hundred publications since earning her doctorate in 2006. She was ranked seventh among the most productive educational psychologists.[6]
- Sirui Wan: 2022 AERA Division C (Learning and Instruction) Graduate Research Excellence Award winner. Graduate of University of California, Irvine.
- Ming-Te Wang: Best known for his work on achievement motivation and engagement. Several early-career awards including Distinguished Scientific Award for Early Career Contribution to Psychology. Earned his doctoral degree in 2010 and has authored about ninety publications.
- Barry Zimmerman: Best known for his work on self-regulated learning. Author of more than two hundred publications, including fourteen books. He received the Thorndike Career Achievement Award in Educational Psychology (APA).

References

Appendix: Meet the Productive Scholars

1 Fong, C. J., Flanigan, A. E., Hogan, E., et al. (2022). Individual and institutional productivity in educational psychology journals from 2015 to 2021. *Educational Psychology Review*, 34, 2379–2403.

2 Gage, N. L., & Berliner, D. (1998). *Educational psychology* (6th ed.). Boston, MA: Houghton Mifflin.
3 Fong, C. J., Flanigan, A. E., Hogan, E., et al. (2022). Individual and institutional productivity in educational psychology journals from 2015 to 2021. *Educational Psychology Review, 34*, 2379–2403.
4 Ibid.
5 Ibid.
6 Ibid.

Index

9 781009 342506